Warren Buffett Wealth

Principles and Practical Methods Used by the World's Greatest Investor

Robert P. Miles

WILEY

John Wiley & Sons, Inc.

Published by John Wiley & Sons, Inc., Hoboken, New Jersey.
Published simultaneously in Canada.

For general information on our other products and services, or technical support, please contact our Customer Care Department within the United States at 800-762-2974, outside the United States at 317-572-3993 or fax 317-572-4002.

Wiley also publishes its books in a variety of electronic formats. Some content that appears in print may not be available in electronic books.

For more information about Wiley products, visit our web site at www.wiley.com.

Library of Congress Cataloging-in-Publication Data

Miles, Robert P.
    Warren Buffett wealth : principles and practical methods used by the world's greatest investor / Robert P. Miles.
        p.   cm.
    Includes index
    ISBN 0-471-46511-9 (CLOTH)
    1. Investments. 2. Buffett, Warren. I. Title.
HG4521 .M4567 2004
332.6—dc22

                                                    2003022243

Printed in the United States of America
10 9 8 7 6 5 4 3

In loving memory to my heroes

Timothy John Miles
Leo McCrossin
Ross Steggles

Contents

Acknowledgments

Although the skills used to write are different than those used in presentations, written and oral forms of communication have both shaped the content of this book. Therefore I am most grateful to the hundreds of associations, service clubs, student groups, nonprofit organizations, bookstores, book clubs, investment clubs, local and international chamber of commerce groups, investment conferences, wealth workshops, universities, and private and public corporations that have invited me to discuss Warren Buffett and Berkshire Hathaway.

Dottie Walters, Felicia Ferrara, Dave Bell, Karen Post, Robyn Winters, and many members of the National Speakers Association have helped make me a better presenter. This book should "wrightfully" be dedicated to Janet Wright. She suggested that I send my Buffett CEO audio CD—recorded live before fifty-seven Canadian CEOs—to Nightingale Conant, the world's largest producer and distributor of audio programs. Dan Strutzel, new product development manager at Nightingale, had just completed a market research poll, and listeners were asking for an audio program about Warren Buffett. This connection led to my recording a six-hour, twelve-session audio series titled *How to Build Wealth Like Warren Buffett: Principles and Practical Methods Used by the World's Greatest Investor*.

If you enjoy this book, an outgrowth of the audio program, full credit belongs to Janet. If you don't take away at least one new idea about wealth or investing using similar principles as Warren Buffett, then the blame belongs to me. Either way I am grateful to Janet and all of her wonderful support, enthusiasm, and encouragement throughout the book creation process.

I was thrilled to be invited to deliver a half-day Buffett Wealth workshop in Australia suggested by Susie Christie and her assistant Donna Bunnell of the Global Speakers Bureau based in Sydney, Australia. Many of the graphs, charts, and tables used in this book were developed for my live speeches in Sydney and Melbourne for the Wealth Workshop clients of Freeman Fox. Their CEO Peter Spann, Australia's foremost wealth educator, and his seminar team led by Lisa Cadigan were a joy to meet.

In the United States, the Financial Forum Speaker's Bureau based in Logan, Utah, and led by Lyn Fisher have been excellent representatives for my speaking engagements. Our friends to the north have invited me to speak many times. Nicole Martel, CEO of Interlogic of Montreal, Canada, asked me to speak at her annual conference designed exclusively for CEOs. Geoffrey Carlton, Michael Lee-Chin, Jerry Santulli, Jeff Hull, Sarah Tucker, and Jessica McKnight from Berkshire Securities and AIC Funds in Canada have been very loyal clients.

Helping the message reach a third continent is Norman Rentrop. Along with his associates Andreas Hahne and Sandra Witscher, Norman helped organize half- and full-day workshops in Bonn, Germany. Norman simultaneously translated my presentation into German for those Europeans unable to understand my English or me.

I'm also grateful for the feedback and insights of Ross Brayton. I'm indebted to Professor Wendy Guo of the University of Nebraska at Omaha for inviting me to present to her students each year. Thanks to Gary Repair, executive producer and director from UNO TV, and his dedicated team for guiding me through the unique world of video program development and distribution—and to executive grip Michael Shearn and his friend John Newman (who only reads the acknowledgments: Hi, John!) for their opinions, support, and encouragement.

Thanks to Ralph Malloy, owner-manager of the 114th Street Omaha Dairy Queen, for his assistance in helping me host the Berkshire Hathaway pre–annual meeting reception and author fest. Jim Ross, manager of the Omaha airport Waterstones Booksellers, has made the DQ reception an extraordinary success and is a ready friend and valuable resource to every Buffett author.

For the past five years Berkshire's wholly owned subsidiary Sees Candy has kindly opened their Los Angeles manufacturing, packing, and shipping facilities and offered a very unique tour each spring, on the morning before Charlie Munger's Wesco Financial annual meeting. Tour leader and long-time Sees CEO Chuck Huggins and his team, led by Customer Service Director Dave Harvey, and the Sees associates at every level have made this event a sweet success.

Helping launch the annual Graham Buffett Book Conference in Los Angeles are Roland Shank, the foremost Buffett-related book collector, and money managers and publishers Rich Rockwood and Adam Jones.

International investment managers François Rochon of Montreal, Canada, and Wayne Peters of Sydney, Australia, inspired and provided several charts in this book. I wish to thank Chris Wholeben and Kristen Friend for their technical support, their Excel and PowerPoint expertise, and their chart creation talent.

Special thanks to The Motley Fool, Tom and David Gardner and Selena Maranjian, for creating a personal finance forum for all investors.

My gratitude goes to the fine folks at Berkshire Hathaway and related subsidiaries: Warren Buffett, his assistant Debbie Bosanek, and Charlie Munger. To Robert Bird and Jeffery Jacobson of Wesco Financial; Bill Child, R.C. Willey Home Furnishings; Harrold Melton, Acme Brick; Barnett Helzberg and Jeff Comment, Helzberg Diamonds; Stan Lipsey, the *Buffalo News*; Susan Jacques, Borsheim's Jewelry; Randy Watson, Justin Boot; Lou Simpson, GEICO; Brad Kinstler, Fechheimer; Al Ueltschi, Flight-Safety International; Kevin Russell, NetJets; and Louie, Irv, and Ron Blumkin, Nebraska Furniture Mart.

Few accomplish much without the aid of a mentor, and the person most responsible for getting me noticed by a publisher has been Janet Lowe, a prolific author. She and Wiley representative Tim Hand were instrumental in publishing my first book. Intellectual property attorney Ken Sweezy guided me through the audio and book contracts without jeopardizing the delicate relationship between an author and a publisher.

Special mention goes to Andy Kilpatrick. His unending dedication to chronicling the story of Warren Buffett and Berkshire Hathaway has been recorded in biannual book updates titled *Of Permanent Value*.

Thanks to John Wiley and Sons: publisher Joan O'Neil and executive editor Debby Englander, along with David Pugh, Greg Friedman, Alexia Meyers, Alison Bamberger, Aditi Shah, and P. J. Campbell. This book really took shape under the capable hands of Ruth Mills, my developmental editor. Every author should be blessed to have someone like Ruth to work alongside.

Friends John Baum, Whit Wannamaker, Lee Bakunin, Hendrick Leber, Nigel Littlewood, Stan Teschke, Camille Roberts, Greg Ekisian, Ken Walters, John Bryant, Tom Hastings, John Cavo, Ben Keaton, John Zemanovich, Will Harrell, and Frank Booker have played a valuable role in guiding me in the right direction. High school buddy, college roommates, and business associates Tim Cleary and Jim Klaserner have made me a better businessman and therefore a better investor.

My family—in particular, my daughter Marybeth—has been especially understanding and supportive. My mother was supportive and strong despite losing a mother, brother, son, and nephew in less than twelve months. To Katie Miles, my niece, whose father was my hero. Thanks to my niece, Sarah, who enjoys reading, writing, telling funny jokes, and doing things s-d-r-a-w-k-c-a-b. My friend Nancy Pellotte and I share the same humor and emotional age as Sarah.

Introduction

"Wealth is the product of a man's capacity to think."

—Ayn Rand

If you invested $10,000 in 1956 with Warren Buffett when he first started his investment partnership, you would be worth today, after all fees, expenses and taxes, over $300 million.

Buffett's amazing success is all the more remarkable because he doesn't own any patents, hasn't developed a new technology or retail concept, or even started his own business. The tools he used are available to everyone in the capitalistic world: extraordinary discipline and adhering to the principles of value investing.

The good news from the man who has created over $100 billion in capital (and he's still working on creating more) is that there is no secret to wealth building by investing in other people's businesses. The promise is that, by using the same principles and methods, you too can create wealth, preserve it, and pass it on to future generations.

This book offers a Horatio Alger story that you may have never thought possible. It's the story of how one man, without the benefit of inheritance, without taking over a family business as a starting point, without doing what everyone else was doing, without inside information or special connections, without a large salary or stock options, created abundant wealth and plans to give it all back to society.

The premise of this book is that by carefully selecting the ownership of a business and owning it for a lifetime—hopefully, several lifetimes—you can create enormous wealth.

To become wealthy is easy: Just be born into it, marry into it, or win the lottery. But most people become wealthy, like Warren, by owning a business and living below your income. For many of us, the best way to own a business is by owning parts of it through the stock market, just as Warren Buffett has done. If you're really good at the investment and management game, you can then use the earnings of your business to buy more ownership in other businesses and eventually the whole business.

Buffett Wealth is not about whom you know, but rather what you know. Buffett Wealth is not how much money you have, but how you invest what you have.

I've written this book to tell you the story of one of the few men to become a billionaire by investing in the stock market—in other words, by investing in other people's businesses, first in part and then eventually in whole by acquiring wholly owned subsidiaries.

I've written two books and given numerous speeches about Warren Buffett. He is a favorite topic and passion of mine, and I hope of yours by the time you finish reading this book. Hopefully, in addition to learning about his character and life lessons, you'll also understand important investment principles and techniques.

Warren Buffett is known as a value investor and a values manager. Fortunately, he is able to choose to work with exactly those people he likes, admires, respects, and trusts. Warren invests in value enterprises but not without a values manager. He encourages his people to always do first-class business in a first-class way.

Buffett's conglomerate, Berkshire (pronounced BerkSure) Hathaway, is publicly traded on the New York Stock Exchange (its class A share [symbol NYSE: BRKA] and class B share [symbol NYSE: BRKB] are the first and second highest price stock on any exchange in the world) and is now the twenty-fifth largest employer, with more than 165,000 employees. His Net-Jets subsidiary can be considered the sixth largest private airline based on the number of corporate jets under management. Buffett maintains all of this with no large headquarters building, no large staff, no management stock options, no funny accounting, no yachts, no Rolls Royces, no mansions or typical trappings of wealth. Warren Buffett enjoys one of the longest CEO tenures: thirty-nine years and counting.

To give you a perspective of Warren's investment record, consider in the last century that the Dow Jones Industrial Average went from 66 to 11,000. The NASDAQ, formed in 1971, went from 100 to close the century at approximately 2,000. Berkshire Hathaway, under Warren Buffett's management and leadership, has added one zero every decade since he first acquired it in 1962. The stock has gone up from 7 to 70 to 700 to 7,000, to over 70,000 dollars per share.

Warren has done all of this without unfriendly deals, without sizeable employee layoffs, without requiring additional capital shareholder contributions, without major management changes or restructurings or investing in promising new-economy stocks or risking capital in turnaround businesses. Remarkably his accomplishments have taken place without issuing management stock options to himself or anyone else, without paying himself more than $100,000 in salary, without enjoying the typical trappings of most CEOs, and without ever selling a single share of his company's stock.

Warren made himself a billionaire and one of the world's richest men; at the same time, he also created enormous wealth for his partners and shareholders. For every dollar in wealth he created for himself, his family, and his foundation, he has created more than two additional dollars in wealth for others.

WHY I DECIDED TO WRITE THIS BOOK

I want to tell you about my background. I started my career first as a student of investing. I made all the classic investment mistakes. I graduated from one of the top business schools in the country without learning about Warren Buffett or the simple concept that all investing is value investing.

After thirty years of making all the wrong investment moves, I finally asked myself: Who is the best at investing and what can I learn from that person? The answer, of course, was Warren Buffett. So I became an avid student of everything he said and everything he had written. In 1996 I purchased his stock when he first offered the B shares (1/30th the share price and economic value of the A shares), and I have since more than doubled my investment.

You might find it interesting how I came to writing about Warren Buffett. I thought the man and his investment vehicle were so profound that I could come up with 101 reasons why you should own it. So over a period of 101 days, on the Motley Fool's Internet discussion boards, I posted a new, unique reason to own his company. For example, consider the fact that Berkshire's stock is the only one to issue an owner's manual and hosts one of the largest annual meetings of any publicly traded company, when some fifteen thousand shareholders from all fifty states and many other countries descend on Omaha, Nebraska. Much to my delight, Warren had read what I wrote on the Internet about him and Berkshire Hathaway; he gave me his permission to publish *101 Reasons to Own the World's Greatest Investment*. I did, and as a real honor, Warren ordered ten copies of my first book to give to his board of directors.

My book—written to other shareholders—struck a chord with other students of the Buffett investment strategies. I self-published it, and a revised edition was later published by John Wiley & Sons.

My next project was interviewing twenty CEOs who all report directly to Warren Buffett, and I wrote *The Warren Buffett CEO*. When I finished that manuscript, I was invited out to Omaha to speak at a personal investment conference. Warren invited me to lunch, and we ended up having a two-hour lunch during which we talked about many different subjects. When we finished, I gave him my four-hundred-page manuscript. He read it in one sitting, and then called me at 6:50 a.m. the following morning to point out that he had found only six factual errors, which he didn't think was too bad for four hundred pages. Fortunately I had a week to fix the manuscript errors. Characteristically, he made no comment on my editorial opinions, only the facts.

Warren again treated me warmly when he recommended this book in his annual letter to shareholders and at his annual meeting in the spring of 2002.

Publication of these two books gave me a new career: as a professional speaker giving presentations on the management and investment principles and practical methods of Warren Buffett. Nightingale Conant, the world's largest producer and distributor of audio presentations, took notice and asked me to create a new audio series titled *How to Build Wealth Like Warren Buffett*, a six-hour, twelve-session program, the first comprehensive audio product available about Warren Buffett. This book is the text version and outgrowth of both my audio and live workshop presentations.

FULL DISCLOSURE

As a disclaimer, I am not authorized, compensated, selected, or approved by Warren Buffett. I do not speak for him; instead, I merely share my observations as a keen observer and fellow shareholder. As a courtesy, and as is my customary practice, I sent a manuscript of this book in advance to him and after production I will send him a finished book.

I've been in Warren's company several times, including two visits to his office, a delightful and spirited two-hour lunch, and a forty-five-minute phone conversation. I helped him celebrate his seventieth birthday, and we have corresponded with many letters. He is so disciplined and focused that, even though he receives as many as two hundred letters a day, he answers his mail the day he receives it.

Please note my natural bias. I am a long-term shareholder of his company, Berkshire Hathaway, but I have never been employed by Berkshire or any of its subsidiaries. I have had the good fortune to meet and interview most of the Buffett CEOs (now over fifty, with three or four more added each year).

Any of the stocks mentioned in this book are not presented as a recommendation to buy or sell. I have nothing to gain or lose if you follow the advice in this book. I hope you will benefit from my experiences and observations—those of a forty-something private investor and investment advisor who made thirty years' worth of investing mistakes, then discovered the methods of the world's greatest.

WHAT THIS BOOK CAN TEACH YOU ABOUT BUILDING WEALTH

I hope you'll want to leave the world a better place—like Warren—by living below your means and giving back some of your money to society. Like Buffett, most of you will find the best way to own a business is by owning parts of it through the stock market. Then, if you end up being smart at the investment and management game, you can use the earnings of your business to buy more ownership in other businesses and eventually the whole business. Actually, investing in a business to build wealth may be easier than starting and managing your own business. That's been Warren Buffett's strategy.

The purpose of this book is to help to find the difference between being *rich* and being *wealthy*. Being rich is having money, which can be temporary in nature and is often fleeting. Riches are about excess and indulgence, whereas being wealthy is having knowledge, personal relationship success, a sense of humor, and a foundation of principles.

This book focuses on the principles of becoming wealthy: creating wealth, sustaining it, and passing it on to future generations for the betterment of society. Whether you adopt only some or all of these wealth principles, Warren said it best: "Money will not change how healthy you are or how many people love you."

A man is rich according to what he has, and wealthy according to who he is. Warren's true wealth is not in how much he's worth but rather his character values, mentor selection, investment principles, management strategies, extraordinary discipline, and gift of genius, combined with the luck of being born in the right time and right place.

It's important also to point out what this book won't do: There are no get-rich-quick schemes or promises. Instead, this is a "get-rich-slow" program. This book points out the Buffett principles and methods as best as I have been able to observe them. Of course, I make no promise that you too will be a billionaire simply by reading this book. The hard work and application of these principles is up to you.

Now a word about what this book will do. I'm reminded of the lady who stood up at a recent Berkshire annual meeting and said, "Mr. Buffett, I only have one B share." And he interrupted her and said, "That's okay, lady, between you and me, we own half the company. What's your question?" You see, with extraordinary wealth and timeless principles, Warren now has a platform and the opportunity to teach and advance investment education. He points out new ways at looking at investments, proven strategies, rare methods not generally talked about or written about. Instead of old terms like "market price," you'll see new terms like "intrinsic value." He takes you from the outside of riches and price to the inside of wealth and value.

This book discusses new ways to look at risk. While most investors believe risk is the volatility of a stock price, Warren's world says risk is simply not knowing what you are doing. Most people think that "long term" is any amount of time you are losing money on your investments, but to Warren Buffett, "long term" is forever. You'll also come across more new terms, like "Mr. Market," a fictional drunken, manic-depressive character representing wild emotional swings in stock market prices, and the difference between growth and value investing, if there is one. The investment philosophy of Warren's college professor was that your investment activity be limited to just twenty lifetime investment decisions. Ownership should take precedence over trading, and intelligent investing (thinking) should supersede emotional investing (acting). Even Aesop, an ancient and wise philosopher some twenty-six hundred years ago, can provide investment guidance for today. We think too little and compute too much.

Combine the unique skill sets of Warren Buffett—confidence; selecting the right mentors; developing the right principles; being frugal, patient, disciplined, and independent; and having extraordinary genius, work ethic, and values—and you too can build Buffett Wealth. We'll talk about stocks being unique, and when they are on sale, for some reason, they are not appealing to the amateur investor. Unfortunately, many people view the stock market like jewelry purchases; the more expensive, the better. Buffett methods are the opposite; the greater the discount to a stock's true value, the greater the interest.

This book is designed for readers unfamiliar or with limited knowledge of Warren Buffett and his investment company. It's written for those with limited time to read his writings available on the Internet at www.berkshirehathaway.com. It's best for those who are tired of using principles and methods that have not produced excellent returns and have not built wealth.

HOW THIS BOOK IS ORGANIZED

Chapter 1 begins with the simple concept of studying the best to be the best. Warren learns from every expert craftsman and in every field of endeavor. Chapter 2 is the brief history of Warren's life and the story of the making of a billionaire from early childhood to adulthood, from $100 to $1 million to $1 billion to many billion. It next describes how Warren's gifts of memory, genius, and skill at numbers have turned into an amazing wealth-building machine.

Chapter 2 offers a timeline of not creating his own business, but rather very shrewd investments in other people's businesses, first in part and then in whole, first through the stock market and then by purchasing them outright.

Chapter 3 asks the rhetorical question, What kind of investor are you? Are you even an investor? Do others easily influence you, or are you an independent thinker? Can you ignore the madness of crowds? All investing must start with self-discovery. The answers to these questions are critical to understanding Buffett's principles and methods.

Chapter 4 dives into the merits of developing an investment philosophy, and Chapter 5 asks whether you know what you own. Warren Buffett does, and he often studies an investment over many decades before he makes a purchase. Many business owners who have sold their businesses to Warren suggest that he knew more about their businesses than the owners and founders of those businesses.

The wealth program described in this book showcases the idea of investing in Main Street rather than Wall Street, as discussed in Chapter 6. Your focus must be on businesses and their valuations, not on markets. Whether a business is an excellent investment has nothing to do with whether or not the Dow Jones Industrial Average is up or down. Contrary to most advice you receive from many financial advisors, Chapter 7 discusses the merits of concentrating your investments in a few stocks and buying to keep, maybe even for a lifetime.

In Chapter 8, you see what you can learn by studying Warren Buffett's investment mistakes; Chapter 9 explores investment, wealth, and Buffett myths. Just what are the five investment principles of the next Warren Buffett? Chapter 10 describes them, and I think you will find that person to be a unique and independent thinker. My favorite chapter is Chapter 11, which offers lessons about life. You can't learn about wealth without also exploring character, integrity, reputation, and thriftiness. This fact may disappoint you or warm your heart, but the second richest man on earth lives no better than the average college student. He just travels better. Chapter 12 reviews how Buffett Wealth has been a journey of a lifetime and how Buffett's billions have been created with the careful application of principles and practical methods over six decades.

Chapter 1

Study the Best to Be the Best

"We are what we repeatedly do. Excellence is therefore not an act but a habit."

—Aristotle

Warren Buffett studies the best in every field of endeavor and from every country. He plays golf with Tiger Woods, tennis with Martina Navratilova, and bridge with two-time world champion Sharon Osberg. He'll talk body-building and politics with Arnold Schwarzenegger, music with Jimmy Buffett, movie-making with Debbie Reynolds, and dance with Michael Flatley. Good friend Bill Gates discusses the latest and future world of technology. The world's best CEOs gather to seek counsel and to listen to Warren at every available opportunity. Politicians stop by Omaha for his endorsement. Presidents, legislators, judiciary members, even the chairman of the Federal Reserve greet him by first name at the annual Washington DC–based Alfalfa Club dinner every January. To be acquired by Warren's holding company is considered an honor.

In fact, not only does Warren study the best, he now has a built-in subsidiary that brings him the best of the best in the world of entertainment, athletics, entrepreneurial success, wealth, power, and corporate chiefs. Buffett's NetJets now shuttles over 5,000 high-net-worth people and the best of the best to over 140 countries in 240,000 flights each year. Net-Jets likes to say that anyone with a net worth of $20 million or more can do no better to enhance their lifestyle, security, safety, and comfort than to purchase an ownership interest in one of their jets. It's the equivalent of having Air Force One without being elected president of the United States.

Radio talk-show (Don Imus) and late-night television (David Letterman) hosts brag about their NetJet plane. Not just athletes, entertainers, and musicians, but even a top religious leader and spiritual advisor to U.S. presidents is attracted to this ultimate service. Even GE, the world's largest conglomerate, owns several NetJet shares to supplement their own fleet and to have the right plane and the right time for the right business meeting—all at a cost that reflects their actual use, not their ownership. As they say, buy a share and gain a fleet.

SUPERINVESTORS—PROOF THAT WARREN BUFFETT STUDIES THE BEST

Of course, Warren also studies the best at investing (which is exactly what you are doing by studying Warren Buffett). He observed, studied, lectured, and wrote that the best investors are those that follow value investment principles.

As a graduate student of economics, Warren studied security analysis under professors Ben Graham and David Dodd. In 1984, on the occasion of the fifteenth anniversary of the last published edition of *Security Analysis* written by Graham and Dodd, Warren Buffett gave a speech at his alma mater, Columbia University, titled "The Superinvestors of Graham-and-Doddsville" (see Appendix).

Warren proposed that those superinvestors (a small group that has been able to solidly beat the market over many years) have read, understood, and followed the value investing principles set forth in the book *Security Analysis* were from the virtual intellectual community of Graham and Doddsville (named by Buffett after the authors of *Security Analysis*).

He has always believed and proved it with this speech that the residents of Graham and Doddsville have achieved and continue to achieve outstanding superinvestor returns by investing in *different* stocks. Buffett asserts that average small investors can compound a portfolio better than the overall market as long as they follow the principles of Graham and Dodd, or value investing. Investors can do this by applying the same principles and methods as Buffett without actually investing in the same stocks.

Value investing, which according to Buffett describes all investing, is the art and science of buying $1 worth of assets for 50 cents. Warren not only identified and named this virtual town of Graham and Doddsville, he is one of the first residents and the rightful mayor. As you will read in Chapter 10, Lou Simpson is now deputy.

So if Buffett studies the best in every field of endeavor, not just investment management, it seems logical that if you, too, want to be an above-average investor, then you should study Warren Buffett and learn from the best.

CREATING MORE THAN $100 BILLION IN WEALTH

To understand the profound accomplishment of Warren Buffett in creating wealth, consider this: $1 million earned and invested each year for 48½ years at 10 percent annual interest equals $1 billion. Not a minor feat by anyone's standards, but Warren Buffett did this 66 times for his shareholders plus 36 times for himself or more than 100 times over his investment career of the past fifty years, and he's not finished. His partner Charlie Munger says, "Warren's getting better with age."

Billionaire Wealth:
  $1 million invested each year @ 10 percent × 48½ years = $1 billion
Multibillionaire Wealth:
  $10 million invested each year @ 10 percent × 48½ years = $10 billion
Buffett Wealth:
  $100 million invested each year @ 10 percent × 48½ years = $100 billion

---

Buffett treats his shareholders like partners. Buffett Wealth is created *with* shareholders, not at their expense. Figure 1.1 shows how first with a $50,000 annual salary and now with a $100,000 salary, with no additional capital investments, grew a personal $3 million investment to over $35 billion—without ever buying or selling a share of his holding company or without issuing stock options to himself.

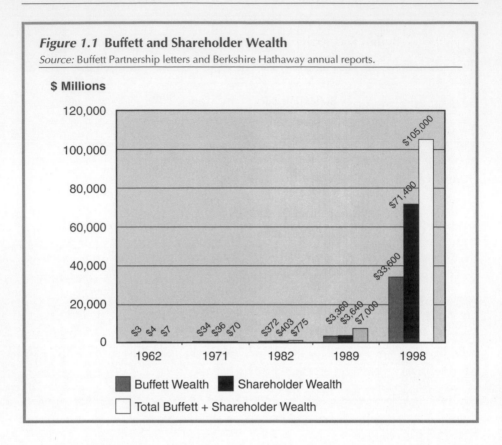

Figure 1.1 **Buffett and Shareholder Wealth**
Source: Buffett Partnership letters and Berkshire Hathaway annual reports.

(Readers should note that aside from his salary, Warren keeps 1 percent of his net worth outside Berkshire, which is an additional $300 million. A 5 percent withdrawal of $15 million annually would be a comfortable lifestyle by almost anyone's standards.)

As Figure 1.1 and Tables 1.1 and 1.2 show, Buffett grew wealth for his partners and shareholders as he created wealth for himself, for his family, and ultimately for the benefit of the world, as his wealth will one day fund the world's largest foundation. In 1962, when Buffett had a net worth of $1.5 million, his partners had $8.5 million, for a total of Buffett and shareholder wealth of $10 million. By 1971, at the age of forty-one, Buffett had $33.6 million and his shareholders had $36.4 million for a total of $70 million. By 1982, Buffett's net worth climbed to $372 million and his partners accumulated $403 million, for a total of $775 million. Buffett achieved multibillionaire status in 1989 with $3.4 billion, his shareholders at $3.7 billion, and total wealth of $7.1 billion.

Table 1.1 Buffett Partnership Annual Returns Compared to DJIA

Source: Buffett Partnership letter dated January 22, 1969. Note that returns are after general partner fees of 25 percent of the gain after an annual 6 percent distribution to the partners.

Year	Buffett Partners	Dow	Value Added
1957	9.3%	(8.4%)	17.7
1958	32.2	38.5	(6.3)
1959	20.9	20.0	.9
1960	18.6	(6.2)	24.8
1961	35.9	22.4	13.5
1962	11.9	(7.6)	19.5
1963	30.5	20.6	9.9
1964	22.3	18.7	3.6
1965	36.9	14.2	22.7
1966	16.8	(15.6)	32.4
1967	28.4	19.0	9.4
1968	45.6	7.7	37.9
Total Return	1403.5	185.7	1217.8
Average Annual	25.3	9.1	16.2

Table 1.2 How Buffett Created Wealth for Himself along with His Partners

Source: Buffett Partnership letters.

Age	Year	Partner Wealth	Buffett Wealth
27	1957	$105,100	$100
31	1961	$7 million	$1 million
32	1962	$10 million	$1.5 million
33	1963	$18 million	$2.5 million
34	1964	$26 million	$3.5 million
35	1965	$44 million	$7 million
36	1966	$54 million	$8 million
37	1967	$68 million	$11 million
38	1968	$104 million	$25 million

In 1998, Buffett became a cultural icon and the second richest man in the world with a net worth of $33.6 billion. His partners had an additional $71.4 billion, for a total of an astonishing $105 billion. No one has ever achieved this level of wealth without *ever* selling a share of his own company's stock, issuing a management stock option, adding additional capital, cornering a new process or patent, or without ever starting and owning one's own business.

Wealth can be gained four ways: inheritance, marriage, lottery, or through the ownership of a business. All wealth, however acquired, must be preserved by ongoing ownership of a business and by underspending income generated. Buffett Wealth comes not from inheritance, marriage, lottery, or the ownership of one business, but instead through the ownership of many businesses—first in part through the stock market, and then by the outright purchase of wholly owned businesses. As you will learn, Warren Buffett has always underspent his income and has never stopped adding to his partners' and his own wealth. He is on track to accumulate over $100 billion personally, and then after his and his wife's deaths, his foundation will distribute over $5 billion per year in perpetuity.

Warren Buffett's holding company, Berkshire Hathaway, owns more businesses and a wider cross-section of industries than any other public or private conglomerate, but it has no divisions or vice presidents in charge of certain business categories. Buffett has created a very unique conglomerate.

Unlike much of the rest of the Forbes 400 list of the wealthiest individuals, Warren hasn't inherited, married into, won by lottery, or created wealth by owning a business. Warren hasn't even created any new investment methods or practices. His investment principles were learned from his mentors and early employers: his father (an Omaha-based stockbroker and U.S. congressman) and his college professor. His extraordinary investment and business success came not from any invention or method, but instead by the persistent application of old, value-based principles that are, rather amazingly, simple common sense and easy to learn and implement.

Buffett's expertise, talent, and skills are to properly value a business, access the values of management (or lack of), purchase the business at a discount to its value, and motivate and retain talented managers. He then redeploys the excess capital to replicate this feat over and over again—a virtual circle of capitalism at its finest. You too can be exceedingly wealthy if you decide to live below your income and learn and follow his methods. Actually, they aren't even his principles and practical methods, but rather the simple teachings and examples of his father and college professor.

Buffett the Multicapitalist

Most people think of a capitalist as employing capital to produce goods and services at a profit. Buffett has redefined "capitalist" into multiple dimensions.

Intellectual Capital   The gift and development of extraordinary intelligence to deploy capital.

Values Capital   The careful selection of ethics and principles to attract and keep capital.

Value Capital   The artful acquisition of resources at a discount to their real value.

Capital   Access to ever-increasing resources to allocate to their best use.

Human Capital   Selecting and associating with people who cause you to perform better.

Social Capital   Having the right connections for the right reasons to move in the circles that bring more and better deals.

Opportunity Capital   Being the first one called when a business opportunity meeting specific acquisition criteria becomes available.

Business Model Capital   Developing a business environment to attract an untold variety of businesses and managements under one umbrella.

Circle of Capital   Successfully allocating the excess capital of one business into the acquisition or expansion of another.

Influence Capital   Able to influence the U.S. Congress to give Salomon Brothers (a partly and previously owned company) another chance and to save the jobs of over eight thousand associates. Also able to influence all branches of government: legislative, judicial, and administrative. Can attract over fifty worldwide media outlets to cover Berkshire's annual meeting, while giving limited access to interviews during the rest of the year.

Note that you can't expect to become wealthy by investing in other people's businesses without doing a substantial amount of reading and research. In order to outperform the average investor, you must read every day and enjoy it. Unfortunately no shortcuts are available. If research isn't your cup of tea, then you may consider yourself a passive investor and might best be served by investing in a low-cost index fund, from which you will achieve the same results as the market with minimum time requirements.

STUDY THE BEST TO BE THE BEST

Why does Warren Buffett study the best in every field of endeavor? Because the traits of the best are universal and can be replicated. The best do one thing well and focus all of their life's energy doing that one thing. One of history's greatest golfers, Tiger Woods, hits five hundred golf balls everyday, just for practice. Ted Williams, considered to be the best hitter ever to play baseball, made a science of hitting and wrote a book with the same title. He carved the strike zone into seventy-seven cells, each the size of a baseball (seven balls across and eleven balls high) and marked each cell according to his ability to hit a ball in that cell. By simply hitting the balls in his self-selected zone and leaving the low-average balls alone, Williams became the best at what he did—hitting a baseball.

If Warren Buffett studies the best in every field of endeavor, why shouldn't you study him, given that he is undoubtedly the best at what he does? If you examine his investment, management, and business record, you quickly learn that no one even comes a close second.

Some aspects of investing can be very similar to gambling. Not knowing what you are doing, not understanding what you own, trading in and out of the market, following the advice of interested parties, being in a hurry to get rich, and relying on luck rather than skill are all signs of gambling. But investing and wealth building as applied by Warren Buffett is very much an art and a science and can be emulated.

Notice that Warren plays bridge in his spare time—a game of skill, not luck, and a game where choosing the right partner can make all the difference between winning and losing. The stock market, investing, and managing a business have the same characteristics. Selecting the right partners is critical. Warren's bridge partner, Sharon Osberg, is a two-time national bridge champion. She is so dedicated to bridge that it has, at many times during her career, taken the place of a full-time job. He carefully selects all of his partners and does not allow his outcome to be determined by chance and luck.

In his constant pursuit of excellence, Warren hosts one of the largest annual shareholder meetings each year in his hometown of Omaha and invites the grand masters of bridge, backgammon, Scrabble, and chess to demonstrate their skills. One master chess player (one of only fifty in the United States) takes on as many as six random chess challengers simultaneously while he is blindfolded, carefully committing each match to memory as it progresses. Patrick Wolff has rarely if ever lost a multiple blindfolded game.

Why showcase the best at games of skill? Because that is what Warren Buffett is, that is what he admires and is attracted to, and that is what is attracted to him. Genius admires genius. Talent recognizes skill. The best seek out and measure themselves against the best.

Following his passion and doing exactly what he was born to do, Warren does not believe in retirement. Jokingly, he says he will retire five years after his death. Asking him to name a replacement and retire would be like asking Picasso to stop painting. Berkshire is his masterpiece and his museum.

He has inspired and handpicked other master business artists to hang their business masterpieces at Berkshire—the Metropolitan Museum of Businesses—and to continue painting. Berkshire owns outright more than one hundred wholly owned businesses, from Dairy Queen to World Book to GEICO auto insurance. It also owns more than $30 billion in common stocks, including Coca-Cola, American Express, and Gillette. His job is simply to provide paint and brushes to the business artists or CEOs. He requests no formal meetings or budgets, offers no advice unless asked, and promises that their master business paintings will not be merged or painted over. He asks each of his business managers to act as if their business is the only asset they and their families own and as if it will not be sold for at least fifty years.

Buffett had a relationship with his first partners that guaranteed them a 6 percent annual return, after which Buffett received 25 percent of the profits.

After closing his partnership in 1969 and turning his attention to acquiring, managing, and building Berkshire into a conglomerate, Buffett has enjoyed a remarkable record, but it should be noted that making $100,000 grow to $100 million during the thirteen years of the Buffett partnership was easier than growing $17 million (Berkshire's average original acquisition cost) to over $100 billion today. The challenge of growing $100 billion to even $400 billion will be Buffett's greatest feat. If anyone can do it, he's the one. Review his extraordinary record compared to the S&P 500 and the value added over the past thirty-eight years, shown in Table 1.3.

Most professional money managers and private investors would be happy to meet and beat the S&P 500, which represents 70 percent of the publicly traded NYSE stocks. To more than double it over more than three decades is nothing short of profound. Notice, too, that he has accomplished this with only one losing year, 2001 (the S&P 500 also lost more that same year).

Warren measures himself annually and appropriately against the S&P 500 index, but he insists on calculating his benchmark by changes in book value (assets minus liabilities), which is most conservative, keeping his focus inside the business and on things he and his managers can control.

If instead he reported on annual changes in stock price (a figure determined by others outside the business and the last two people to buy and sell the stock), he would show more swings in valuations, more annual losses, and of course, a mind-blowing annual rate of return.

Tracking historical stock market prices is more volatile than tracking annual changes in book value. As Table 1.4 dramatically shows, a 30 percent average annual rate of returns from 1965 through today is worthy of analysis and study. Berkshire's CEO has written many times that he prefers book value to reflect intrinsic value (the valuation of a company based on the discounted cash flow of its owner's earnings over its useful life).

NEW-ECONOMY WAY OF INVESTING, OR TECHNOLOGY VERSUS BUFFETT

Not long ago the stock market was on an unchecked path to extraordinary increases, now known as the tech bubble or a period of irrational exuberance.

Most pundits and market participants were suggesting that because Berkshire had achieved a yearly low in March 2000, Buffett had lost his

Table 1.3 Buffett's Performance vs. S&P 500

Source: www.berkshirehathaway.com. Value added (Column 4) is Column 2 minus Column 3.

| Year | Annual Percent Change | | |
	Buffett	S&P 500 plus div	Value Added
1965	23.8	10.0	13.8
1966	20.3	(11.7)	32.0
1967	11.0	30.9	(19.9)
1968	19.0	11.0	8.0
1969	16.2	(8.4)	24.6
1970	12.0	3.9	8.1
1971	16.4	14.6	1.8
1972	21.7	18.9	2.8
1973	4.7	(14.8)	19.5
1974	5.5	(26.4)	31.9
1975	21.9	37.2	(15.3)
1976	59.3	23.6	35.7
1977	31.9	(7.4)	39.3
1978	24.0	6.4	17.6
1979	35.7	18.2	17.5
1980	19.3	32.3	(13.0)
1981	31.4	(5.0)	36.4
1982	40.0	21.4	18.6
1983	32.3	22.4	9.9
1984	13.6	6.1	7.5
1985	48.2	31.6	16.6
1986	26.1	18.6	7.5
1987	19.5	5.1	14.4
1988	20.1	16.6	3.5
1989	44.4	31.7	12.7
1990	7.4	(3.1)	10.5
1991	39.6	30.5	9.1
1992	20.3	7.6	12.7
1993	14.3	10.1	4.2
1994	13.9	1.3	12.6
1995	43.1	37.6	5.5
1996	31.8	23.0	8.8
1997	34.1	33.4	0.7
1998	48.3	28.6	19.7
1999	0.5	21.0	(20.5)
2000	6.5	(9.1)	15.6
2001	(6.2)	(11.9)	5.7
2002	10.0	(22.1)	32.1
Overall Gain	214,433.0	3,663.0	
Average	**22.2**	**10.0**	**12.2**

Table 1.4 Annual Changes in Berkshire's Stock Price

Source: Barron's. August 11, 2003, Legg Mason, National Quotation Bureau, Bloomberg.

Year	Year-end Stock Price*	Berkshire	S&P 500**	Difference
1966	$17.50	(8.0)	(11.7)	3.7
1967	20.50	15.7	30.9	(15.2)
1968	37	82.7	11.0	71.7
1969	42	13.5	(8.4)	21.9
1970	39	(7.1)	3.9	(11.0)
1971	70	79.5	14.6	64.9
1972	80	14.3	18.9	(4.6)
1973	71	(11.3)	(14.8)	3.5
1974	40	(43.7)	(26.4)	(17.3)
1975	38	(5.0)	37.2	(42.2)
1976	94	147.3	23.6	123.7
1977	138	46.8	(7.4)	54.2
1978	157	13.8	6.4	7.4
1979	320	102.5	18.2	84.3
1980	425	32.8	32.3	0.5
1981	560	31.8	(5.0)	36.8
1982	775	38.4	21.4	17.0
1983	1310	69.0	22.4	46.6
1984	1275	(2.7)	6.1	(8.8)
1985	2470	93.7	31.6	62.1
1986	2820	14.2	18.6	(4.4)
1987	2950	4.6	5.1	(0.5)
1988	4700	59.3	16.6	42.7
1989	8675	84.6	31.7	52.9
1990	6675	(23.1)	(3.1)	(20.0)
1991	9050	35.6	30.5	5.1
1992	11,750	29.8	7.6	22.2
1993	16,325	38.9	10.1	28.8
1994	20,400	25.0	1.3	23.7
1995	32,100	57.4	37.6	19.8
1996	34,100	6.2	23.0	(16.8)
1997	46,000	34.9	33.4	1.5
1998	70,000	52.2	28.6	23.6
1999	56,100	(19.9)	21.0	(40.9)
2000	71,000	26.6	(9.1)	35.7
2001	75,600	6.5	(11.9)	18.4
2002	72,750	(3.8)	(22.1)	18.3
2003	†75,300	3.5	11.9	(8.4)
Average		**29.9**	**11.5**	**18.4**

*Class A shares
**Includes dividends
†Aug. 15 price

touch and was out of step with the market. But he stood to his value prin-ciples and said he didn't invest in anything he didn't understand.

In fact, he went further with his beliefs, principles, and technology in-vesting and said if he were teaching a class on investing, he would have stu-dents perform one company valuation after another. As a final exam he would ask his students to value an Internet or dot-com company. Anyone who turned in an answer he would flunk, because the world's greatest capi-tal allocator doesn't think it is possible to value an enterprise that is not making money, doesn't have a competitive advantage, and has an uncer-tain future.

Sometimes the best way to silence the critics is to stick to your guns and let time and experience play out.

Figure 1.2 illustrates that old-economy and old-school Buffett handily beat the new-economy and new-school approach as represented by the NASDAQ, which largely reflects new issues and technology companies.

THE DOWN-MARKET TEST

The true measure of a successful investor is not a comparison of perform-ance against the NASDAQ or the Dow Jones Industrial Average (DJIA) or even the S&P 500 Index, but rather how well a portfolio performs during down markets. Table 1.5 ranks the Buffett Partnership performance by value added (the last column) and points out that during the years that the Dow was losing money, the partnership was adding the greatest value. Con-versely, when the Dow was achieving 38.5 percent growth during 1958, Buffett was not able to add value.

The down-market record continues if you review Table 1.6, which ranks Berkshire's value added over the S&P 500 Index from 1965 to 2002.

Other measurements of Buffett's profound investment, management, and business success are summarized in Figures 1.3, 1.4, 1.5, and 1.6. Be-cause Warren invests in companies with earnings that are growing over time and which are not as vulnerable to competition, these figures show rather dramatically how he has built a snowball of earnings. Berkshire buys companies with earnings, and with those earnings buys more companies. The type of industry doesn't matter; the quality of those earnings do.

As shown in Figure 1.3, in 1967 Berkshire's earnings before tax and before distributions to minority shareholders was $1.4 million. Earnings in

Figure 1.2 Buffett (Old Economy) versus NASDAQ (New Economy)
Source: bigcharts.com.

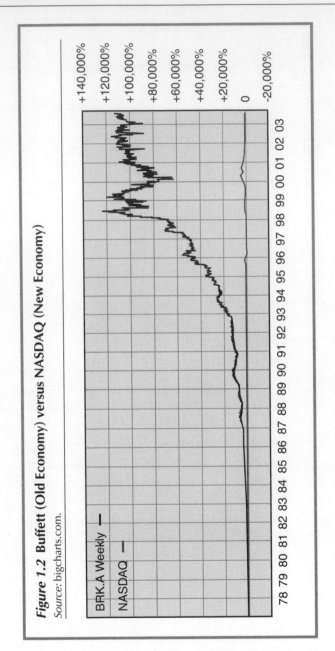

Table 1.5 Buffett vs. DJIA, 1957–1968, Most to Least Value-Added Years
Source: Buffett Partnership letters, 1957–1968.

Year	Buffett Partners	Dow	Value Added
1968	45.6	7.7	37.9
1966	16.8	(15.6)	32.4
1960	18.6	(6.2)	24.8
1965	36.9	14.2	22.7
1962	11.9	(7.6)	19.5
1957	9.3	(8.4)	17.7
1961	35.9	22.4	13.5
1963	30.5	20.6	9.9
1967	28.4	19.0	9.4
1964	22.3	18.7	3.6
1959	20.9	20.0	0.9
1958	32.2	38.5	(6.3)

Table 1.6 Buffett vs. S&P 500, 1965–2002, Most to Least Value-Added Years
Source: www.berkshirehathaway.com.

Year	Buffett	S&P 500 with Dividends	Value Added
1977	31.9	(7.4)	39.3
1981	31.4	(5.0)	36.4
1976	59.3	23.6	35.7
2002	10.0	(22.1)	32.1
1966	20.3	(11.7)	32.0
1974	5.5	(26.4)	31.9
1969	16.2	(8.4)	24.6
1998	48.3	28.6	19.7
1973	4.7	(14.8)	19.5
1982	40.0	21.4	18.6
1978	24.0	6.4	17.6
1979	35.7	18.2	17.5
1985	48.2	31.6	16.6
2000	6.5	(9.1)	15.6
1987	19.5	5.1	14.4
1965	23.8	10.0	13.8

(continued)

Table 1.6 (continued)

Year	Buffett	S&P 500 with Dividends	Value Added
1989	44.4	31.7	12.7
1992	20.3	7.6	12.7
1994	13.9	1.3	12.6
1990	7.4	(3.1)	10.5
1983	32.3	22.4	9.9
1991	39.6	30.5	9.1
1996	31.8	23.0	8.8
1970	12.0	3.9	8.1
1968	19.0	11.0	8.0
1984	13.6	6.1	7.5
1986	26.1	18.6	7.5
2001	(6.2)	(11.9)	5.7
1995	43.1	37.6	5.5
1993	14.3	10.1	4.2
1988	20.1	16.6	3.5
1972	21.7	18.9	2.8
1971	16.4	14.6	1.8
1997	34.1	33.4	0.7
1980	19.3	32.3	(13.0)
1975	21.9	37.2	(15.3)
1967	11.0	30.9	(19.9)
1999	0.5	21.0	(20.5)

Figure 1.3 **Berkshire Total Annual Earnings**
Source: Berkshire Hathaway annual reports.

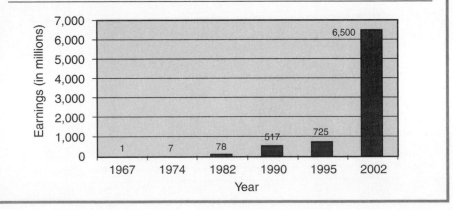

1974 were $7 million. Earnings continued to grow from $78 million in 1982, to $517 million in 1990, to $725 million in 1995, and to $6.5 billion in 2002. In essence, Berkshire's capital architect has created an unlimited source of cash and a brilliant earnings business model.

Although revenue growth has never been a goal or measurement metric, it is interesting to see the dramatic growth in Berkshire's sales over time (see Figure 1.4). With Buffett's business model, sales will continue to grow because there is no restriction on the type of business or industry that Warren will add to the Berkshire Empire.

When present management took over in 1967, Berkshire Hathaway was a textile mill in New Bedford, Massachusetts, with $40 million in revenue. Through shrewd investments of its small capital base and earnings, management grew sales to $102 million in 1974, to $480 million in 1982, to $3 billion in 1991, to $4.5 billion in 1995, and to $43 billion in 2002.

Warren is unique in measuring himself annually against changes in book value (the simple calculation of assets minus liabilities), as shown in Figure 1.5. He then compares this annual percentage against the S&P 500 with dividends to determine if he has added value or not. Buffett has not only added value. He has done the remarkable, by more than doubling the returns of the S&P 500.

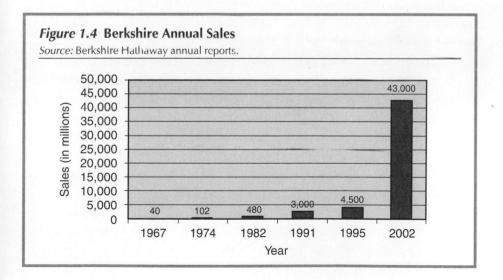

Figure 1.4 **Berkshire Annual Sales**
Source: Berkshire Hathaway annual reports.

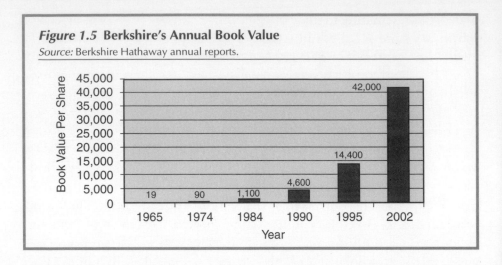

Figure 1.5 **Berkshire's Annual Book Value**
Source: Berkshire Hathaway annual reports.

Berkshire Hathaway is the largest domestic publicly traded corporation not included in the S&P 500 index. The reason is that management controls such a significant amount of stock and shareholders sell so infrequently that the stock is considered illiquid. If it is added to the S&P 500 index, which it will be one day, the price will skyrocket as mutual funds, institutions, and indexes add it to their portfolios.

Buying earnings of companies at attractive prices with outstanding management and with remarkable competitive advantages have all led to mind-boggling increases in book value.

Another metric that Warren Buffett never reports or comments on is the actual market price of his stock. He reports on the value of his business because he can control purchases, ongoing management, asset purchases and sales, liabilities, and other things that affect changes in book value. Conversely, he ignores the share price because often it has nothing to do with what is going on inside the business. Value is inside. Price is outside.

Nevertheless, changes in the share price of Berkshire stock have been nothing but extraordinary, as shown in Figure 1.6.

You may have seen a stock's prices go from single digits to double digits and sometimes to triple digits, only to be split because Wall Street likes to lower the market price to make it more psychologically appealing. Stockbrokers like splits because they are compensated by the number of shares traded. It is fascinating to study the following charts by www.bigcharts.com, shown in Figure 1.7. Berkshire has never split its stock because management wants to attract owners rather than traders.

Most large corporations issue management stock options, which offer a natural incentive for managers to manipulate earnings, issue quarterly guidance targets, and talk about their stock price. Without stock options, Berkshire has no incentive to talk up its price.

When the Buffett Partnership first started buying shares of textile maker Berkshire Hathaway, shares were purchased for $7, giving the enterprise, with 1,017,547 outstanding shares, a total valuation of a little more than $7 million. Then, given what was going on in the business, changes in book value, and Berkshire's underlying intrinsic value, the share price has steadily marched up. According to Andy Kilpatrick's book *Of Permanent Value*, the market price of Berkshire's stock has gone from $70 in 1971, to $775 in 1982, to $7,000 in 1989, and to more than $70,000 per share in 1998.

Compounding $7 to $70 is easier than growing $70,000 to $700,000. Even though the percentages are the same, the law of large numbers increases the degree of difficulty. This result once again shows the advantage of the small investor. Using the same principles and practical methods, the same portfolio outperforms the larger one every time. The Buffett Partnerships closed with approximately $100 million in 1969, achieving superior returns to the much larger Berkshire Hathaway, with a market value over

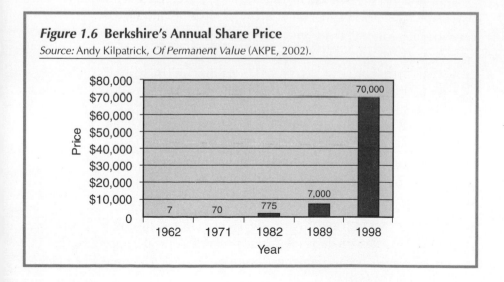

Figure 1.6 Berkshire's Annual Share Price
Source: Andy Kilpatrick, *Of Permanent Value* (AKPE, 2002).

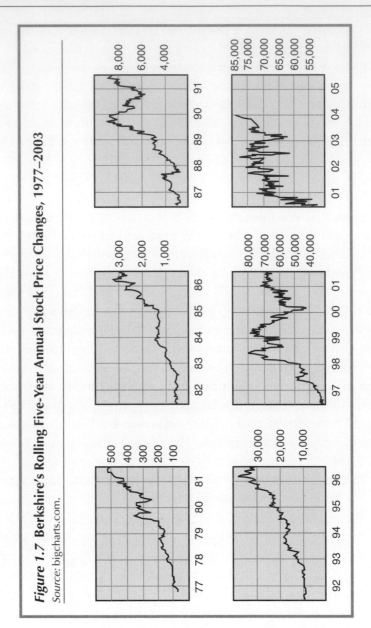

Figure 1.7 Berkshire's Rolling Five-Year Annual Stock Price Changes, 1977–2003
Source: bigcharts.com.

$100 billion today. Growing a small $10 million to $100 million is easier than it will be to increase $100 billion in market capitalization to $1 trillion. This is the most encouraging statistic for those investors willing to spend the time and effort to employ Buffett's methods. The small investor, equipped with the same Buffett principles and strategies, has far more investment opportunities than an investment company worth over $100 billion— even if the world's greatest capital allocator is at the helm.

CONCLUSION

To summarize, first you must study the best to become the best. Warren is the best at creating wealth by investing in other people's businesses. No one comes a close second. Warren studies the best in every field of endeavor. Wise investors study and understand Warren Buffett.

Second, wealth is created through owning a business. Wealth is also best preserved through owning a business. These concepts are the essence of capitalism. Warren has become the world's foremost capitalist by deploying earnings from various enterprises into the ownership of more businesses in order to generate more earnings to redeploy—a virtual snowball at the top of an economic mountain with enough time to create a huge, ever-expanding, and momentum-increasing capital avalanche.

Third, the best athletes become the best at focusing all of their gifts, time, and energy on becoming the best in their sport. Likewise, unless one has the benefit of inheritance or marriage, great fortunes have been created by an entrepreneur who focused all of his or her gifts, time, and energy on *one* business. Only one person has created billions in wealth by not only investing in someone else's business but many assorted businesses. His gift is one of identifying the right businesses and managers in which to invest. Others can do this—simple in theory and practice, but not easy. At a recent news conference, Buffett announced that if he were managing money in the millions instead of billions, he could compound money at an even faster rate—probably twice as fast—which has always been and will always be the average-investor advantage.

Warren Buffett hasn't invented anything new and doesn't own any patents. He has never started a business and has never taken on the day-to-day management of one. The Oracle of Omaha is so good that he doesn't even need to talk with management, access inside information, or even visit company headquarters of the businesses in which he invests. Assuming, however, that you study, understand, and employ the same Buffett principles, you too can achieve outstanding market-beating results. Knowledge counts more than experience and business contacts.

In the next chapter, we explore the timeline from a small boy growing up in Omaha, Nebraska, through his education years, and into his business life as an early hundred-aire, thousand-aire, millionaire, billionaire, and finally multibillionaire. His life is one of extraordinary wealth built on exemplary character traits.

Chapter 2

The Making of a Billionaire: A Timeline of Warren Buffett's Wealth-Building Lifetime

"Try not to become a man of success, but rather try to become a man of value."

—Albert Einstein

That it has taken a lifetime for Warren to build significant wealth for himself and others comes as no surprise. His wealth, because it was built on classic principles, came easy but certainly not quickly.

Warren Buffett, through his partnership, first began buying the stock of Berkshire Hathaway, a New England textile mill with $39 million in revenue in 1967, in the early to mid-1960s for prices ranging from $7 to $17 per share. Buffett and company took over management in 1965 by buying the majority of shares for less than $20 million. Over the next four decades, he grew that original investment into over $100 billion by adding little additional capital. This chapter describes the making of a billionaire—by describing every significant financial event in Warren's life, from birth to one million, then to one billion in net worth and more.

BLESSED WITH EXTRAORDINARY WEALTH-BUILDING TALENT

Maybe American author, poet, and philosopher Ralph Waldo Emerson said it best: "Man was born to be rich, or grow rich by use of his faculties, by the union of thought with nature. Property is an intellectual production. The game requires coolness, logical reasoning, promptness, and patience in the players."

As this chapter tells, Warren Buffett was not born to riches, but he was blessed with extraordinary talents. His enduring wealth, which he created during his lifetime and which he has structured to benefit future generations, was solely developed by intellectual application. He is cool, rational, decisive, and patient. This mesmerizing story tells of a man who started with his own labor and his own money and who, by the constant application of natural talent in a capitalistic system, becomes one of the world's wealthiest. The total wealth he has created is greater than the gross domestic product (GDP) of Iraq, Ethiopia, and Costa Rica, and greater than the combined GDP of Cuba, North Korea, and Yemen.

Warren Edward Buffett was born August 30, 1930, to Howard and Leila Buffett in Omaha, Nebraska. He jokingly says that he was conceived during the fall of the 1929 stock market crash because his stockbroker father had so little to do then. With a chuckle, he claims that "the irrational behavior of investors at that time is now part of his genetic code."

Warren likes to say that he and many of us have won the ovarian lottery (another way of saying he was born lucky) with just a 2 percent probability of being born white, male, and American. One simply cannot overlook the timing of being born right in the middle of a democratic and capitalistic society. Had he been born one hundred years earlier, or in a poor third-world country, or with skills other than being able to allocate capital, he would not be the subject of some thirty books, with more on the way. He was gifted with unique skills to value companies, coupled with being born during the time period that would enjoy the greatest economic expansion and would be capitalism's finest hour to date. One simply cannot underestimate the luck of being born in the United States, home of 4 percent of the world's population but one half of the world's capital and publicly traded companies, with a political and legal system that disproportionately rewards capital allocation talent over most other occupations, and during a century that experienced a sevenfold increase in the standard of living.

His good friend and Microsoft founder Bill Gates likes to tease that if Warren had been born a few centuries earlier, without the skills to run or hear very well, he would have been some wild animal's lunch. Or if Warren had been born a woman during a time that women were occupationally restricted, instead of allocating capital, as he was born to do, he would have most likely been a housewife, teacher, secretary, or nurse.

That Warren's father operated a stock brokerage company in Omaha and later became a U.S. Republican congressman from Nebraska was also good fortune. Although his father left him without an inheritance, he knew his son didn't need one. What his father did leave him was an affinity for stocks, confidence to make his own name, deeply rooted character traits, and natural political savvy that has served him well. His father also gave him a deep streak of independence, which Warren demonstrated by selecting a different political party than his father. Both have a frugal nature, but Warren's father was known to be quite serious, and his son could be a stand-up comic.

A 20 PERCENT RETURN ON INVESTMENTS—AT AGE SIX

By age six, this boy, whose grandfather and great-grandfather owned a small corner grocery store in his hometown of Omaha called Buffett and Son, was already an enterprising merchant. Warren purchased a six-pack of Coke bottles for 25 cents and sold them individually for a nickel each, setting a lifelong benchmark of a 20 percent investment return. While other kids were busy playing in the streets during hot summer nights, this industrious elementary-school student was wise enough to buy Coke from his grandfather's grocery store and hard working enough to go door-to-door selling it for a cool profit. Chapter 5, "Know What You Own," describes how this early business venture would stand him well, as his company would end up some fifty years later as the largest shareholder of Coca-Cola.

Very early in life Warren was fascinated with numbers, math, money, and coins. His sisters remember Warren carrying around at a very early age a metal moneychanger attached to his belt. To this day he can do complex math problems in his head, does not have a calculator or computer in his office, and has an overflowing assortment of gifts and mementos of stacks of play money on his desk. From the first years of his life to this day, he has been completely consumed by making money and seeing it grow.

By age eight, he began reading books about making money and business. *A Thousand Ways to Make $1,000* was an early favorite, and he read it many times. By age ten, this would-be billionaire checked out every book from the local Omaha library about investing, finance, and the stock market. Make no mistake about his gifts of memory, advanced verbal abilities, and skill with numbers; as evidence, note that he skipped a grade in elementary school.

One of Warren's first work experiences at his father's stockbroker office was marking the prices of stocks on the blackboard with chalk, which was known as "marking the board" in an age before electronic display ticker tapes. By June 1942, at eleven years old, Warren purchased his first stock while marking the board. He purchased six shares of City Service Preferred, three shares for himself and three shares for his older sister, Doris, at a cost of $38 per share. These three shares represented most of his wealth at the time, or approximately $100. The price soon fell to $27, but shortly thereafter it climbed back up to $40. Warren sold their stock, but he learned an important and early lesson when almost immediately after he sold it, the stock price shot up to over $200 per share. He probably didn't know it at the time, but this experience of selling too soon and selling based on price instead of value would form a cornerstone in his investment philosophy.

By age thirteen, already displaying an insatiable thirst for knowledge, Warren knew he wanted to be associated with the stock market. In fact, he declared to a friend of the family that he would be a millionaire by the time he turned thirty. He went further to say to Mary Falk, the wife of his father's business partner, while spooning her homemade chicken soup, that if he didn't become a millionaire, he would jump off the tallest building in Omaha.

FIRST JOB AND FIRST BUSINESS VENTURE—AT ONLY AGE FOURTEEN

He moved with his family to Washington DC for high school while his father served in Congress. He wasn't particularly happy in the nation's capital and yearned for his hometown of Omaha. His loyalty for and love of his city of birth would exhibit itself through all of his adult life.

He was, by all accounts, an ambitious and industrious teenager. This bespectacled lad with the crew cut took on five newspaper routes and delivered some five hundred newspapers. Warren soon was making $175 a month delivering the *Washington Post*.

Even today Warren enjoys delivering newspapers with his grandson. He recently admitted that it is the perfect job because you can think about whatever you want to think about while on your route.

Just as his early experience with Coca-Cola would later serve him well, so, too, would his boyhood experience with the *Washington Post*. His holding company would also end up becoming the largest outside owner of the very paper he delivered as a youngster.

He had a used-golf-ball business, which involved many youngsters in the neighborhood. At fourteen years old, he invested $1,200 of his savings, earned from his newspaper routes and other boyhood ventures, into forty acres of Nebraska farmland, which he then leased out. This investment became the first indictor that this savvy and confident fourteen-year-old could pursue and complete sophisticated and adult business deals even though he wasn't living in the state at the time. Also this venture declared, probably unintentionally and at an early age, his lifelong love of his home state of Nebraska. Characteristic of this teenage absentee real estate deal, he often invests today without even visiting the home office or state of the wholly owned subsidiary.

In his senior year of high school, Warren and a good friend, Don Danly, purchased for just $25 a used pinball machine that had an original price of $300. (As you will learn, this transaction would not be the last time he purchased a dollar of assets for less than 10 cents. He has performed this magic his whole life.) Their new company was named after a fictitious Mr. Wilson to give the teenagers an air of credibility and authority and was therefore called the Wilson Coin Operated Machine Company. The boys strategically placed their machines in nearby Washington DC barbershops.

The first night, at 5 cents a play, the machine returned somewhere between $2 and $4, an investment return that has been almost impossible to match. The boys always told the barbers that they would need to check with Mr. Wilson for placement of their machines and blamed him for any unpopular decisions they had to make, like why they weren't able to replace older machines with newer ones. At its peak, this business owned seven machines placed in different locations and earned $50 a week; the teenagers sold it later in the year for $1,200 to a war veteran. Once again, this experience would serve Warren well, when four decades later, his company became the largest shareholder of one of the world's largest vending-machine operators, The Coca-Cola Company.

As a side note, even today, as a gift from a shareholder, Warren has the name of his boyhood vending machine business displayed on his auto license plate holder: the Wilson Coin Operated Machine Company.

Buffett's Dividend Policy Formed as a Teenager

Warren Buffett's investment vehicle, Berkshire Hathaway, is well known for not paying a dividend. His stated policy is that he will pay out a dividend if he is not able to create one dollar in market value for every dollar retained.

On the occasion of Warren's seventieth birthday party, several shareholders along with his teenage buddy and business partner Don Danly (now deceased) surprised him with an original version of one of his first business ventures: a pinball machine.

This machine, made of wood, was from an era before side flippers. The player put in a nickel (remember those days?), received five metal balls, pulled back the spring loaded pin, shot a ball and held the sides of the machine to guide the ball into the higher scoring holes.

When Warren was presented with the machine of his youth, he pulled off the front panel to check the tilt just like an old pro, put in a nickel, and skillfully moved the machine back and forth.

After the first nickel play, Warren quipped, "This pinball business is just like Berkshire; you put money in and you don't get anything back."

Warren graduated high school at age sixteen and had a self-made net worth of $6,000. He was then and is still now living way below his income and net worth. By age sixteen, he had already read one hundred business books. Even today, he continues to be a ravenous reader and often consumes a book in one sitting. At one point in his life, he read as many as five books per day. He recently quantified his reading as five times more than the average reader and, most likely, five times more than the average investor, with just about every publicly traded annual report read and on file in his stockroom. His high-school yearbook said he was good in math and, following in the footsteps of his father, that he would be a future stockbroker. His parents paid for his college, allowing him to save and invest his growing fortune.

COLLEGE YEARS: THE BEGINNING OF THE VALUE INVESTING PHILOSOPHY

Warren enrolled originally at the University of Pennsylvania, but he later transferred and graduated in 1950 with a bachelor of science in economics from the University of Nebraska, in Lincoln. He has always had an affinity towards Nebraska, maybe because his parents met at this same university and campus. As a college senior, he read *The Intelligent Investor*, written by his future graduate school professor, employer, and lifelong mentor, Benjamin Graham. Reading this book was like an epiphany, the beginning of an investment philosophy that is simply known as value investing. Its central idea is that an investment is best when the buyer is most businesslike and invests without emotion, fear, or by following trends or fads.

By age nineteen, Warren's wealth was $9,800. He applied to but was rejected by Harvard Business School for graduate study in economics. Although he was disappointed, this setback turned out to be another gift, because he learned that the author of *The Intelligent Investor*, Benjamin Graham, taught at Columbia, and he was accepted and enrolled there. As good fortune would have it, both Ben Graham and David Dodd were professors at Columbia; they were co-authors of the 735-page book *Security Analysis*, which Buffett recommends for all participants in the stock market who need to learn how to properly value companies *before* they can determine if the price offered is attractive.

In 1951, at the age of twenty-one, Warren discovered that his mentor, Graham, served as chairman of the board of directors of GEICO auto insurance. If Graham was involved with this investment, Buffett instinctively knew he had to learn more about it. Warren took the train from New York City to Washington DC and learned firsthand from an executive working on a Saturday all about the direct auto insurance business. This early experience would also help him understand the company that he would one day own in its entirety.

One of the principal ingredients of building Buffett Wealth is to know so much about an investment that you are able to figure out its intrinsic value: how it makes money, the durability of its earnings, what its weaknesses are, opportunities for future growth, the strength of its competitors, and the honesty and competence of its management.

Warren's visit to GEICO's headquarters would help him understand all of these factors and more. With this hard work he would later know that this investment was attractively priced in relation to its true value; as a result, he invested in it all of his net worth, or $10,282. Without this hands-on research, college-age Buffett would not have the confidence to invest 100 percent in one stock, another key principle to his wealth-building success. He sold his GEICO stock one year later for $15,259 only because he found a more attractive stock, another investment method employed by super-investors.

Warren knew so much about GEICO that he wrote a research report for *The Commercial and Financial Chronicle* at the age of twenty-one titled, "The Security I Like Best." His research taught him that GEICO earned five times more than its competitors mainly because of its business model of direct selling without an agent. He knew this company so well that in 1976 Berkshire bought one third of the company for $45.7 million, which would later grow to one-half ownership because of stock buybacks or re-purchases by the company. In 1995 Berkshire bought the other half that it didn't own for $2.3 billion, adding it to an ever-growing list of wholly owned subsidiaries.

Warren graduated with a master's degree in economics in 1951. He wanted to work on Wall Street, but both his father Howard and his mentor, Graham, urged him not to. The two most influential men in Warren's life had lived through the Depression and intimately understood the ups and downs of the stock market. They both advised the young and ambitious graduate to seek job security and work for a large noninvestment-related company. Both of his mentors thought the stock market was over valued. He would ignore their advice.

Warren offered to work for Benjamin Graham for free doing stock research and analysis, but Graham refused, even though Warren was the only student to earn an A+ in Security Analysis from Graham. Warren jokingly said that his professor did a quick cost-benefit analysis and determined that even if Warren worked for free, it would not be a very good deal. Actually the real reason he wasn't initially hired is that the Graham Newman partnership had a policy of hiring Jews to counterbalance the lack of employment opportunities elsewhere on Wall Street. So instead, Warren returned home to Omaha and, as luck would have it, began dating Susan Thompson, his sister's college roommate.

SELECTING THE RIGHT MENTORS AND HABITS

"Tell me who your heroes are and I will tell you what kind of person you will be," Warren suggests to student audiences. He goes on, "At first the chains of habit are too light to be felt and then later, too heavy to be broken." Just as heroes define you, so do your habits.

To capture his listeners' imaginations, Warren further suggests to students to select a classmate that they would want to have 10 percent of their future earnings. Chances are it isn't the peer with the most intelligence, the best athlete, or even the best looking. The likely choice is the classmate with the right mentors, the right habits, and the right values and principles. Integrity stands for the most, and your peers know best whom they can trust.

Continuing the exercise, Warren suggests that students identify in their minds the person they would sell short, or the person who they would least like to have 10 percent of their future earnings. That person may be the peer with the least amount of integrity and character.

He recommends the practice of observing and writing down those characteristics and traits that you admire, and as long as you start soon enough, all of them can be part of your makeup and mind-set. Similarly, if you make a list of habits you admire, you too can have those same habits. Building character is not a function of station in life, privilege, status, parentage, or wealth, but rather the simple choices that everyone has available to them.

At an age when most teenagers are selecting sports and entertainment heroes, Warren's internal and instinctual guide had him select his father and Ben Graham as his mentors. Instead of baseball star Joe DiMaggio and or musical entertainer Elvis, Warren chose a stockbroker and politician and a value-oriented professor, from whom he received his values, principles, ethics, and bargain recognition skills.

We all make choices regarding mentors and habits. Those choices define us. Fortunately we can change. Change, however, is easier when we are young, which may be why Warren talks exclusively to college students. Selecting the right mentors and developing extraordinary work and discipline habits have ultimately led to Warren's having the respect of hundreds of thousands of partners, shareholders, employees, managers, suppliers, and even competitors.

EARLY CAREER: STOCK BROKER

Warren began working as a stockbroker at his father's small local company, Buffett and Falk, and he began teaching a night class at the University of Omaha, coincidentally titled Investment Principles. At twenty-one, the students were twice his age. But Warren wasn't focused solely on his financial success. He married his sister's college roommate Susie in 1952. They moved into a modest apartment (only $65 a month), and a year later had their first of three children. It was rumored that he brought along and reread Graham's *Security Analysis* during his honeymoon automobile trip to California.

While working for his father, Buffett kept in touch with Graham and sent him his stock research and stock picks, which included his first pick: GEICO auto insurance. Then, in 1954, Ben Graham called Warren and offered the twenty-four-year-old a job at his partnership located in New York City. Buffett's starting salary was $12,000 a year—at the time less than the average major league baseball player earning $13,800, but considerably more than the starting salary of $5,000 for a New York schoolteacher. Two years later, Graham decided to retire and folded up his partnership.

With two years' apprenticeship under Graham, Buffett was now ready to step out on his own investment partnership in his favorite hometown. Since leaving college six years earlier, Warren's personal net worth had grown from $9,800 to more than $140,000—by underspending his income and making extraordinary value investments, some back then priced at one times earnings (or paying $1 for stocks earning $1 per year), absolutely amazing for a twenty-six-year-old.

Table 2.1 offers a timeline that shows Buffett's accumulation of wealth, beginning at age eleven, when he bought his first shares of stock (which netted him $114), to age seventy-two, when his wealth was valued at more than $36 billion.

Table 2.1. Buffett Wealth by Age
Source: Buffett Partnership letters and Berkshire annual reports.

Age	Significant Event/Investment	Wealth
11	Purchases three shares of Cities Service Preferred at $38	$114
13	Declares he will be millionaire by age thirty Makes $175 month delivering newspapers	
14	Purchases forty acres of Nebraska farmland for $1,200 Eventually earns $5,000 from newspaper route	$5,000
16	Purchases used pinball machines for $25 Begins venture named the Wilson Coin Operated Machine Company Sells company for $1,200 Graduates high school. Enters college	$6,000
19	Graduates college in three years Reads Ben Graham's *The Intelligent Investor*	$9,800
20	Begins master's degree from Columbia University Taught security analysis by Ben Graham	

Table 2.1. *(continued)*

Age	Significant Event/Investment	Wealth
21	Takes train to GEICO auto insurance to learn about the company from management	$19,738
	Graduates Columbia with master's in economics and begins work as a stockbroker for his father's Omaha company	
	Begins teaching Investment Principles at local college	
24	Begins work for $12,000 a year as a security analyst for Ben Graham's company, Graham Newman, in NYC	
26	Graham closes partnership; Warren moves back to Omaha	
	Begins investment partnership with $100 of his own money and $105,000 from family and friends and working from a home office	$140,000
27	Purchases Omaha home for $31,500. Still owns and lives in it today	$315,000
28	Doubles partners original investment	
30	Reaches boyhood goal and becomes a millionaire	$1,000,000
32	Buffett partners worth $7.2 million	
	Begins buying Berkshire Hathaway for $7 per share	$1,400,000
33	Buffett Partners become largest shareholders of Berkshire	$2,400,000
34	Begins buying American Express for $35 per share, a $13 million investment	$3,400,000
35	Buffett Partners worth $26 million	
	Buys 5 percent of Disney for $4 million	
	Takes control of Berkshire Hathaway	$7,000,000
36	Buys for the first time a business in its entirety—Baltimore department store Hochschild, Kohn & Co.	$8,000,000
37	Buffett partners worth $65 million	
	American Express investment worth $33 million	
	Begins transforming Berkshire into an insurance company; purchases National Indemnity for $8.6 million	$10,000,000
38	Buffett partners earn $40 million, now worth $104 million	
39	In thirteen years, Buffett partners earn 29.5 percent per year	
	Closes Buffett partnerships; pays out shares of Berkshire Hathaway to partners	
	Warren owns nearly one-half of Berkshire stock or 483,000 shares	
	Purchases Illinois National Bank for $15.5 million	$25,000,000
40	Becomes chairman of Berkshire and begins writing letters to shareholders	
	Berkshire earns just $45,000 from its original textile business and $4.7 million in insurance, banking, and investments	

(continued)

Table 2.1. *(continued)*

Age	Significant Event/Investment	Wealth
43	Purchases 15 percent of The Washington Post Companies for $11 million	$34,000,000
44	Loses almost one half of his net worth with a declining stock price	$19,000,000
47	Purchases the *Buffalo News* for $32.5 million	$67,000,000
49	Salary $50,000 and Berkshire trades at $290 share	$140,000,000
52	Berkshire shares trade at $775	$376,000,000
53	Berkshire shares trade at $1,310; joins Forbes 400 richest Purchases 80 percent of Nebraska Furniture Mart for $55 million	$620,000,000
55	Closes original Berkshire textile mills	
56	Berkshire shares $3,000 each; becomes billionaire	$1,400,000,000
58	Buys 8 percent of Coca-Cola for $1 billion; Berkshire becomes its largest shareholder Berkshire's price $4,800 per share	$2,300,000,000
59	Berkshire at $8,000	$3,800,000,000
66	Berkshire at $35,000; Buffett named world's richest	$16,500,000,000
72	Berkshire at $75,000 Now owns one hundred diverse wholly owned businesses	$35,700,000,000

LAUNCHING A LIMITED INVESTING PARTNERSHIP

So Warren returned home to Omaha from New York City and launched a small investment partnership, limited to family and friends. This home-based business consisted initially of only seven partners, who contributed a total of $105,000. Buffett himself invested only $100. Without a formal office, a secretary, or even a calculator, the Buffett partnership would earn 29.5 percent per year over the next thirteen years without ever experiencing a down year. Warren's oldest child and only daughter, Susie, likes to tell the story that when she was young, she thought her father was in the home-alarm business because he worked at home and was a security analyst.

In 1957, with his wife about to have their third child, Warren purchased a five-bedroom stucco house on Farnam Street. It cost $31,500, representing 10 percent of his net worth. He still lives in the same house today. This investment is telling of a would-be billionaire, whose core philosophy is to save, invest, and buy only when it represents 10 percent of one's net worth, instead of what most of us do, which is to save 100 percent of a 20 percent down payment on a house and sign up for thirty years of debt for the other 80 percent we don't own. It's also telling that this home represents Warren's philosophy to "buy to keep" and "not for sale at any price." With no intention of ever selling, he will die owning that home, just as he will die owning his company, Berkshire Hathaway.

With his principles and philosophy, Buffett has attracted like-minded shareholders. Most have a cost basis of $17 and have owned the stock for over twenty-seven years. With his communication and corporate policies, Warren does everything possible to attract and keep owners of his stock that plan to die owning Berkshire.

Warren surprised no one when he reached his goal of becoming a millionaire by age thirty. By 1962, the Buffett partnership, which had begun with $105,000, was worth $7.2 million. He moved into a nearby office high-rise (also on Farnam Street, some twenty blocks from his home), where he still operates today with very few employees. In the early 1960s, he discovered, like most of his investments, with careful reading and research, a textile manufacturing firm based in New Bedford, Massachusetts, called Berkshire Hathaway. He began buying the stock for $7 per share, which was a substantial discount to its $17 in book value with very little debt: a prime example of value investing. By 1963, the Buffett Partnership was its largest shareholder.

BUILDING A PORTFOLIO OF STOCKS

In 1965, Buffett began to purchase stock in the Walt Disney Company, after meeting with Walt personally. Like GEICO back then, Warren preferred to meet with management before making a substantial investment. Today he learns all that he needs to know by reading public documents and doesn't need to talk with management or visit. Warren's initial purchase was 5 percent of Disney, for $4 million. It is interesting to note that if he had had the money, Warren could have purchased all of Disney for $80 million compared to a market value of $40 billion today.

Had he held on to that initial investment in Disney it would be worth $2 billion today or an 18 percent annual return on investment (not including dividends). It is profound to imagine that the price of the whole company then ($80 million) would buy today only a roller coaster at one of its theme parks. At the time of Buffett's investment, Disney had spent $17 million on its Pirates-themed amusement ride for Disneyland and had already produced some two hundred animated movies, so it wasn't difficult for Warren, or anyone else taking the time to do the research, to see the true value. Recognizing the same value today, he would undoubtedly buy the whole company, which is his preferred choice if he has the cash available. That same year, he took control of Berkshire, which would become his holding company and investment vehicle.

By age thirty-six, Warren was worth $7 million. One year later, his net worth was $10 million, and his investment partnership was worth $65 million. Rather amazingly, at the age of thirty-eight, his partnership earned more than $40 million in one year, bringing the total value to $104 million in 1968.

In 1969, following his most successful year, Buffett closed the partnership and liquidated its hundred-million-dollar portfolio to his partners because he felt that he could no longer find excellent value investments in a runaway bull market while partner expectations were sky high. (One of the secrets to Warren's success is to constantly lower the expectations of his partners/shareholders.) Among the assets paid out to his partners were shares of Berkshire Hathaway. Warren's personal stake stood at $25 million. He was only thirty-nine years old, and he owned nearly one half of Berkshire.

At this time he also started writing the annual letters to Berkshire shareholders, which have become the most widely read of all publicly traded reports, probably because of Buffett's extraordinary success at building wealth for himself and his shareholders and for his simple explanations, honesty, and down-home humor. He had thirteen years experience writing to his partners and telling them what was going on inside their partnership, so it was natural for him to continue writing to his shareholders, whom he has always treated as partners. Buffett's annual letter has become the tool for him to explain corporate philosophies and ultimately attract the type of owners that he desires.

Another defining moment for Buffett was shifting from building wealth through his partnership to instead building wealth within a publicly traded corporation. He went from knowing and selecting his partners to having a company open to anyone and everyone. Under a partnership, the general partner could select the partners he wanted. With a public corporation, owners selected him, and his job was to have the right ones select and the right ones stay. He does this by corporate owner–related principles and communications, mainly his annual letter to shareholders.

That same year Berkshire earned $45,000 from textile operations and more than ten times that—$4.7 million—in insurance, banking, and investments. Here was still another defining moment: Warren began to take the earnings from his insurance and operating companies and use the proceeds to purchase other businesses, which created a huge circle of wealth. In essence, this method is how he built his company to what it is today.

In a nutshell, Berkshire invests in businesses that have earnings, and it takes those earnings and reinvests in more companies with even greater earnings. He manages each wholly owned business and its manager like it was partly owned or similar to a stock portfolio. Berkshire also has over $40 billion in insurance float (premiums paid before claims are made against it or money available for investment) to invest in other enterprises, creating even more earnings. Some call Berkshire a capital allocating machine.

Consider this: In 1967 Berkshire had $40 million in sales (mainly textiles) and $1 million in earnings. More recently the company would produce $66 billion in sales and over $6 billion in annual earnings. Buffett now needs to allocate over $150 million in weekly cash flow.

In 1971, the NASDAQ, representing mostly technology stocks that Berkshire has avoided, was launched starting at 100. Berkshire was selling for $71 that same year. In 1973, with a declining stock market, Berkshire purchased and became the largest shareholder of The Washington Post Companies, approximately thirty years after Warren was an independent newspaper boy. The Post Companies is an investment that he still owns today, and the annual dividend of $9 million paid to Berkshire is almost equal to its original purchase price.

A year later, in 1974, during the oil crisis, Warren lost half his net worth in a bear market. By 1979, with the stock market recovered, Berkshire was trading at $290 per share, bringing Warren's net worth, at the age of forty-nine, to $140 million, though he was still living on a salary of $50,000 per year, without ever selling a share of Berkshire or using stock options to gain more.

Within four years, by investing in excellent value stocks and using the float from his insurance companies and the earnings of his wholly owned subsidiaries, Berkshire had $1.3 billion in its corporate stock portfolio. Berkshire began 1983 at $775 per share and ended up at $1,300 per share. Warren's personal net worth was $620 million at that time, and he was more than half way toward becoming a billionaire. He joined the newly formed Forbes 400 richest list.

BECOMING A BILLIONAIRE

In 1985, because of cheaper foreign labor and overseas competitors, Buffett closed the Berkshire Textile Mills, the original business, which by then was worth nothing more than its name. A year later, Berkshire hit $3,000 per share, making Warren a billionaire at the age of fifty-six.

Also, by 1988, at the age of fifty-eight, Warren took his boyhood business of selling Coke full circle: he began buying stock in The Coca-Cola Company, eventually purchasing up to 8 percent of the company for $1 billion. He is now the largest shareholder of a boyhood business (which, if you remember, earned him 20 percent returns on his money back in 1936). Coke was buying back its own stock at that time, and Warren was impressed with the Coca-Cola management. He began to accumulate the stock at $5 per share. Unlike technology stocks, he understood the contents of a can of Coca-Cola, understood how the business made money, recognized its worldwide competitive advantage, and like all the other brilliant investment moves he has made, knew that earnings would continue and likely increase.

Contrary to widely held beliefs, he didn't contact Coca-Cola management or receive any inside information on his billion-dollar purchase. All of his information and research was obtained from sources available to the general public. It didn't make sense for him to contact management, since Coke was buying back its own stock and Warren wanted to buy as much as he could. When he was finished buying what is now 200 million shares of Coke, management was very relieved to learn that it was Berkshire and Buffett and not some other takeover artist or greenmailer. (The name "greenmail," derived from "blackmail," represents a situation where an unfriendly takeover attempt is terminated with a premium price, usually higher than the current stock price.) Although he respected management or he would not have purchased the stock, management also knew that Warren would not seek control of the company or request any management changes. Instead he was offered and accepted a seat on the board of directors and continues to support, encourage, and help management, not hinder it. His oldest son, Howard, is a board member of Coca-Cola Enterprises, its bottling operation.

Coke owns 70 percent of the worldwide soft-drink beverage business, selling over one billion eight-ounce servings per day. Buffett looks to invest in franchise stocks with wide competitive moats around them. If you offered him $100 billion to take away the soft drink leadership of Coke, he would give you the money back and tell you it couldn't be done. Buffett purchased Coke because it was an excellent value investment that happened to have excellent managers. He understood the business, and the business dominated its market.

Note the irony in the full circle of the businesses in Warren's investment life. Coca-Cola, the *Washington Post*, and GEICO each played a role in Warren's youth, and he owned each as an adult. He also came full circle with ownership of a textile mill, taking the earnings and investing them in other businesses, which generated earnings to help acquire more businesses.

By 1988, he owned many diverse businesses, adding four to five more each year. He was also a billionaire many times over, and he was known as "the Oracle of Omaha," "the Prophet of Profit." Warren is followed and studied more than any other successful financier in time, and he is listened to with the same degree of interest as the chairman of the Federal Reserve. Just the mere rumor, true or untrue, that Buffett is buying a certain stock will send it up. Some have even resorted to floating the Buffett rumor in order to bring attention to their stock or a Wall Street deal.

With a 29.55 percent average annual return for thirteen years with the Buffett Partnerships and a 22.6 percent average annual return with Berkshire over the past thirty-eight years compared to 11 percent for the S&P 500, there is no close second place to Buffett's fifty-year investment record.

He has grown sales of Berkshire Hathaway from some $40 million to more than $66 billion today. Warren Buffett is undoubtedly the greatest architect of economic value ever known in a free capitalistic society. He is a genius, born with the great luck of time and place, combining math and business skills with character traits of patience, discipline, confidence, frugality, rationality, and fierce independence. While these traits are common, they are difficult to achieve in practice, particularly in an economic environment of commercialism and consumerism.

Moreover, Buffett reached his peak during the greatest capitalistic expansion ever known (with the Dow Jones Industrial Average starting the century at 66 and closing its one-hundred-year run at 11,000), with investment principles fit perfectly for all economic conditions. J. P. Morgan said the principal judgments in business are those concerning character. Warren is a living and breathing example that you, too, can create wealth over your lifetime, with simple investments in old-economy stocks, and without compromising your character or your principles.

CONCLUSION

This chapter offered a timeline of how Warren built his wealth. Hopefully it has been an inspiration to you, to show that you, too, can build wealth if you follow many of the principles and practical methods of Warren Buffett.

The takeaway exercises for this chapter are to:

- Begin investing and building wealth early.

- Have confidence.

- Understand accounting and how business works.

- Set goals.

- Save, invest, and live below your income.

- Read and study businesses over many decades before you invest.

- Be a *business* analyst, not a *market* analyst.

- Concern yourself with what is going on *inside* a business, and free yourself of any concern with what is going on in the outside markets.

- Learn to *value* businesses and purchase pieces of them for below what you think they are worth.

- Make a list of traits that you admire in others, and before you know it you will become the person you want to be.

- Create another list of character traits that you don't admire, which will also remind you of the person you don't want to be.

- Write down the habits you want to develop; for example, hard work, integrity, persistence, daily reading, answering the phone with a smile, responding to correspondence the same day you get it, having a positive outlook, devising creative solutions to every problem, listening, asking, resisting unsolicited and self-interested advice.

- Select your mentors carefully. They say A managers hire A people, and B managers hire C people. If you build a team of people who are bigger than you, before you know it you will have a team of giants. Follow Warren's example, and let your mentors guide you throughout your wealth-building endeavors. Maybe you have had the Buffett luck of having a father or mother that you respect and admire, who has helped you establish the right foundation with principles and values. If not, maybe some other adult figure in your life has become your mentor and guiding light. Hopefully you have come across a teacher, instructor, boss, or professor who has also helped you recognize what you have a passion for and what turns you on.

- Finally, look at what point in Warren's biography you can best relate to, and think about all the things you did in your own childhood that were enterprising. Maybe, like Warren, you had a newspaper route, a used golf ball business, experience helping your father, and/or a simple vending machine enterprise. Then, identify what passions you have that could create wealth. We'll pursue those in future chapters like Chapter 5, "Know What You Own," and Chapter 6, "Invest in Main Street, Not Wall Street."

The next chapter asks the question, what kind of investor are you? Do you enjoy the day-to-day process of investing like Warren Buffett does? Or do you prefer to delegate the reading, research, and decisions needed to become an extraordinary superinvestor?

Chapter 3

What Kind of Investor
Are You?

"The most difficult thing in life is to know yourself."

—Thales

Your answer to the question in the chapter title determines your ability to create wealth. This question is probably the first and most important one that you should ask yourself when learning how to build wealth like Warren Buffett. The answer is even more important.

This chapter describes various types of investor personalities and various approaches to investing. You need to ask yourself if you are a *passive* investor (i.e., not wanting or enjoying the day-to-day activity of evaluating investments) or an *active* investor (i.e., a hands-on, fascinated, energetic participant who enjoys extensive reading and learning about all things related to finance, business, the economy, and the investment world). Ask yourself if you are an *investor* (a long-term owner of a business) or a *trader* (a short-term owner of a stock). It was an important revelation to Warren Buffett, while still a teenager, to understand the single most important building block to his phenomenal wealth: the difference between a stock market *speculator* and a business *owner*.

STOCK SPECULATORS VS. BUSINESS OWNERS

An owner is concerned with what's going on *inside the business*—with its employees, customers, strategic plan, growth and sales, expense and cost reduction, as well as increasing profits and earnings. In contrast, a speculator is more concerned about what is going on outside the business or the *stock's market price*: the speculator buys something today in order to sell it later for a higher price. "The sooner, the better" is the motto of every trader and speculator. Speculators focus on the price, and owners focus on the business. Speculators are *market* analysts; owners are *business* analysts.

By definition, Buffett never purchases from speculators, turnaround specialists, or managers selling a business to the highest bidder (at auction). Under Buffett's acquisition criteria, management must come along with every deal (Berkshire has no managers in waiting). The managers of the business are just as, if not more, important than the price paid for the business. The world's greatest investor is attracted only to those self-defined businesses managed by those who care more for long-term business and employment survival than short-term highest price.

An effective way to tell the difference between an owner and a speculator is to simply look at his or her office. The goods and services of a business surround an owner. Warren's small office displays framed stock certificates, including American Express and its predecessor Wells Fargo, numerous commemorative bottles of Coke, books, annual reports, and in the corner, an old-fashioned glass-bubble ticker-tape machine.

Another true sign of owner mentality is displayed on the front of Warren's desk; a stack of business cards with a toll-free number for GEICO auto insurance. This business owner surrounds himself with what he owns. A box of Sees chocolates greets visitors and is sampled by the small staff. Coke products are available by a fountain dispenser in the file room, next to file cabinets holding annual reports from just about every publicly traded corporation, including Coca-Cola. Shaw Carpet is in the hallway and office suite of his executive offices. Warren doesn't even have a calculator or computer in his office (although he has one at home for research and to play bridge on the Internet).

In contrast, a trader and speculator's office typically has a computer screen, maybe several, with flashing ticker symbols and the latest stock picks ready to be sold at the click of a mouse. A trader is likely to have an addictive personality, is quite possibly superstitious and prefers games of luck over games of skill. "Calling a trader an investor," writes Buffett, "is like calling a person who engages in frequent one-night stands a romantic."

VALUE INVESTING VERSUS FOLLOWING THE MADNESS OF CROWDS

Many differentiate between being a value investor or a growth investor. Warren says they are joined at the hip. After all, what is investing but laying out money today in order for a greater return later on? If you take away just one thing from this book, let it be the concept that *all* intelligent investing is value investing.

You may want to ask yourself a few questions to determine if you are an owner or a trader. Are you concerned with the present and future earnings of a business, or are you evaluating only its price? Are you influenced by reading and research? Or do others influence you? Warren Buffett and most value investors are by nature independent thinkers and get little satisfaction by being with the "in" crowd. They do their own research and read nonstop. They observe others but do not follow, taking great delight in choosing their own path.

An important step is to do some self-discovery to determine your investment expectations, your time frame, and your risk tolerance.

The old school of investment thought, asset allocation, and risk is that when you are young you should invest much more heavily in the stock market than in bonds, and this emphasis should shift the older you get and the closer you are to retirement. Marital and life factors are also a factor; that is, whether you are single, married with children, or retired should all play a part in determining your asset allocation and the number of businesses you would like to own.

The Buffett School of thought is that no matter what your life factors are, you should buy quality and buy cheap, whether the value is in fixed income (bonds) or stock. The Buffett School wisdom is that risk is not in the volatility of the investment but rather the lack of knowledge of the participant or simply not knowing what you are doing.

Table 3.1 compares the market, which is the collective action of over 50 million investment participants in the United States alone plus the rest of the world, versus the methods and principles of the world's greatest investor.

WHY YOU NEED TO INVEST IN A BUSINESS

The Barnes Foundation of Philadelphia provides an excellent example of how the ownership of a business created wealth and how the foundation's

Table 3.1 **Market's versus Buffett's Approach to Investing**

Market	Buffett
Crowd	Individual
Emotional	Intelligent
Price	Value
Diversification	Concentration
Speculator	Owner
Traitor	Loyalist
High costs and taxes	Low costs and taxes
Trading	Reading
6 months of ownership	Lifetime ownership

strict rules against business ownership bankrupted the very fund set up to ensure its perpetual longevity. This example, offered by François Rochon of Giverny Capital, has become an excellent lesson to those pursuing wealth creation, wealth transfer, and wealth preservation. As Ralph Waldo Emerson wrote, "It requires a great deal of boldness and a great deal of caution to make a great fortune, and when you have it, it requires ten times as much skill to keep it."

The Barnes Foundation was established in 1922 by the eccentric Dr. Albert C. Barnes to "promote the advancement of education and the appreciation of the fine arts." Little did he realize that by restricting the foundation to government bonds only, his foundation inadvertently has promoted the advancement and education and the appreciation of stock investments.

Dr. Albert Barnes created wealth by starting a pharmaceutical business and developing a blockbuster drug. He discovered, patented, and manufactured an antiseptic product called Argyrol, a silver-based compound used to fight eye infections. Near the beginning of the last century, the medication was used throughout the world, until the introduction of antibiotics, to prevent blindness in newborn infants. Because of his business ownership and patent, Barnes was a millionaire by the time he was thirty-five.

Barnes's business success allowed him to further his interest in art. Because he read every book on the subject of art and art appreciation, Barnes was able to buy art like a value investor, for pennies on the dollar. He bought unheralded masterpieces for bargain prices.

In 1922, Barnes created and funded the Barnes Foundation in Philadelphia and transferred 710 paintings—including many by Picasso—

from his personal collection, along with an endowment of $10 million to maintain it in perpetuity. The eccentric millionaire also established strict rules for his foundation. Having sold his business prior to the 1929 stock market crash and having witnessed many fortunes wiped out as a result, he stipulated that his foundation could only invest his foundation's endowment in government bonds. Little did Barnes realize at the time that because of inflation, this no-stock-investment mandate would almost destroy his foundation, the very capital designed to preserve his art collection and museum and pay for its annual operating costs (see Figure 3.1).

It is interesting to compare more than fifty years later, after his death from an auto accident in 1951, what would have happened to the operating fund of the Barnes Foundation if instead of $10 million being invested in bonds, the foundation invested its capital in stock assuming a 10 percent annual return and 3 percent annual increases in the museum's operating costs (see Figure 3.2).

The Barnes Foundation includes an extraordinary number of impressionist and postimpressionist masterpieces, including 181 works by Renoir, 69 by Cézanne, 60 by Matisse, and others by Picasso, Modigliani, Monet, Manet, and Degas. The collection of more than 2,000 pieces is valued in excess of $6 billion, some estimate as high as $25 billion. Under strict rules the foundation cannot sell any of its paintings to pay its bills.

Just as Barnes created his initial fortune by investing in ownership of a business, his foundation has seen its wealth grow with the ownership of

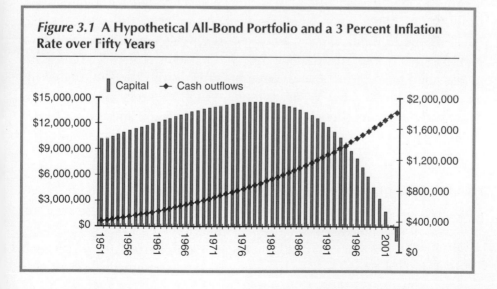

Figure 3.1 A Hypothetical All-Bond Portfolio and a 3 Percent Inflation Rate over Fifty Years

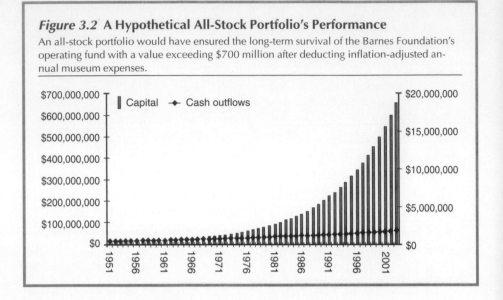

Figure 3.2 **A Hypothetical All-Stock Portfolio's Performance**

An all-stock portfolio would have ensured the long-term survival of the Barnes Foundation's operating fund with a value exceeding $700 million after deducting inflation-adjusted annual museum expenses.

master artworks. Recently, since the foundation cannot sell any of its paintings, the Barnes Foundation has rather creatively raised money for its operating expenses by loaning several of its works for a world tour.

Just like Buffett believes in investing in old-economy, everyday, common companies, products, and services, Barnes also believed in investing in art that reflected everyday life. Table 3.2 illustrates the similarities of Barnes and Buffett. Yet, although Barnes and Buffett had many similarities, Table 3.3 highlights, more importantly, their significant differences, which have allowed Buffett to grow four times the wealth over fifty years since Barnes's death. Dr. Barnes thought he was reducing risk by restricting his foundation to fixed income investments only. Instead he bankrupted his foundation, but fortunately his investment in master artwork has appreciated beyond the inflation rate.

IDENTIFYING YOUR INVESTOR PERSONALITY

Do you need income or capital growth? Maybe you're seeking low taxes? All investing starts with self-analysis and knowing yourself. Are you a risk taker? Are you conservative? Are you an ethical investor? Maybe you're contrarian? Or maybe you're just starting to invest. Maybe you have a lump

Table 3.2 Similarities between Barnes' and Buffett's Approaches to Investing

Barnes	Buffett
Read, research and understand so much about the art that you know what price is an excellent value	Read, research, and understand so much about the business that you know what price is an excellent value
Invest in art depicting the everyday common life of man	Invest in businesses used in the everyday common life of man
Preserve wealth and enjoy capital appreciation by long term investment in classic art	Preserve wealth and enjoy capital appreciation by long term investment in classic businesses
Invest in art that has stood the test of time	Invest in businesses that have stood the test of time
Created a museum to showcase his art and preserve it for future generations	Created a virtual museum (Berkshire Hathaway) to showcase his businesses and preserve each one for future generations
Strict rules against selling any art	Strict rules against selling any businesses
Museum built and showcases worldwide artists in Barnes's hometown of Philadelphia Museum open to the public but with restrictions	Berkshire built and showcases worldwide businesses in Buffett's hometown of Omaha; Berkshire open to the public but with restrictions
More for the individual than for the institutions	More for the individual than for the institutional investor
Bringing art, art appreciation and art education to the common man	Bringing investment, wealth appreciation, and wealth education to the common man
Wealth preserved and expanded by long-term ownership of master artwork	Wealth preserved and expanded by long-term ownership of master business managers and their business

sum or an inheritance, or you have a little or a lot to lose. Many variables determine what kind of investor you are. What is your personality? Do you get up early and run? Do you read all the financial information? Do you fly off to work? Would you rather sleep in, spend time with your family, and casually observe business and prefer to look at your investments annually?

Table 3.3 **Differences between Barnes' and Buffett's Approaches to Investing**

Barnes	Buffett
Sold his patent and business	Never owned a patent or operated a business; has never sold a single share of Berkshire stock; will never sell his business. Prefers to buy businesses and never sell them. Prefers to invest in businesses that have a patent, leadership, and a durable competitive advantage.
Wealth created by the ownership of a patent and the investment in master artwork	Wealth created by the ownership of many businesses, first in part and then in whole
Invested in the artwork only; did not purchase artist, succeeding artists, or the ongoing product of the artist.	Invested in the artwork (business), the painter (CEO), the succeeding painters (managers), and the earnings of the artwork (business)
Wealth is 100 percent from the ownership of rare artwork	Wealth is capital appreciation of the businesses purchased, plus succeeding management, plus expanding canvas of business opportunity, plus current and future earnings
Foundation designed to ensure the survival of Barnes's museum is strictly forbidden from investing in stocks	Culture to ensure the survival of the Berkshire museum is given complete flexibility in investing in businesses (public and private), bonds, cash, commodities and any other investment that can be purchased at a discount to its underlying value
Inflation plus fixed income investments plus time have destroyed the $10 million foundation established to last forever	Inflation plus business ownership plus a steady stream of ever-increasing earnings plus time have created enormous wealth for Berkshire shareholders

Answers to these questions reveal your investing goals and risk comfort level.

Consider the many categories of investors:

- *Faddists* want to know the latest trend. They are fun to watch and listen to because their investment style and principles change frequently.
- *Fortune Tellers* do what their psychic suggests or they read charts or

tea leaves. They are also known as *Chartists* because they look to charts to determine the likely movement of a stock's price.

- *Delegators* turn their investments over to somebody else to make the day-to-day decisions on the activities of their portfolios.
- *Validators* like to look over and approve or reject every decision that is made. They enjoy micromanaging their stockbrokers, investment managers, mutual fund managers, and corporate managers.
- *Technicians* believe that investing is more science than art. They are also known as *Mechanical Investors*, interested in the quantitative or measurable aspects of investing, with no regard to the qualitative aspects, such as management integrity.
- *Contrarians* purposely take the opposite approach no matter what the market conditions.
- *Guru Followers* approach investing with the belief that somebody wiser than they can guide them to financial heaven. They hang on every word and blindly follow every dictate of their chosen leader. If the guru goes astray, they simply choose another to follow.
- *Mountain Climbers* like to get up above and look down at the macroeconomics of what is going on in the markets. They concern themselves with what interest rates are doing and whether or not it's a bear or bull market. They are also known as *Market Analysts*.
- *Random Walkers* approach investing with the deeply held belief that whatever is known about a stock is already reflected in its price. They are also known as *Efficient Market Theorists*, believing that little can be gained from the active study of stocks and determining their true value in relation to the public price offered.
- *Lemmings* or *Momentum Players* simply follow the crowd. This group is notorious for trying to determine, sometimes in vain, sometimes with great success, what the general market is doing. They buy when everyone else is buying and sell when everyone else is selling.
- *Copycats* or *Shadowers* mimic every move that someone else is making. They are also known as *Tippers*, waiting for the latest stock tip without understanding the true essence of their investments.
- *Valuers*, which is the group that Warren Buffett belongs to, dig deeply into businesses to discover what they're really worth and determine whether or not they would like to be an owner. Valuers read. They do their own research. They listen to others but think for themselves. They always attempt to buy a dollar of assets for 50

cents, or one dollar of annual earnings for one dollar. They are a hard-working bunch, reviewing hundreds if not thousands of investment ideas before selecting one to own.

Some are *Diversifiers*, preferring to own many investments to reduce their perception of risk. Others are *Concentrators* who pile on to three or four of their best ideas. Many believe that investing should be complicated to work best. Few think that the simple approach is best.

As you can see there are as many types and combinations of investors as there are personalities. The most important thing is to match your personal traits with your investing style. And you may find that you are a combination of several styles. Most importantly, no one road leads exclusively to financial success.

PASSIVE INVESTING: A SUCCESS STORY

The most important thing is to ask yourself if you are a passive or active investor. If you are truly a passive investor, you might simply enjoy owning a mutual fund, or better yet, a low-cost index fund where a computer selects stocks for you and automatically represents what is going on in the market. Passive investors may not do any more research after they have chosen their course of action. They may simply be delegators and have better results than those who actively work their investments on a day-to-day basis. Passive investors are not necessarily following blindly but may instead carefully review their manager on an annual basis and make changes accordingly.

Passive or inactive investing, although not a method used by Warren Buffett, may be one of the smartest pathways to take.

One of the best examples of passive investing and delegating is the story of Don and Mildred Othmer. They had the good fortune to grow up in Omaha and to know of Warren. Each invested $25,000 with him in the early 1960s. Without adding to their original investment or spending their ever-increasing wealth, their investment grew to $800 million. The Othmers didn't want to read about investments or do the research. They didn't enjoy the process of evaluating companies and determining when to buy and when to sell. They delegated completely and were not able to call and question their investment manager. They were not valuators per se but hired a valuator to invest for them.

Don had been a professor of chemical engineering at Brooklyn Poly-technic University, and he and Mid didn't have any children. After their deaths, the Othmers bequeathed Don's employer $200 million, which was four times its endowment at the time and equaled about $100,000 per student. In addition, Long Island College Hospital in Brooklyn received $160 million. The University of Nebraska and the Chemical Heritage Foundation in Philadelphia each received $100 million. And there were even more recipients of the Othmers' largesse.

Their philanthropy was all possible because the Othmers were passive investors who focused on what they were good at, what they enjoyed, and their own passions, and they significantly lived below their means. The original cost basis for their shares was just $42, and it grew to some $40,000 per share when they passed away. They lived comfortably but not ostentatiously. Had one of them lived a few more years, they would have died with a billion-dollar estate and certainly as some of the richest passive delegators.

Without the Buffett Wealth, they would still be a success story. Don was born poor in Omaha and had a lifelong frugal streak. He earned money in his youth by picking dandelions and walking a farmer's cow to and from pasture. He enrolled at the University of Nebraska and ultimately received a Ph.D. from the University of Michigan. He developed forty patents for Kodak, and he also had many patents on his own. He became a professor, a consultant, and an editor of *Chemical Engineering News*, but he had absolutely no influence over his investment manager.

After Don and Mid passed away, Warren said, "We have a lot more of them to come." In other words, more Berkshire Hathaway shareholders will be passing along a great deal of the Buffett Wealth. The Othmers offer a great example of how Warren has created $2 for others from every dollar in wealth he created for himself, and how most of it will be returned back to society. More about the future of Buffett's wealth in Chapter 11.

WHAT IS ACTIVE INVESTING?

Let's clarify further the difference between being a passive investor and an active one.

A passive investor decides not to spend time or energy on investing. A passive investor may make this choice deliberately or by default. Passive investors, like Don and Mid Othmer, may have realized that they get more enjoyment and can make more money pursuing their chosen career. Certainly passivity has different degrees—from reviewing quarterly and annual results of your mutual fund, to attending the annual meeting of the companies you own, to a detailed conference with a certified financial planner every five years.

You may decide or have already decided to be an active investor and have committed yourself to studying the best by reading this book and others. An important distinction for you to understand, though, is between being an active investor and being an active trader. Buffett is an active investor but doesn't actively trade. He thinks about the investment business and choices available every day. He has a passion for the process and the business of investing.

An active investor's primary activity must be reading—a little bit of talking with other investors, managers, suppliers, customers, and competitors on the phone, but mainly doing a lot of research and independent thinking on your own. Many confuse activity with results. Sometimes when it comes to investing, the best thing you can do is to do nothing.

Buffett likes to make baseball analogies when referring to the active investment process. He says, "There are no called strikes with investing." You can sit with the bat on your shoulders all day long—all year long for that matter. You don't have to swing. Wait for the fat pitch, he advises, and then hit it out of the park. Unfortunately most active investors do not have the patience to be a super-investor.

Another benefit of active investors is that, unlike most other occupations, they never need to retire. As long as they love it and were born to value companies and allocate capital, they will probably become better with age (most athletes wish they could say that).

Passive or active—no matter what kind of investor you are, you should never put money in an investment you don't understand (a topic that is discussed in more detail in Chapter 5, "Know What You Own").

AVOID EMOTIONAL INVESTING

Always review your investment plan periodically, especially after major life changes like graduating college, getting married or divorced, having children, sending your kids to college, selling your business, and retiring. Many of your investment decisions depend on how soon you need the money. Active investors need to read, research, and understand before they act. Successful active investors are rational and logical investors, not emotional ones.

Professor Graham said, "In the short run, the stock market is a voting machine. But in the long run, it's a weighing machine." What he meant is that in the short term, stock movements are determined by popularity or lack of it. Markets in the short term are auctions, and the price is determined by the last ones to buy and sell. But in the long run, it's all about the earnings or the weight of the business you own. "Price is what you pay," says Warren, "and value is what you get."

Here's an interesting exercise. Point to yourself. Where did you point? Most people point to their heart. Few people, when given this exercise, point to their heads; so, too, it is with investments. We buy homes and automobiles based on our *emotions*, and we run into trouble doing the same thing with our investments. You need to know what kind of investor you are and purchase your investments with your head, not your heart.

Stocks and investor behavior are very unique. When stocks are on sale we stay away, and when they are overpriced we buy them all day long—which is really the exact opposite of what consumers do with any other product on the market, whether it's cars, clothes, groceries, or electronics.

Famed investor Peter Lynch once said, "If you can't convince yourself, 'When I'm down 25 percent, I'm a buyer,' and banish forever the fatal thought of 'When I'm down 25 percent, I'm a seller,' then you'll never make a decent profit in stocks. Profit in stocks goes to those who buy stocks on sale. There's no such thing as a risk-free investment." Active investors should buy stocks at wholesale prices, when they are temporarily out of favor.

Three words that summarize the investment philosophy developed by Graham and applied brilliantly by his star pupil are "margin of safety." Graham used this example: If you were a bridge engineer, you would make sure you built a thirty-thousand-ton bridge to carry ten-thousand-ton vehicles across it. With investments he would suggest buying with such a certainty of return that you can sleep very well at night. More specifically, buy a dollar of assets for 50 cents and/or a dollar of annual earnings for a dollar. Speculators do high-wire acts without the benefit of a net. They drive eleven-thousand-ton portfolios over ten-thousand-ton bridges. They are in a hurry, and their recklessness eventually becomes their downfall. You should view your investment portfolio the same way: Make sure you have a margin of safety, no matter what kind of investor you are.

WHAT IS VALUE INVESTING?

Value investing is about the careful review and calculation of a company's book value and intrinsic value and its relationship to market value. How do you tell the difference? Well, *book value* is the simple subtraction of assets from liabilities. *Intrinsic value*, on the other hand, is the challenging and artful calculation of how much the business will earn over its lifetime. Unfortunately, intrinsic value is not constant and changes all the time. Finally, *market value* is simply the stock price you are quoted or that you read in the paper.

Selena Maranjian wrote *The Motley Fool Money Guide*, in which she did an excellent job explaining the elusive calculation of intrinsic value. She gives the following example:

> What would you pay for a machine that generates $1 a year for 10 years? You wouldn't pay $10 because you would just be getting your money back over 10 years. You wouldn't pay $9 today to get $1 a year for 10 years, which would be a return of 11.1%, or 1% a year. What you would pay is determined by how much you seek in return on your investments. If you seek an 11% annual return, which happens to be the long term rate of return on equities over the last several decades, you would offer approximately one penny per day for a year, or $3.52 for this machine.

Selena goes on to explain that, in 1990, you could have purchased stock in GE for $6 a share, and in ten years, you would have gotten $6 back in the form of dividends. But you would also have a stock that had appreciated to $150 a share.

Value Investors and Baseball

In researching many of her books on value investing, Ben Graham, Warren Buffett, and Charlie Munger, author Janet Lowe discovered that value investors share a love of baseball. It is a game built on statistics and features active managerial moves as different information is discovered. Baseball requires patience of the participants; consider that it is one of the few ballgames played as a team that doesn't have a clock keeping time. Warren has studied the best baseball hitter of all time, Ted Williams, and often uses baseball analogies to make his investment points. Warren is a quarter owner of his local professional baseball team, the Omaha Royals. When he first interviewed his back-up capital allocator, Lou Simpson, they talked about investment principles and the Chicago Cubs.

Ultimately, companies are valued by their earnings. Warren thinks about stocks as though they are bonds. The only difference is that bonds have the price and the annual rate printed on the front of them. Stock certificates do not have the return printed on their face; each shareholder must figure out future returns and what price they are willing to pay for a piece of those earnings. Bonds are easier to value compared to stocks. If a ten-year bond is offered with a $1 a year return at a price of $20, then the buyer is agreeing to a 5 percent rate of return. With stocks, you need to figure out their intrinsic value without the same benefits that bonds enjoy. But for Warren, the challenge and fun are in the calculations.

After understanding how to value a stock, the second most important thing is to know how to think about stock prices. As Figure 3.3 illustrates, if you purchase a stock below its intrinsic value you have what Ben Graham referred to as a Margin of Safety.

DO YOUR OWN RESEARCH, AND BE AN INDEPENDENT THINKER

"There are two requirements for success in Wall Street," said Ben Graham during an interview. "One, you have to think correctly; and secondly, you have to think independently."

When he was asked how he learned so much about stocks, Warren said he went to the library and started with the As; he read the annual re-

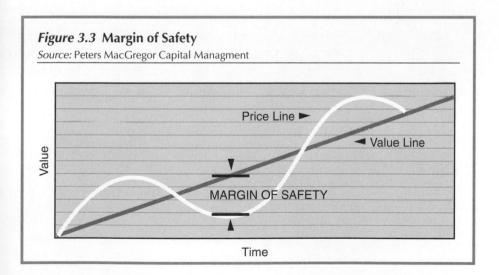

Figure 3.3 Margin of Safety
Source: Peters MacGregor Capital Managment

Price Line ►

◄ Value Line

Value

MARGIN OF SAFETY

Time

port of every public company. Ask yourself how often you follow the financial news and whether or not you enjoy being an active (daily involvement) investor, or if you prefer to be a passive investor (quarterly or annual review). Keep in mind, though, that all brilliant investors are independent thinkers.

Once asked if he subscribes to any investment newsletters, Warren quickly said no. He makes up his own mind. Each year in his annual report he lists his acquisition criteria and tells his readers and shareholders that he isn't interested in getting advice on any publicly traded stocks. He already knows about them and has formed an opinion. He does solicit letters about private companies that may be for sale that fit his simple investment criteria: $50 million in consistent annual earnings, little debt, managers in place, simple business, and an offering price.

Buffett does subscribe to Valueline (a stock data and rating publication) and many daily newspapers and business publications. He references Valueline for the top-half data, not the bottom-half editorial. He makes up his own mind as to the value of a business and if it is trading at a discount to that value.

If you follow the market, you will probably achieve the same results as the market. You must act differently to see different results (good or bad) than the market. You must do your own research and make up your own mind. You must reject the madness of crowds. The best route to average returns is to follow the market, which is the collective groupthink of 50 million investors. Follow the same research and you will see the same results.

Independent researchers and thinkers have no gurus and subscribe to no investment newsletters. They make their own decisions. Buffett's mentor was Ben Graham; as a mentor he became, and is still in many ways, a guiding light. The independent decision maker always maintains responsibility over all investment decisions. So if you are or decide to become an active trader, remember to make your own decisions and take full responsibility for their outcome. Be a leader. Resist the temptation to follow the stock tips of interested parties.

One of the more common investment errors is to track and buy the highest performing mutual funds, only to see them become the lowest performing in succeeding years. Purchasing the hottest mutual fund or selecting the same stocks held by the hottest mutual funds is not independent research or thought.

Before Berkshire's purchase of wholly owned subsidiary Scott Fetzer (principal businesses include Campbell Hausfeld Air Compressors, World Book Encyclopedia, and Kirby Vacuum) the business broker in charge of positioning the business for sale put together what is called a "book," which gives the prospective buyer a pro forma intended to help the buyer understand what the business is "really" worth and persuade the buyer into a higher price. In this case the investment banker collected a fee up-front of $2.5 million to find a buyer and put together the "book."

Scott Fetzer's broker was having no luck finding a buyer, so Buffett, after doing his own research and making up his own mind as to how much he thought Scott Fetzer was worth, bought the business. The investment banker wanted to feel better about its nonrefundable fees and asked Warren and his partner Charlie Munger if they wanted to read the "book," to which Charlie responded, "I'll pay $2.5 million not to read it." Now that's independent research and thought!

DEFINING RISK

How you define risk may give you insight into the kind of investor you are. Many believe that risk is how much an investment will swing in value. As a result, they put their money in low-volatility investments, which give the appearance of low risk but may present a higher risk. Others believe that risk is owning only a few investments, so they diversify. Instead of owning a lot of a few (more on that in Chapter 7), they buy a few of a lot.

Buying two of everything has the feel of less risk than buying a lot of one. Warren calls a person who has this approach "the Noah's Ark investor": you buy two of everything, and you end up with a zoo for a portfolio.

Many investors confuse conservative with safe and low risk.

Risk, as defined by Warren, is not knowing what you are doing. Most people diversify, or as Peter Lynch said, "de-*worse*-a-fy," out of ignorance. If you know how to value businesses and buy them at attractive prices, then you want to buy more of what you understand and own, not more of something else less attractive.

Some active traders believe that you can reduce risk by trading more frequently. Like the game of hot potato—so the thinking goes—the longer you hold something, the more likely you are to be burned.

Not so, according to the Buffett School of investing. Warren bought Coca-Cola because it was a quality investment that was available at an attractive price in relation to its real value. Owning a huge share of it reduced his risk. According to the world's greatest investor, owning Coke for a few hours, a few days, or even a few months, like most day traders do, would be risky.

You need to exercise patience. Recall that it was more than fifty years after understanding Coke that he invested in it. He follows and understands most investments for decades before his purchase, and when he buys he buys big.

Another way to reduce your risk is to understand your investment. If you don't understand it, then you are engaging in risky business. You may get lucky. You may not fully understand how you made money, but eventually you will suffer the consequences of your lack of understanding. Warren calls this your circle of competence: staying with what you know and understand and ignoring everything else.

Not admitting your mistakes and lacking humility are more ways that investors increase their risk. Arrogance has broken many high-flying investors. The world's best investors all make mistakes (Chapter 8 highlights Buffett's). The most important thing is to acknowledge mistakes and learn from them. Better yet, let others make them and learn from them.

As discussed in this chapter, risk is also measured by whether or not you have a margin of safety with your investments. Reckless speculating or placing investments with a low probability of return is akin to gambling.

A dangerous hidden form of risk is having high expectations with your investments. If the long-term stock market has returned 11 percent and you expect 22 percent, you are setting yourself up for high-risk investment behavior. You need to lower your expectations. If you go to the plate seeking a home run every time, you will undoubtedly strike out and be frustrated. Find partners, managers, and businesses you're going to buy stock in who consistently underpromise and overdeliver.

Another risky maneuver is to follow the conventional wisdom taught by most university-level finance classes. A popular instructional approach is to teach efficient market theory—that the market knows everything that needs to be known about an investment and that it is already reflected in its stock price. In other words, thinking doesn't pay.

Efficient market theorists would have you buy the market and therefore help you perform in an average fashion with your investments.

Risk is increased by the chartists who follow the movement of a stock or a market's price. Chartists focus on past price action over value. "The dumbest reason in the world," says Warren, "is to buy a stock because it is going up. It doesn't have to be at a rock bottom," he goes on to say. "You just need honest and able people [running the company]. Do not gamble, but watch for unusual circumstances. Excellent investment opportunities come about when superior businesses experience a one-time event that depresses the stock price in relation to its intrinsic value."

Buying the same stocks as Mr. Buffett will not guarantee you the same results or reduce your risk. In most cases you learn about his purchases and stock sales one year after the fact. Just because Bill Gates and Warren Buffett enjoy playing bridge doesn't mean that if you play bridge, you too will be a billionaire. This belief is illustrated by the person who visited America and toured the Carnegie libraries and wrote, "You can't believe how much money there is in libraries." The tourist obviously did not know that Andrew Carnegie made his fortune in steel and circled it back to society through library donations. You need to understand the underlying value principles of why you are making an investment and then hold it for the long term.

Market watchers follow and talk about the market. It's either a red day or a green day, depending on what the market is doing. They are *market* followers and market analysts. Warren, on the other hand, does not follow the market and would be happy if the market closed for several years. He follows *businesses* and considers himself a *business* analyst. His craft is to determine what a business is worth over its life, and he simply tries to buy it cheaper.

Jumping into new-age investments, technology, and businesses with much promise, but without earnings is very risky behavior.

All of Warren's wealth has been made in old-economy stocks: beverages (Coca-Cola), newspapers (*Washington Post*), and auto insurance (GEICO). He also invests in wholly owned businesses, like bricks (Acme), carpets (Shaw), paint (Benjamin Moore), chocolate candy (Sees), ice cream (Dairy Queen), encyclopedias (World Book), and cowboy boots

(Justin), because they all can be valued. He simply goes out ten years to determine what a company will earn and discounts that back to today. If he can't figure out where a company will be in ten years, he can't value it. As the head librarian of a college once said, "Warren Buffett is a great future investor." Companies without earnings cannot be valued.

Investing without considering management is risky. Is management running the business for the benefit of shareholders? Warren's acquisition criteria are simple. He's looking for a big purchase, $50 million in annual earnings now. He's looking for consistent earnings, no debt, management that comes along. Remember, he said, "Buying a retailer without management is like buying the Eiffel Tower without an elevator." He's looking for a simple business. He won't do any unfriendly deals. He's looking for a fair price, and he will make his mind up in five minutes or less.

Buying because you have the money is risky. Sometimes the best investment activity is no activity at all. From 1985 to 1988, Warren Buffett purchased no stock, and no major stock changes in his investment portfolio have occurred for the past ten years. Value investors sleep well and live long. As he says, "Don't own it for ten minutes if you don't intend to own it for ten years."

Investing by following the market is fraught with risk. Some never invest because of many of the following market events or risks during a billionaire's lifetime. Table 3.4 lists nearly seventy market events over Buffett's lifetime that would prevent a market follower from ever investing, and if a market analyst did invest, he or she would quickly sell because of these market risks.

Warren Buffett reduces risk by being a business analyst, not a market analyst. Just because there was an energy crisis in 1973 did not prevent him from investing in the Washington Post. Nor did the market collapse of 1973 and 1974 cause him to sell what has been a wonderful long-term investment.

THE RELATIONSHIP BETWEEN OWNERSHIP AND VALUE INVESTING

Ownership and value are consistent in every area of life. Remember, Warren purchased his first and still current home with only 10 percent of his net worth, in contrast to most home buyers, who pay 100 percent of a 20 percent down payment and borrow 80 percent more than they have.

Table 3.4 Buffett's Age, DJIA, and Events over Buffett's Lifetime

Source: DJIA—Dow Jones Industrial Average

Age	DJIA	Market Events	Business Events and Buffett's Time Line
4	104	Great Depression	Coca-Cola forty-eight years old
5	144	Spanish Civil War	
6	180	Economy struggles	Bought six cans of Coke for 25 cents; sells for 5 cents each
7	121	Recession	Nebraska Furniture Mart opens
8	155	War imminent in Europe and Asia	
9	150	War in Europe	
10	131	France falls	National Indemnity founded
11	111	Pearl Harbor	Purchases first stock
12	119	Wartime price controls	
13	136	Industry mobilizes	Delivers Washington Post
14	152	Consumer goods shortage	Used golf ball business
15	193	Postwar recession predicted	
16	177	Dow tops 200: "Market too high"	Used pinball machine business
17	181	Cold War begins	
18	177	Berlin blockage	
19	200	USSR explores atomic bomb	Reads The Intelligent Investor
20	235	Korean War	Studies under Graham
21	269	Excess profits tax	Visits GEICO and invests 100 percent of his assets
22	292	U.S. seizes steel mills	
23	281	USSR explodes hydrogen bomb	
24	330	Dow tops 300: "Market too high"	Joins Graham in NYC as junior stock analyst
25	485	Eisenhower has heart attack	
26	499	Suez Canal crisis	Begins Partnership with $105,000 from partners and $100 of his own money
27	436	USSR launches Sputnik	
28	584	Recession	Doubles partners' investment

(continued)

Table 3.4 (continued)

Age	DJIA	Market Events	Business Events and Buffett's Time Line
29	679	Castro takes over Cuba	
30	616	USSR downs U-2 spy plane	Becomes millionaire
31	731	Berlin Wall erected	
32	652	Cuban missile crisis	Initial purchase of Berkshire for $7 per share
33	763	JFK assassinated	
34	874	Gulf of Tonkin incident	Buys 5 percent of Amex for $13 mil
35	969	Civil Rights Marches	Buys 5 percent of Disney for $4 mil. Takes over Berkshire management
36	786	Vietnam War escalates	Buys first business in its entirety
37	905	Newark race riots	Purchases National Indemnity for $8.6 mil
38	944	USS Pueblo Seized: "Market too high"	
39	800	Money tightens, market falls	Buys Illinois National Bank Closes Buffett partnership
40	839	Conflict spreads to Cambodia	
41	890	Wage and price freeze	NASDAQ index begins
42	1020	Largest trade deficit in U.S. history	Sees Candy acquired for $25 million; now earns three times purchase price
43	851	Energy crisis	Purchases 15 percent of *Washington Post* for $11 million
44	616	Steepest market drop in forty years	
45	852	Clouded economic prospects	
46	1005	Economy slowly recovers	Buys one third of GEICO
47	830	Market slumps	Purchases *Buffalo News*
48	805	Interest rates rise	
49	839	Oil skyrockets — 10 percent–plus unemployment	
50	964	Interest rates hit all-time high	

Table 3.4 (continued)

Age	DJIA	Market Events	Business Events and Buffett's Time Line
51	875	Deep recession begins, Reagan shot	Same DJIA as age 34 (17 year bear market)
52	1047	Worst recession in forty years; debt crisis	
53	1259	Market hits record: "Market too high"	Acquires Nebraska Furniture Mart for $55 million
54	1212	Record U.S. federal deficits	
55	1547	Economic growth slows	Closes Berkshire Hathaway Textile Mills
56	1896	Dow nears 2000: "Market too high"	Purchases World Book, Kirby Vacuum. Becomes billionaire
57	1939	The Crash—Black Friday	
58	2169	Fear of recession	
59	2753	Junk bond collapse	Largest owner of Coca-Cola
60	2634	Gulf War: Worst market decline in sixteen years	
61	3169	Recession: "Market too high"	Enters shoe business with H. H. Brown
62	3301	Elections: market flat	
63	3754	Business continues restructuring	Takes over Dexter Shoe for 2 percent of stock or $420 million
64	3834	Interest rates are going up	
65	5117	"The market is too high"	Helzberg Diamond acquired
66	6448	Fear of inflation	Buys balance of GEICO for $2.3 billion
67	7908	Irrational exuberance	Dairy Queen added
68	9374	Asia crisis	NetJets acquired
69	11497	Y2K	Enters energy business with Mid American Energy
70	10787	Technology correction	Purchases Acme Brick
71	10022	World Trade Center, Pentagon terrorist attacks	Buys Fruit of the Loom
72	8342	Iraq war	

Bankers and real estate brokers are quite happy when we trade our homes on average every six years.

Is it a coincidence that one of the best-known value investors and one of the richest people in the world still lives in the same home he purchased over forty years ago? Also, consider his automobile: Warren selects the car he's going to purchase by its weight and its margin of safety (driver and passenger airbags), and he drives it for ten years. His office and his staff are simple, small, and effective. You can learn from the best, or you can make your own mistakes. Warren has chronicled his mistakes, and you can read about them online at www.berkshirehathaway.com. He freely admits that he used to invest with his glands instead of his head.

CONCLUSION

The takeaway exercise for this chapter is simply to define what kind of investor you are or want to be. This self-analysis and knowing yourself is the best long-term advantage. No matter what you want to accomplish, you need a plan. If you were going to build a house, you would need detailed plans. You need the same thing in order to build wealth. Your plan starts with knowing yourself. What is your investor profile? Buy reading glasses. Keep it simple. Table 3.5 offers a simple questionnaire to get you started.

Table 3.5 **Probing Questions to Assist You in Defining Your Investment Strategies**

All investing starts with self-analysis. Do the self-discovery to determine what kind of investor you are. Read through the list below and fill out an in-depth description of yourself in relation to investing.

Your investment expectations are:

_____

_____

_____

_____

_____

_____

Table 3.5 (continued)

The time frame that you have to invest is:

On a scale from 1 to 10 (with 10 high), your risk tolerance is:

Your current life situation is (single, married, a parent, or retired):

Do you need income or capital growth? low taxes?

Are you a risk taker? Conservative? An ethical investor? Contrarian? Just starting?

How much do you have to invest? Do you have a lump sum, an inheritance, a little or a lot to lose?

Describe your personality in relation to investing. Do you get up early and run, read all financial-related information, and fly off to work? Or do you sleep in, like to spend time with your family, casually observe business, and prefer to look at your investments annually?

The most important thing is to ask yourself is if you are a passive or an active investor. Which are you?

Warren can teach you his whole portfolio management course in a few weeks. That's the easy part. Knowing yourself and having the discipline to apply it is the hard part. Admit your mistakes and make fewer, better decisions. Ask yourself: Can you go three years without trading? "Activity" and "trade" are usually in the name of many brokerage companies. They are set up to encourage you to follow the opposite principles of Warren and to be a speculator and trader. Maybe that's the kind of investor you don't want to be. These brokerage houses are not named Ameri-*wealth*, E-*Asset*, or Scott-*Earnings*. They all have "trade" in their names and make money off of your trading activities.

Buy storybook stocks—like Coca-Cola, an old-economy business that has been around for more than one hundred years. The average year of origin for the companies that Warren Buffett has invested in is 1909, twenty-one years before he was born.

Seek excellence. Be like a prospective business purchaser and talk to the company's employees, managers, customers, and even its competition. Invest for the long term. Expect your business relationships to last a lifetime.

Stocks are simple. Buy shares in great companies with management of the highest standards for prices that are less than the companies are worth. Take the time to ask yourself just what kind of investor you are. You can build wealth, but first you must build knowledge, particularly about yourself.

Now that you have defined what kind of investor you are, let's move on to the next chapter and talk about developing an investment philosophy. This step is critical in learning to build wealth like Warren Buffett.

Chapter 4

Developing an Investment Philosophy

"Philosophy begins in wonder."

—Plato

Investment philosophy is the cornerstone of all successful investing.

Warren's wealth was largely the result of an investment philosophy that he learned from his professor Benjamin Graham. By the age of twenty-one, Warren knew Graham's philosophy and principles so well that he was able to teach them at a nearby local college.

Chapter 3 explored your investor personality, definitions of risk, speculation versus ownership, active compared to passive investing, intelligent against emotional investing, and the merits of value investing and independent thought.

In this chapter, we talk about how you can develop your own investment philosophy—your guiding principles. Once you know what kind of investor you are, you're ready to design a plan, which is critical to any serious project. For example, you wouldn't start constructing a home without a plan; if you did, your home might look like a tree house. Yet with a plan, a serious and experienced homebuilder could build a mansion. Similarly, with an investing plan, your investment road map could build you enormous wealth.

WARREN BUFFETT'S INVESTING PHILOSOPHY

Warren began developing his investing principles first with the guidance of his father and redefined them later under the watchful eye of his mentor, Benjamin Graham. Buffett's investment philosophy can be presented as simply as these two rules:

- Rule number one: Don't lose capital.
- Rule number two: Don't forget rule number one.

Warren has said, "Lethargy bordering on sloth should remain the cornerstone of an investment style." In other words, active investors should perform three activities every day: read, research, and think.

Warren's investment principles can also be summed up as follows:

- Know what you own.
- Research before you buy.
- Own a business, not a stock.
- Make a total of only twenty lifetime investments.
- Make *one* decision to own a stock and be a long-term owner.

Your acquisition criteria for a stock should be the same criteria you would use if you were buying the whole company. Warren Buffett used to invest with the cigar-butt method, where he would look for old-economy stocks that only had one or two puffs of earnings left in them—businesses like Berkshire Hathaway textile mills, trading at a few times earnings with a lifespan of twenty years or less.

The cigar-butt method has now evolved into buying wonderful businesses at fair prices. Gillette is an excellent example. Purchased in 1989 for $600 million, Buffett's holding company now owns 11 percent or $3 billion of the world's largest razor blade company. Gillette was purchased for $6.25 per share and has achieved a 12 percent return on capital over the past fourteen years. More importantly, it recently earned $1.25 per share or 20 percent of his purchase price. Warren is comforted with the thought that every night 2.5 billion men go to sleep and grow whiskers and that Gillette owns 70 percent of the worldwide shaving market.

You should look to buy a wonderful business or stock at a fair price. Warren has always attempted to buy a dollar's worth of assets for 50 cents. Even by 1967, anyone could have purchased Berkshire Hathaway for

$20.50 per share while it had a book value of $32 per share. With an average cost basis of $17, the Buffett partners enjoyed a 50 percent discount to book value. From 1967 to 1970, Buffett and his shareholders earned $18.60 per share, more than the average purchase price. Today what Berkshire earns in one day is what it earned 30 years ago in one year.

Buffett buys to keep, and he buys so well that he doesn't have to sell. Keep in mind the twenty investment decisions of a lifetime developed by Warren's professor Benjamin Graham. If you think about that advice, you will slow down your trading activity and speed up your reading, research, and thinking.

Warren's philosophy is simple. Work out how much a business will pay you between now and until judgment day. Discount that back to today, and attempt to buy the business or stock cheaper. Warren is always buying businesses for less than he thinks they are worth.

If you bought Berkshire stock in 1968 for $37, for example, you would have earned the purchase price back within two and a half years.

Present Value Calculations or Discounted Cash Flow

It probably doesn't surprise you, but Warren can perform complicated discounted cash flow calculations in his head without the aid of a calculator or computer. How much would you pay for an investment that earns $1 per year for ten years, with no earnings after that and no remaining value? The answer depends on your expected rate of return. Let's say you require 11 percent return on your investment. You would be willing to pay $5.89, or roughly six times earnings. Warren can do this in his head.

In his 1977 letter to shareholders, Warren laid out his simple investment philosophy:

We select our marketable equity securities in much the same way we would evaluate a business for an acquisition in its entirety. We want the business to be (1) something that we can understand, (2) with favorable long-term prospects, (3) operated by honest and competent people, and (4) available at a very attractive price. We ordinarily make no attempt to buy equities for anticipated favorable stock price behavior in the short term. In fact, if their business experience continues to satisfy us, we welcome lower market prices of stocks we own as an opportunity to acquire even more of a good thing at a better price.

Buffett's purchase of the Illinois National Bank in 1969 illustrates these principles. Banking is a business he understands. Illinois National had favorable long-term opportunities. It was managed by its founder, Gene Abegg, in such a way that it was one of the most profitable banks in the country. Most importantly Warren was able to buy it at less than book value and at seven and a half times what it was earning.

PHIL FISHER'S INFLUENCE

California-based investment manager and author Philip Fisher was a pioneer of modern investment theory. His book, originally published in 1958, *Common Stocks and Uncommon Profits* has become a classic guide written for the layperson on valuing companies based on their growth potential. Fisher influenced Buffett to consider the value of excellent managers and brand equity, which could lead to rapid earnings growth over the years. This approach added more principles to Buffett's philosophy, in addition to the Graham School of pure asset and balance sheet valuation.

Graham was East Coast and old school. Fisher was West Coast and new school. Graham was quantitative with principles that considered only that which could be measured, like balance sheets and income statements. Fisher introduced the qualitative aspects of investing: the hard-to-measure factors of people, management, brand, and other competitive advantages that would make you pay more for a company. Unlike Graham, Fisher believes in interviewing management and measuring the scuttlebutt (thoughts and opinions of a company's competitors, suppliers, and employees).

Warren likes to say he is 85 percent Benjamin Graham and 15 percent Phil Fisher. "I am an active reader," says Warren, "of everything Phil Fisher has to say."

Fisher's investment philosophies are simple and straightforward:

- Invest for the long term.
- Diversify your portfolio through proper asset allocation.
- Blend passive with active management.
- Know your costs and keep them low.

Here are Fisher's eight investment principles:

1. Buy companies that have disciplined plans for achieving dramatic long-range profit growth and have inherent qualities making it difficult for newcomers to share in that growth.
2. Buy companies when they are out of favor.
3. Hold a stock until either (a) there has been a fundamental change in its nature (e.g., big management changes), or (b) it has grown to a point where it no longer will be growing faster than the economy as a whole.
4. Deemphasize the importance of dividends.
5. Recognize that making some mistakes is an inherent cost of investment. Taking small profits in good investments and letting losses grow in bad ones is a sign of abominable investment judgment.
6. Accept the fact that only a relatively small number of companies are truly outstanding. Therefore, concentrate your funds in the most desirable opportunities. Any holding of over twenty different stocks is a sign of a financial incompetence.
7. Never accept blindly whatever may be the dominant current opinion in the financial community. Nor should you reject the prevailing view just for the sake of being contrary.
8. *Understand* that success greatly depends on a combination of hard work, intelligence, and honesty.

These principles have worked in the past half-century and when applied properly will work just as well into the next century. As Fisher wrote, "Sustained success requires skill and consistent application of sound principles."

In Chapter 10, we talk about the investment principles of Lou Simpson, CEO of capital operations for GEICO auto insurance, a wholly owned Berkshire subsidiary, and the backup to Warren Buffett. Principles are principles because they don't change. No new philosophy is needed during changing market environments. Two diseases that are always present in the market are fear and greed. Benjamin Graham called this phenomenon "Mr. Market" and portrayed this character as a manic-depressive, constantly swinging from fear to greed and back to fear. However, you can contain Mr. Market with the right investment philosophy. Most of all, you need the right temperament, and you can become an expert at investing by having a written investment philosophy. All successful investors—Warren

Buffett, Lou Simpson, and Phil Fisher—have well-developed investment principles.

CREATE A WRITTEN INVESTING PLAN

If successful investors have one thing in common, it's a set of investment principles that don't change much after they've been developed. Just like business and personal goals, they are achievable and always written. Your goals might be to invest in the new economy, the old economy, technology, Internet companies, initial public offerings, you name it. Well-defined investment principles cover them.

In spite of the fact that some people suggest that today's investing environment is different or may require a different approach or a new philosophy, that's not really true. Principles are principles because they don't change. They may evolve, but they don't change. If they changed, they wouldn't be principles. Ben Franklin may have said it best: "If principle is good for anything, it is worth living up to."

Put your principles in writing. There's something about writing that helps crystallize your thinking and helps you with a guidepost during major market swings from the inevitable greed to fear and back again. Mr. Market can only be tamed if you follow your written beliefs. Investment principles help you with the right temperament as well. It's kind of like teaching. In order to write, you first need to comprehend, and there's no better teacher than experience.

Very few individual investors have written investment beliefs and philosophies. Famed investor Peter Lynch of the Fidelity Magellan Fund, noted for achieving 29 percent annual returns during his thirteen-year tenure, suggests writing down on one page why you are buying a particular stock and then later write down why you are selling it. The act of writing makes all investors think more clearly and be more intelligent and less emotional. Philosophies are like goals: They should be written, reviewed, consulted, and followed. Whatever decisions you make should always be in line with your goals. Unwritten investment beliefs tend to change like the wind.

In the United Kingdom, the government requires pension funds to write and publish investment principles. Many mutual fund families have online services to help beginning investors with an investment plan.

Although it is slanted towards mutual funds (because that is what they sell), the Vanguard mutual fund family of index funds has a "How to create your investment plan" online at www.vanguard.com under the "planning and advice" tab. Their five-step investment plan is as follows:

1. Identify your goals and time horizon.
2. Determine your investor personality (by answering an investor questionnaire).
3. Understand asset classes.
4. Select your investments.
5. Know when to change your asset mix.

Formulating a written set of investment principles has several advantages:

- You know immediately if an investment idea fits into your investment plan.
- The mere exercise of writing helps you determine just what you are looking for with your investments.
- You can compare your philosophies with others.
- A written philosophy helps you evolve and emerge as an investor. You can look back over time and see just how far you have come with your principles.
- By reading someone else's investment philosophy, you can better understand where they have come from and where they are going.
- Finally, if you share your principles with others, they are able to better guide you towards investments that meet your criteria. Others may be able to point out some weaknesses in your principles, or help you better explain them.

READ AND STUDY OTHER PEOPLE'S INVESTING PHILOSOPHIES

You should read about developing an investment philosophy. The second best thing you can do is to read what other successful investors like Warren Buffett have done, and discover for yourself why there's such a great interest in him and his company, Berkshire Hathaway. You might ask, what is the first best thing you can do? Follow that philosophy.

Challenged to summarize his investment philosophy in just three words, Graham wrote, "margin of safety."

The best book on this topic is titled *Developing an Investment Philosophy*, by Philip Fisher. It's published as part of Wiley's investment classic *Common Stocks and Uncommon Profits*, and includes *Conservative Investors Sleep Well*. This three-part book should be half of your investment library— the other being Graham's *The Intelligent Investor*. Fisher's *Developing an Investment Philosophy* suggests that you

- Examine businesses, not markets
- Ignore the madness of crowds
- Disregard efficient market theorists (popular among college finance professors)
- Avoid market timing

MAKE YOUR INVESTMENT PLAN AND PRINCIPLES PERSONAL

One of the best things you can do is make your investment principle and philosophy personal. You can mimic someone else's philosophy, which is what we do by default when we invest in a company or a mutual fund, or you can develop your own. Your best philosophy is one that you develop yourself. Although reading and studying other philosophies is a wise approach, copying another's belief word for word is generally not a good idea. The problem with imitation is that the imitator doesn't truly understand what he or she is copying. Original thought is always recommended.

Some make the mistake of adopting Buffett's investment philosophies and shadow his every move without determining if these moves fit their own principles. The folly with this strategy is threefold: you may be at a different stage in your life than him, you have many more investment opportunities with greater impact, and you need to decide for yourself which principles work for you.

What about the origins of a philosophy? First, you have to have an interest in investing. Like Warren, it usually starts at a young age, and either you have more of an interest in saving and investing or, more commonly, you are interested in spending and consuming. Rarely do you see a saver become a spender or a consumer become an investor.

One father may attempt to teach his teenage daughter about investing, but every time he brings up the subject her eyes glaze over. She may patronize him for a short while, but what she really wants to talk about is music, dancing, friends, boys, and school. No matter how much he tries to talk about investing, it's going to be very difficult to make a young family member who is a spender and consumer into an investor and saver.

Another West Coast father has had the opposite effect on his children by encouraging them to invest, giving them an annual balance sheet and income statement, and bringing them to Omaha to meet and listen to Mr. Buffett. Each child has their own investment business name and have done remarkably well. Their father, like Warren's father, has facilitated their understanding and investment education, but it had to come from within.

Once the interest is there, you can read all you want about investment principles, but nothing beats real-life experiences. It takes time, experience, and mistakes—a lot of them for many of us—to develop an investment philosophy. Investing is an evolution—a process that with a philosophy can bring great financial rewards, and most important, a peaceful night's sleep.

Fisher's book titled *Conservative Investors Sleep Well* explains that because they have a written investment philosophy, understand what they are investing in, have purchased a business/stock below what they think it is worth, and make money when the market realizes the investment merits of their decision, conservative investors can rest without worry at the end of the day.

You must have independent thought. A proper investment philosophy must prove your ability to move against the grain and to think independently. All great investors, professional and individual, have a common characteristic of ignoring the crowd. People who say they believe in a guru—even if they say the guru is Mr. Buffett—immediately red flag themselves as group thinkers. Independent thinkers make no mention of gurus in their investment philosophy.

Gurus are followed blindly and can do no wrong. Followers don't understand the underlying principles and do not make their own decisions. Mentors, on the other hand, are teachers, coaches, and counselors who guide those who have selected them to make their own decisions and follow their own philosophy.

You must have patience. No investment belief can be proven in the short term. Phil Fisher asked his clients to give him at least three years to prove himself as an investment manager. Too many of us are unfit for investment decision making because of our short-term nature and unrealistic expectations. If Fisher wanted three years from his clients for proper evaluation, he also gave his investees, the stocks that he purchased, three years to prove their merit as well. Few of us can demonstrate that kind of stock fidelity.

TEST YOUR INVESTING PHILOSOPHY

It's also important to look at declining markets, to test how strongly you believe in your investing philosophy. Certain experiences shape each investor and his or her philosophies, and nothing better can happen to an investor than to buy a stock that declines. This decline tests your investment confidence about the stock more than any stock price increase. Rising markets always spawn more investment "geniuses."

Successful homebuilders know that the best time to enter home building is during bad times. Without that foundation of the struggle and the necessity of running a tight ship, a homebuilder won't be able to suffer the inevitable poor home-building market. Declining markets test your investment philosophy. Will you change your principles during bad times? If so, were they really your investment philosophies? With the greatest bull market during the 1980s and 1990s, experienced and successful investors look past that time period to the 1973–74 oil embargo or the 1964–81 seventeen-year bear market to test how an investment principle held up during declining markets. It's how you and your principles stand up during these trying times that prove their real strength. Unless and until your philosophy has been tested by fire, you really don't have a proven method.

Arrogance and self-righteousness have humbled many a bull market performer. One just has to look back a few short years to witness the great bubble of runaway investment valuations that had no merit or sustainability to see how once golden-boy investment wizards were tamed and humiliated.

Buffett's philosophy of value investing was tested many times during market declines of his stock; from 1972 to 1974 he lost 60 percent of his net worth in stock market price declines of his stock. But that didn't prevent him from making two of the best long-term and significant investments: The Washington Post Company and Sees Candy. Purchased for $11 million and $25 million, respectively, they are now each billion-dollar assets.

Your measure as an investor is how your philosophies hold up during turbulent times. The true test of a jet pilot is not how well he or she does when flying along with perfect weather and on auto pilot, but rather how he or she flies a fully loaded four-engine plane with just one engine, during a major storm, landing on a snow-covered unfamiliar runway with zero visibility and not enough fuel to do it more than once.

Back testing, the uncanny knack for looking to the past to prove your investment results, doesn't work. Unfortunately, the investment world is full of Monday-morning quarterbacks able to call the perfect play for yesterday's game. Back testing just about any investment philosophy isn't a true test. Just about any fifth-grader can look at the past and weave a brilliant investment scenario. This is like painting the Mona Lisa with paint-by-numbers. Any historical investment market can be redrawn with a perfect investment philosophy that will buy the lows and sell the highs. You can't short-circuit your formative experiences by back testing. You can't truly understand major things in life by living vicariously through others. As most country songs say, you don't know romance until you've experienced it, and you don't know what a broken heart feels like until yours has been broken. Developing your investment philosophies works the same way.

Mistakes are also important when you're developing your investment philosophy. Explaining your mistakes and how you have learned from them makes you a better investor. Detailing how your investment mistakes have made you a better investor should be part of every investment plan. Explain how you have grown and evolved as an investor. The admission of mistakes and how you have picked yourself up from them are the measure of the investor, not your successes. Ninety-eight percent of us are ready to tell the world about all of our genius moves in buying pieces of businesses. Yet only the rare individual talks about a decision that seemed like a sign of genius but was far from it. Most years Warren writes to his shareholders and admits what he calls the mistake du jour. (We discuss mistakes more thoroughly in Chapter 8.)

Great investors do post-mortems. Explain how you thoroughly analyzed your decision to buy stock in a company and later changed your mind and sold it. Tell about your get-rich-quick schemes that no one else has ever heard of or tried.

Detail how you thought you would supplement your family's income by actively trading in the stock market. Did you confuse activity with results? Did you think that Internet stocks were different from investing in railroads? The best investment philosophy is born out of your mistakes. It becomes a sign that you have learned from experience.

You should also compare your own investment philosophy against other investors, private and professional, who have a well-developed and written set of their investing principles. The best comparison is against those who have used their beliefs to beat the market over long periods of time, like the super-investors of Graham and Doddsville. Your results should be compared to how much value you added to the S&P Index, an index of the five hundred largest domestic corporations in the United States. If your investment beliefs don't add value, then you should reconsider your investment philosophy.

Are there exceptions? Yes. Fisher proved there are exceptions to every rule, and he did admit to acting against his written investment philosophies. He had the three-year rule. He asked his clients to give him the same amount of time to prove his investment talents and believed in treating the stocks he invested in the same. Only on one occasion did he break his three-year rule and sell his stock in an under-performing company before three years. How many of us who have written investment philosophies can admit to breaking them just once? Even Mr. Buffett modified his cigar-butt principles of buying companies that had one or two puffs of earnings left in them to include Fisher's advice to pay up for quality brands like Sees Candies and Coca-Cola, and to consider the qualitative (people, management, and other hard-to-measure qualities) side of investing. Even the best of the best evolve and amend.

CONSIDER MARKET SWINGS WHEN MAKING YOUR INVESTMENT PLAN

A complete investment plan addresses market timing and the efficient market theory. Some investment beliefs work well in the short term and are even taught at major universities. Look at all of the major universities that fall prey to sponsoring investing contests that include short-term trading. Even the *Wall Street Journal* is guilty of comparing the success of investing professionals versus choosing stocks by throwing darts over a ridiculously short period of time. Most financial self-interested suppliers offer these games and promote what is contrary to sound investment principles. Serious investors instinctively ignore them.

Just about any investment theory works in the short run, and most beliefs are brilliant during raging bull markets. Millions have been swimming naked without defined principles or with a poor investment philosophy, only to be revealed when the investment tide moves out. Your written investment philosophy should speak to these issues. Do you believe in market timing? If not, do you have a minimum holding period like Fisher (three years) or like Buffett (ten years)? Second, do your beliefs address efficient markets? Do you believe opportunities exist because Mr. Market doesn't properly value a stock that you have researched and thus understand its intrinsic value? What do your principles say about the anticipation of a declining market? Do you sell or do you stay the course?

Doing a few things well is important. Nobody can be good at everything, and no investor can properly follow more than a few stocks. Ben Graham called this your circle of competence. Phil Fisher calls this doing a few things well. Make sure your principles define your competence, and don't fall prey to the friction or transaction costs of the Wall Street brokerage community, which emphasizes overdiversification, active trading, and reaching beyond your circle of competence.

Our founding father and second president Thomas Jefferson may have said it best: "In matters of style, swim with the current; in matters of principle, stand like a rock."

CONCLUSION

Remember, principles are principles because they don't change with the latest fad, the so-called new economy, technology, the Internet, dot-com fads, initial public offerings, or whatever the future friction agents (also known as "fiction agents") may bring our way. Don't be shamed into changing your principles because of name-calling or someone or everyone suggesting that you have failed to change. One day, you'll probably notice that the people bragging about swimming with the majority are, when the tide goes out, naked without well-defined, individual, written investment principles.

Phil Fisher has lots of ideas that together compose his investment philosophy. Think about these three:

1. Concentrate your investments in world-class companies managed by strong management.
2. Limit yourself to companies you truly understand: five to ten are good; more than twenty is asking for trouble.
3. Select the very best and concentrate your investment.

Table 4.1 summarizes how to develop your own investment philosophy as described in this chapter.

Table 4.1 Creating Your Investment Philosophies

Create an investment strategy and stick to it through up times and down times in the market. Several Warren Buffett–modeled investing philosophies are:

- **Put Your Investment Philosophy in Writing.** Mr. Market can only be tamed with written beliefs. Investment principles help you with the right temperament as well. Like teaching, in order to write, you need to first comprehend. There's no better teacher than experience.

- **Read about Developing a Philosophy.** Second best to writing is reading about other successful investors, which is why there's great interest in Warren Buffett and Berkshire Hathaway.

- **Make Your Philosophy Personal.** You can mimic someone else's philosophy or you can develop your own. Your best philosophy is the one you develop for yourself. Original thought is always recommended.

- **Understanding the Origins of a Philosophy.** You can read all you want about investment philosophies, but nothing beats real-life experiences. Investing success takes time, experience and mistakes—a lot of mistakes to develop an investment philosophy. Investing is an evolution. It's a process that with a philosophy can bring great financial rewards and peaceful nights' sleep.

An investing philosophy requires certain principles in order to achieve success. Investing is and always has been a combination of science and art. It's also an act of faith because it's about the future, and by definition the future is unknown. Faith is merely the belief in a positive future outcome. Worry is faith in a negative future outcome.

- **Be Prepared for Declining Markets.** Certain experiences shape the investor and his/her philosophies, and nothing better can happen to an investor than to buy a stock that declines. Your measure as an investor is how your philosophies hold up during turbulent times.

- **Accept the Fact That Backtesting Doesn't Work.** Unfortunately, the investment world is full of Monday morning quarterbacks. Backtesting just about any investment philosophy isn't a true test. Warren suggests that making decisions on the past is like driving a car by using the rear-view mirror. Remember to invest looking in front of you.

- **Learn from Your Mistakes.** Explain your mistakes and how you have learned from them. The admission of mistakes and how you have picked yourself up from them is the measure of the investor. The best investment philosophy is born out of your mistakes, serving as a sign that you have learned from experience.

Table 4.1 (continued)

- **Be an Independent Thinker.** A proper investment philosophy must prove your ability to move against the grain and to think independently. Independent thinkers make no mention of gurus in their investment philosophy.

- **Be Patient.** No investment belief can be proven in the short term. Phil Fisher asked his clients to give him at least three years to prove himself. Unfortunately most of us, including the professionals, simply rent stocks instead of owning them indefinitely like Warren Buffett does.

- **Compare Your Strategy and Results against Others.** All philosophies should be compared against others who have a well-developed and written set of them. The best comparison is against those who have used their beliefs to beat the market over long periods of time. Your results should be compared to how much value you have added to the S&P index over time. If your investment beliefs don't add value, then you should reconsider your written philosophy.

- **Recognize That Exceptions Exist to Every Rule.** Even the top investors must on some occasions act against written investment principles. Phil Fisher (actually on only one occasion) broke his three-year rule and sold a company before three years.

- **Ignore Market Timing and Efficient Market Theorists.** Your written investment philosophy should speak to these issues. Do you believe in market timing? If not, do you have a minimum holding period? Do your beliefs address efficient markets? Do you believe opportunities exist because Mr. Market doesn't properly value a stock that you have researched and understand its intrinsic value? What do your principles say about an anticipation of a declining market? Do you sell or stay the course?

- **Do a Few Things Well.** Nobody can be good at everything and no investor can properly follow more than a few stocks. Make sure your principles define your competence.

- **Keep in Mind the Most Important Thing.** Whatever your investment philosophy, whatever your beliefs, have a written set of investment principles. Remember what Mr. Buffett says about principles. They are principles because they don't change with the latest fad.

Based on the suggestions above, take some time to write out your investment philosophies in the space provided below.

_____

_____

_____

_____

_____

The takeaway exercises—and the benefits—of this chapter are to challenge you to do the following:

- Read about other investors' philosophies (mutual fund websites are an excellent source) and read Phil Fisher's *The Development of an Investment Philosophy.*

- Come up with some original investment philosophy unique to you.

- If you haven't already done so, write down your investment beliefs and philosophies.

In the next chapter, we discuss how Warren Buffett came full circle by investing in his early childhood businesses and therefore intimately knows what he owns.

Chapter 5

Know What You Own

"One of the greatest pieces of economic wisdom is to know what you do not know."

—John Kenneth Galbraith

Once you have determined your investor personality and developed your investment philosophy, you are ready to understand what you are going to or have already invested in.

Creating Buffett Wealth starts with knowing what you own. Without that knowledge, there is no wealth. When the Internet, dot-com, and technology bubble burst after a period of widespread irrational investor behavior, Warren was asked what he thought or what he would say to all those people who lost money, many their life savings. Resisting the opportunity to say "I told you so" because he had long preached against investing in anything that you do not understand, he simply said, "If you know what you own, you will be fine."

You run into trouble if you own for any other reason. Momentum investors were hit the hardest because they were investing in something that was going up in price (not in value) and they didn't really understand it.

The world's greatest investor is often quoted, "I don't understand technology so I don't invest in it." With an IQ far exceeding the average Wall Street participant, what he is really saying is that he doesn't understand the ridiculously high valuations of technology companies, so he doesn't invest in them.

Remember that risk comes from not knowing what you are doing.

"The only time to buy that which you don't understand," Warren says with a smile, "is on any day with no 'y' in it." In other words, never buy what you don't know.

Some of the best advice from the Prophet of Profit: "For some reason, people take their cues from *price* action rather than from *values*. What doesn't work is when you start doing things that you don't understand or because they worked last week for someone else. The dumbest reason in the world to buy a stock is because it is going up. Investment must be rational. If you don't understand it, don't do it. I want to be able to explain my mistakes. This means I only do the things I completely understand."

What attracts Buffett to old-economy stocks like Berkshire textile mills is that he knows what he owns. Textiles have been around since Adam and Eve, and so have insurance and banking. His list of boring but essential subsidiaries now exceeds one hundred and includes just about everything needed in the home. The companies were founded on average in 1909 and are primarily managed by families for the benefit of families.

Wealth building requires that you know the valuation of what you are buying, you know management, the competition, and you understand what would be an attractive stock purchase price. It's no different if you're buying a piece of a business by investing in that company's stock or if you're buying a business outright to be the sole owner of that company.

There's no real difference on valuation, price, or management influence whether you're buying an appliance, a home, an automobile, or a mutual fund. The process is just like dating and the engagement process when you're selecting a mate. You should know what you're getting into. Warren jokingly says that when selecting a mate, you should look for someone who has very low expectations. He enjoys it when his wife says, "Oh, Warren, I'm so surprised."

Remember the story of GEICO auto insurance from Chapter 2? While still in college, on a weekend research mission, he found out that his professor Benjamin Graham was chairman of GEICO auto insurance. So he took a train from New York City to Washington DC, and he spent the day learning about the business of direct auto insurance. He wanted to find out the essence of the business; GEICO eliminated the middleman and passed the savings on to their customers.

He first made a small investment in GEICO in 1951 for $10,282 (it represented 100 percent of his net worth at that time, and he sold it a year later for $15,259), then he bought a third of the company, in 1976 for $45.7 million and became a director. He then bought the rest that he didn't already own in 1995 for $2.3 billion. GEICO is an excellent example of Warren knowing what he owned. He knew the company's management, he knew its customers, and he knew its competition. He knew what an excellent value it would be, and he also knew what price he'd be willing to pay. Ultimately, value investing is buying a business for less than you think it is worth.

This type of research is possible for small investors. One private investor bought stock in a national fabric retailer. He made a sizeable fortune because he knew what he owned, bought a substantial amount in relation to his net worth, bought at a deep discount to its real value, and was able to monitor his investment by visiting the local store in his area, usually on Saturday. What is going on locally is probably going on nationwide. Although he doesn't buy fabric and isn't a customer, he understands what he owns. Retail fabric is not very difficult to know. He visits his local manager, he examines the quarterly earnings, he reads the annual reports, and he attends the annual meetings. He knows who the company's customers are, and he knows its competitors.

This investment strategy is available to all investors who are willing to do the hard work of research and the weekly visits to the local branch of the national retailer to talk with the manager to see how sales are going. Restaurant investments offer this same opportunity to know what you own, to be a customer, and to extrapolate local numbers into systemwide statistics. You can count cars in the parking lot and figure out one-hour sales volume and determine annual revenue. You can talk with the competitor down the street and they will tell you everything you always wanted to know but were afraid to ask.

Be careful where you get your advice, particularly if you're listening to the so-called experts or talking heads on television. Keep in mind that you don't know what their self-interest is, because they may suggest buying something and often do, just because the price has gone down. Some unscrupulous financial talk-show guests sometimes resort to advising selling a stock they have just shorted (a bet in a stock price decline) and are just as likely to recommend a stock that they have just purchased. Whatever you purchase, remember to evaluate that stock's intrinsic *value*. Again, you really need to know what you own.

According to the Buffett School of investing, students need to know only two things: (1) how to value a business and (2) how to think about market prices.

If Warren were to teach a business school class about wealth building and the stock market, he would simply have the students do one business valuation after the other. He would ask them if they knew what they owned. He would ask them to keep their stock valuations and portfolios simple. As mentioned earlier, he would have just one final exam: He would ask all the students to value an Internet company, and he would flunk any student who turned in an answer. The world's greatest investor thinks it is impossible to value a business that hasn't earned money and is in an industry that is changing so rapidly that figuring out who the winners will be is difficult. The degree of difficulty with the new economy is too great, even for the financial industry's sharpest mind to evaluate and value it.

Some believe and teach the concept of efficient market theory: that which is known about a stock is already reflected in its stock price. This approach in essence tells investors (and students) that the market offers no opportunities and that it doesn't pay to read, research, and know what you own.

Graham said, "In the short run the market is a voting machine, and in the long run it is a weighing machine." Figure 5.1, updated from Robert Shiller's *Irrational Exuberance*, shows price as the voting machine and earnings as the weighing machine. One of Buffett's famous quotes is, "Price is what you pay and value is what you get." If you know what you own, you are more likely to purchase an excellent value.

INVEST IN COMPANIES WHOSE PRODUCTS OR SERVICES YOU UNDERSTAND

Quite often, we regionalize our investments. We think we know and understand the local industry and the company where we work. Investors from Arkansas invest in Wal-Mart. Californians buy Silicon Valley stocks. Seattle residents feel comfortable with Microsoft and Boeing; Texans invest in the oil industry. New Yorkers feel they know the media and advertising.

However, you don't want to invest in autos just because you drive one or because you live in Detroit. Nor should Floridians buy Disney or orange juice manufacturers. It's more than just knowing something about the companies that you're investing in and the products those companies make or the services those companies provide. You also need to know that the stock you're buying is an excellent value and that the company is part of a growing industry.

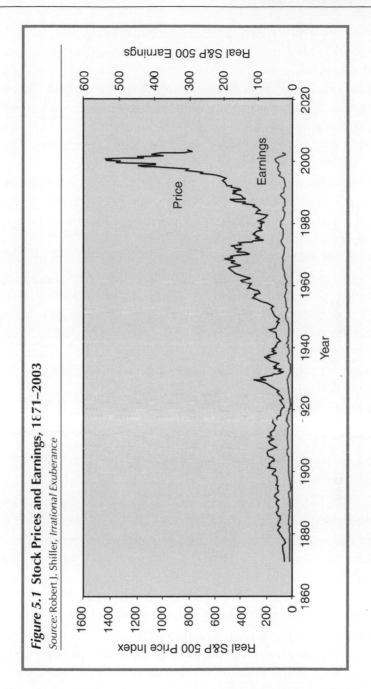

Figure 5.1 Stock Prices and Earnings, 1871–2003

Source: Robert J. Shiller, *Irrational Exuberance*

A good test is to ask yourself if you could explain your investments to a ten-year-old. That may help you determine whether or not you really know what you own.

The wild swings in share prices are really your friend. Be careful of groupthink that is so prevalent in the stock market. Warren is often quoted as saying, "You are neither right nor wrong because the crowd agrees or disagrees with you. You are right if your principles, research, data, future projections, and reasoning are right."

The major university head librarian who said about Buffett, "You know, Warren is a great future investor," meant that he is able to predict the future stream of earnings of a business and industry and buy it at a discount to its real value for the long term.

All investors must look into the future. In 1979 in *Forbes* magazine, Warren said, "The future is never clear. You pay a very high price in the stock market for a cheery consensus. Uncertainty is the friend of the buyer of long-term values." Buying when everyone is selling and selling when everyone is buying is the old adage on how to make money in the stock market, but that's easier said than done. However, if you know what you own and understand why it is such an excellent value, then you position yourself to take natural advantage of the adage.

Learning to understand what you own is a matter of learning to ask the right questions. Remember the story of the fellow standing next to a dog and a stranger approached and asked, "Does your dog bite?" The fellow said, "No," so the stranger reached down and petted the dog and the dog bit him! Alarmed, the stranger said, "I thought you said your dog doesn't bite." The man said, "Well, that's not my dog." The moral of this story is to know to ask the right questions to truly understand.

Berkshire's largest investment of a partly owned business or stock is Coca-Cola, and it provides an excellent example of knowing what you own. As a young lad Buffett sold bottles of Coke door to door in his neighborhood, and as a teenager he was in the vending machine business with his pinball machines, but he didn't rely entirely on these early experiences to understand his billion-dollar investment.

For all of his early years and most of his adult life, Warren drank Pepsi-Cola; some even say that at one time if you cut his vein, Pepsi would come out instead of blood. So he personally understood the competition.

Next he read everything he could about The Coca-Cola Company: how it was founded, grew, and expanded, and its market share, international expansion, and management. Like GEICO thirty-five years earlier, Buffett could have written an extensive stock analyst's report of the security he likes best: Coca-Cola. After careful and thorough reading and research, he noticed that Coke's management was buying back its own shares. The last thing he wanted to do was tip his hat and let management know he was interested in buying. So he quietly purchased $1 billion of the stock.

Like the average investor, Warren had no exclusive or insider information. Unlike the average investor, he studied and understood what he was buying. The soft-drink beverage business is not a very difficult business to know. Figuring out when it is selling at an excellent value compared to its future earnings is the genius part.

Coca-Cola earned 42 cents per share in 1989, so Berkshire paid 15½ times what it was then earning with an average price of $6.50. Book value was $1.18 per share, so it paid 5½ times book. Buffett was paid back with actual net earnings in nine years, nearly one half of the projected earnings payback time. Meanwhile, book value has quadrupled, the stock price has climbed seven times, Coke earns three times more than when it was first purchased, and management continues to buy back its shares (10 percent since Buffett's purchase), which gives the shareholders in essence a nontax dividend making the remaining 90 percent of shares more valuable.

Today Coke sells over 1 billion servings (out of a total of 50 billion) a day and continues to enjoy worldwide leadership of the soft-drink beverage industry. So with just 2 percent of the world market, Coke has enormous growth opportunities ahead.

This type of analysis is all very easy to do in hindsight and over a decade later. The difficulty is being able to see the wonderful investment opportunity in advance, which is what makes Warren Buffett's talent so profound.

Notice how patient Buffett is and how thoroughly he understands what he is doing. A half-century after he was selling Coke door to door and more than a century after it was first formulated, he made a substantial purchase.

The husband of famed author and mystery writer Agatha Christie was an archaeologist. "That was the best occupation for a husband," said Agatha, "because the older things get, the more interested he becomes." Warren invests like an archaeologist—the older things become, the more interested he is.

In *Fortune* magazine in 1993, Warren said, "if you offered me $100 billion to take away the soft drink leadership of Coca-Cola, I would give you the money back and tell you that it couldn't be done." He jokingly says that with Coke, he has put his money where his mouth is. "Coke is exactly the kind of company I like. I like products I can understand. I don't know what a transistor is, but I appreciate the contents of a can of Coke."

There is certainly more to Buffett's methods than knowing the product and understanding how it makes its money. Snapple is a good product, and when it first went public the stock traded up to an unsustainable level. An early investor could drink and know and understand Snapple, but an investor must also know whether the intrinsic value (earnings generated from the business during its lifetime) make for an excellent purchase.

Just because the world's greatest stock picker selected Coke some fourteen years ago at a split-adjusted price of $6.50 per share doesn't mean that a purchase today at a price of over $50 per share is an excellent value. What was an excellent value in 1989 doesn't translate into an excellent value today. Things change, and a company's intrinsic value is never constant.

Today, Warren's office is jammed with commemorative Coke bottles, an old-fashioned bottle Coke machine, and a restaurant-style fountain dispenser in the file room. Often you will find a Styrofoam cup smack dab in the middle of his desk filled with Cherry Coke.

In *Forbes* magazine a decade ago, Warren said, "Bill Gates is a good friend and I think he may be the smartest guy I've ever met. But I don't know what those little things do." He meant computers. So, as a result, he doesn't invest in technology. He uses a computer at home to play bridge (one of his few indulgences, but his shareholders benefit because it keeps his mind active and sharp), and he also uses the computer to read and research. But he doesn't invest in technology.

When New Coke came out at about the time Warren made a substantial investment in Coca-Cola, Warren was quoted as saying, "A great investment opportunity occurs when a marvelous business encounters a one-time, but solvable problem. You just need to know the business to recognize this." Warren went on to say, "Time is the friend of the wonderful business and the enemy of a mediocre one."

Because he knew Coke and understood the products, he knew the New Coke fiasco would be a one-time problem offering the investor an excellent price compared to value. Warren jumped at the opportunity. He instinctively knew that time and a dominant worldwide market share were on the side of his Coke investment.

KNOW ACCOUNTING

If you really want to know what you own, you need to know and should learn accounting, because accounting is the language of business. Every investor should understand Generally Accepted Accounting Principles (GAAP) along with these important finance concepts and features:

- Compound interest
- Present and future value
- Inflation
- Price versus value
- Financial statements

Compound Interest

Albert Einstein called compound interest the eighth wonder of the world. The early Buffett Partnership letters have many examples of compound interest. Table 5.1 shows how $100,000 would compound at 5 percent, 10 percent, and 15 percent over ten, twenty, and thirty years.

In 1963 and at the age of thirty-three, to help his partners understand the joy of compounding, Buffett used the following example: Queen Isabella invested $30,000 in Christopher Columbus's western exploration. Had she and her heirs invested in something other than Columbus, by 1963 with a 4 percent annual compound rate of return, Isabella would have $2 trillion. Forty years later she would have $9.6 trillion, which is roughly all of the value of the publicly traded stocks in the new world that Columbus discovered.

Table 5.1 Compound Value of $100,000 with Different Interest Rates and Time Periods

	5%	10%	15%
10 years	$162,889	$259,374	$404,553
20 years	265,328	672,748	1,636,640
30 years	432,191	1,744,930	6,621,140

A year later the Buffett partners were given the example of the purchase of the Mona Lisa. Francis I of France paid $20,000 for Leonardo da Vinci's painting in 1540. Instead, had he invested the same $20,000 in a 6 percent after-tax investment, his estate would be worth $1,000,000,000,000,000,000,000 or $1 quadrillion (a million billion) by 1964. Today the initial investment would be worth $10 quadrillion if Francis I invested in something other than the Mona Lisa.

Another example to his partners was the sale of New York City by the Manhattan Indians in 1626 for $24. Some believe it was a bargain, until you compound $24 over 338 years at 7 percent after tax to get a present value of $205 billion (that's $2.8 trillion today).

A father, who is also an investment manager, wanted to teach his young daughters the power of compound interest. So he set aside $20 per week or $1,000 per year for them to see how at the end of eighteen years at 10 percent annual compound interest their investments would be worth $45,600 each. Asked how he knew his daughters understood compounding, he chuckled, "Because they asked me why we didn't invest $40 each per week."

You can see why Einstein called compound interest the eighth wonder of the world. All investors need to know is the power and joy of compounding.

Present and Future Value

Present value is what something is worth today and future value is what something is worth in the future. In order to calculate present or future value you need the n (number of years or periods) and the i (interest rate). A simple Texas Instrument business analyst calculator makes it simple.

For example, the present value of $10, ten years from now, at 10 percent interest is $3.86. Conversely, the future value of $3.86 invested for 10 years at 10 percent is $10.

You also need to be able to calculate the present value of a stream of payments. The present value of $1 per year for ten years at 10 percent is $6.15. This is the discounted cash flow analysis done by experienced investors. So a business earning $1 with the likelihood of continuing those earnings is worth $6.15 in ten years if your expected rate of return is 10 percent. The trick is to understand how predictable those annual earnings are, how honest the managers are, and whether those earnings are likely to grow, shrink, or disappear based on your knowledge of the industry and its competitors.

Inflation

The joy of compounding quickly turns into the sorrow of compounding when you understand the impact of inflation (and taxes) on your investment returns. Inflation is the power of compounding in the reverse. It steals away your earning power and represents how much more you need to pay for goods and services. A 3 percent investment in an environment of 3 percent inflation gives the asset holder a net gain of zero, no matter how long you hold the investment. Many investors actually experience a negative return with a 4 percent bank CD or fixed income instrument like a bond, with a 3 percent inflation rate and a 2 percent tax rate (if it is invested in a taxable account).

Price versus Value

Stock market participants need to know the difference between price and value. Price is determined in an auction environment and is set by the last seller and buyer. This may be higher or lower than the value of the stock. The shrewd investor needs to determine the value (based on the present value of its future earnings) to determine if the price is attractive or unattractive. Remember that intrinsic value is never static and changes constantly with market forces.

The more you understand Buffett, the more you move away from talking about price and instead focus on value. Price is one-dimensional, a component of value, and is determined by the last two people who agree to sell and buy. Price is about the present. Value is multidimensional and involves the unpredictable future.

Financial Statements

Successful investors must be able to read quarterly and annual reports of the companies in which they invest. There is no other way to know what you own.

Balance sheets show assets minus liabilities, which equals the book value or worth of the business. You need to note how this value changes over time, both before you own it and after you purchase it.

The income statement is the earnings from the business. Ultimately income gives a stock its value. Continuing the example above, if a stock is earning $1 per year and is likely to continue earning it into the future and the expected rate of return is 10 percent, then the stock should be priced at $6.15. If you understand the company, then a price below $6.15 is a bargain and a price above it is unattractive.

HOW TO LEARN MORE ABOUT POTENTIALLY SUPERIOR INVESTMENTS

Fortunately or unfortunately (depending on how you choose to look at it), the average investor has a virtually unlimited amount of investment choices and combination of choices. Just in the United States, there are nine thousand publicly traded stocks and an equal number of mutual funds. Throw in bonds, bank CDs, insurance products, privately held businesses, real estate, and commodities, and you can see how the average investor is easily overwhelmed. The simple answer is that you only need to choose five or six world-class investments (more on that in Chapter 7). The difficult question is which ones to choose and when to buy them. Successful active investors look at a minimum of one hundred stocks before choosing one investment target.

Warren Buffett often uses baseball metaphors to illustrate some aspects of his investing philosophy and strategy. In speaking about the various choices facing the average investor, Buffett suggests that, in baseball, you can be called out for not swinging at three hittable pitches. With investing, there are no called strikes. The market can lob you fat pitches all day long and there is no penalty for not swinging. You can stand at the plate all day long, all week, month, year or decade, and not swing and not be called out.

You can wait for the fat pitch when the fielders are asleep and hit it out of the ballpark—the fat pitch being those companies that no one is paying attention to and that are trading at a price less than its value, in industries that will enjoy steady future growth.

To continue the baseball analogies, Warren surrounds himself with players and managers who are .400 hitters and he leaves them alone. In his 1986 letter to shareholders he said this: "Charlie and I know that the right players will make almost any team manager look good. We subscribe to the philosophy of Ogilvy & Mather's founding genius, David Ogilvy: "If each of us hires people who are smaller than we are, we shall become a company of dwarfs. But, if each of us hires people who are bigger than we are, we shall become a company of giants."

Warren says that on a typical day, "First I get up and I tap dance into work. And then I sit down and I read. Then I talk on the phone for seven or eight hours. Then I take home more to read. Then I talk on the phone in the evening. We read a lot. We have a general sense of what we're after. We're looking for seven-footers. That's about all there is to it."

Obviously he's being modest and minimizing the genius of what he does. He does enjoy his work and chooses every person who he works with. Warren has said many times that he enjoys what he does so much that he would work for free.

Like every super-investor, he reads five times more than the average investor, and he has been known to read a four-hundred-page book in one sitting. He reads annual reports cover to cover and every day he reads the *New York Times*, the *Washington Post*, and the *Wall Street Journal*. However, he doesn't subscribe to investment newsletters. He does subscribe to Valueline for its research data on publicly traded stocks.

He talks to his various CEOs (approximately fifty report directly, with three to four more added each year) by phone about their respective businesses. They have a direct line, and if he is traveling he will return their messages within hours. His main responsibility is to approve all of the major capital expenditures within each wholly owned subsidiary.

He enjoys the insurance calculations performed by Ajit Jain, CEO in charge of one of his reinsurance companies, so he talks with him every day. The two of them figure out what premium is necessary to cover a potential insurance claim like a California earthquake or career-ending injury to the world's highest paid baseball player.

Active investors can work just as hard to read about various investments. Buffett is looking for just one good idea a year because he has more money than ideas. Most smaller investors have more ideas than money, and that is a huge advantage.

Potentially superior investments can be found by looking for companies that are buying back their stock. In 1976 Berkshire purchased a third of GEICO stock for $46 million. Because management was buying back its stock, Berkshire's investment grew from one third to one half without further investment. Same thing with Coca-Cola, Berkshire initially bought 6 percent of the company, which has now grown to 8 percent, in part because of management share buybacks.

Many stock market participants concern themselves with the wrong activity. They buy, sell, trade, and listen to the investment pitches and swing away. Instead, your activity in investing, Warren suggests, should be reading, research, and thinking, so that you know what you own, not buying, selling, and trading. He says, "We don't get paid for activity, we get paid for being right."

SEVEN TIPS ON HOW TO KNOW WHAT YOU OWN

#1: Invest Rationally, Not Emotionally

Rational investing is one of the main ideas Buffett got from Graham. Stock market investing is best where it is most rational. Remember to think of stocks as businesses, and buy them like you were buying the whole business—with careful consideration and research. Mr. Market is irrational, swinging from manic irrational exuberance to depression, from greed to fear, investing with emotion. Mr. Buffett is rational, investing intelligently and always based on value. Instead of heavily traded, new economy, sexy businesses, this super investor looks for ignored, old-economy, and boring enterprises.

#2: Focus on Domestic Investments

In terms of international investing, Warren suggests that it's hard to know the political, currency, market, and cultural risks of companies that are based in countries other than the one in which you're living and investing. For example, to the students at the University of North Carolina in Chapel Hill in 1995 Warren said:

> We love the kinds of companies that we can do well in international markets, obviously, particularly where they're largely un-

tapped. Would we buy Coca-Cola if, instead of being [located] in Atlanta, the company [were located] in London or Amsterdam or someplace else? The answer of course is yes. Would I like it quite as well? The answer is a tiny notch less, because there might be nuances in corporate governance factors or tax factors or attitude towards capitalists, or anything else that I might not understand quite as well, even in England, as I might in the United States. If I can't make money in a $5 trillion market [right here in the United States], it may be a little bit of wishful thinking to think that all I have to do is get a few thousand miles away, and I'll start showing off my stuff.

#3: Define Your Circle of Competence

What are you capable of understanding? A successful active investor looks at most investments and says, "It's outside my circle of competence." Know what you don't know and be honest with yourself.

The world's most successful investor often gives this advice: "Draw a circle around the businesses you understand and then eliminate those that fail to qualify on the basis of value, good management, and limited exposure to hard times. It's not how large, but how well defined the circle is, particularly at the perimeter. Don't compare yourself to someone else's larger circle with a fuzzy edge."

In the 1995 annual meeting of Berkshire Hathaway, Warren described how he came to be an outstanding investor:

> I would take one industry at a time and develop some expertise in a half a dozen companies in that industry. I would not take the conventional wisdom now about any industries as meaning a damn thing. I would try to think it through. If I were looking at an insurance company or a paper company, I would put myself in the frame of mind that I just inherited the company and it was the only asset my family was ever going to own.
>
> What would I do with it? What am I thinking about? What am I worried about? Who are my competitors? Who are my customers? Go out and talk to them. Find out the strengths and weaknesses of this particular company versus the other ones [in the same industry]. If you have done that, you may understand the business better than the management.

Warren is extremely thorough at evaluating companies. For example, one of Warren's managers, who sold his business in its entirety to Berkshire for $1.5 billion, said that he and Warren met for only an hour and a half to structure the deal. But the manager realized during that time that Warren Buffett knew more about his business than he did—and this manager had founded the company!

Warren has commented on how his "know what you own" philosophy applies to all stocks, not only the old-economy stocks in which he himself invests:

> Our principles are valid when applied to technology stocks, but we don't know how to do it. If we are going to lose money, we want to be able to get up here next year and explain how we did it. I'm sure Bill Gates would apply the same principles. He understands technology the way I understand Coca-Cola or Gillette. I'm sure he looks for the same margin of safety. I'm sure he would approach it like he was owning a business, not just a stock. So our principles can work for any technology. We just aren't the ones to do it. If we can't find things within our circle of competence, we don't expand the circle. We wait.

#4: Know a Lot about a Little

Even Buffett recognizes a limit on what you can know. For example, when speaking to the students of his alma mater, Columbia University, a few years ago, he said, "Anyone who tells you they can value . . . all the stocks on the board must have a very inflated idea of their own ability, because it's not that easy. But if you spend your time focusing on some industries, you'll learn a lot about valuation."

Being able to value companies properly is the key to Buffett Wealth. The only way to do that is to focus on what you know and own.

#5: Forget Missed Opportunities

Even the world's greatest investor has missed out on some golden investing opportunities, including pharmaceuticals, cellular, cable, software, and telecom. Being part of every fantastic investment is not possible, and one can get very wealthy by focusing on opportunities ahead instead of missed pitches behind.

#6: Read and Research

By reading five times more than everyone else, you will naturally recognize and welcome opportunities as they show themselves to you. To be a successful investor and build the kind of wealth that Warren Buffett has, you must be an investigative journalist. Bob Woodward, who works for the *Washington Post* and of Watergate fame, once asked Warren Buffett how he analyzed stocks. Warren said, "Investing is like reporting. I told [Woodward] to imagine he had been assigned an in-depth article about his own newspaper. He'd ask a lot of questions and dig up a lot of facts. He'd know the *Washington Post*, and that's all there is to it." In other words, you should be curious.

#7: Be Book and Street Smart

One of the great things about the stock market is that it knows no race, religion, age, gender, education, or country. It is meritocracy at its best. An Asian immigrant living in Canada without a high school diploma can achieve Buffett Wealth. Investing is naturally diverse and holds no prejudices. It embraces all, preferring irrational behavior (because Wall Street makes more money off of them) but rewarding intelligent investors.

Warren has benefited from his higher education with a master's degree in economics (the equivalent of an MBA today) from an Ivy League school. He supports and recommends good quality public education and universities, although he does suggest that it's a waste of time to get a PhD in economics. He said, "It's like spending eight years in divinity school and later finding out that all you needed to know is the Ten Commandments." But you need to know what you're looking for. Know what kind of investor you are.

CONCLUSION

The takeaway exercises for this chapter are:

- Review your portfolio and determine if you know what you own. Do you understand how each company makes money? Can you explain it to elementary-school students in a way that they would understand?

- Study and know simple accounting. Be able to read balance sheets, income statements, quarterly earnings reports, and annual reports.

- Know how to calculate the present value of a future stream of income. Keep your math simple, suggests Warren. Don't do calculations with Greek letters in them. Most complex calculations are confusing and prevent you from really knowing what you own.

- Be reasonable and have realistic goals. You only need to own stock in a few outstanding companies.

- Know your circle of competence. The businesses in which you own stock should be those you fully understand. Keep these inside your circle. Maybe you'll recognize other companies that you don't understand that you shouldn't put inside your circle. With these businesses you should ask yourself, what is it that you are capable of understanding? Remember what Warren said: Draw a circle around the businesses you understand, and then eliminate those that fail to qualify on the basis of value, good management, and limited exposure to hard times.

- Read the annual reports of the businesses that you invest in or want to invest in. You should be an investigative journalist and know what you own.

The next chapter discusses investing on Main Street, not Wall Street. Chapter 6 may change your focus from your computer screen to your corner retailer. You may begin to believe, as Warren does, that the stock market could close for a few years, and it would not cause you to do anything differently.

Chapter 6

Invest in Main Street, Not Wall Street

"Wall Street predicted nine out of the last five recessions!"
—Paul A. Samuelson

Knowing what you own makes you focus your investment attention on Main Street. It's the everyday boring businesses that have attracted Warren Buffett, not the sexy start-up with the latest and greatest technological invention.

The premise of this chapter is that more wealth has been created on Main Street than on Wall Street. Warren Buffett created billions by investing in everyday common businesses found on Main Street USA. Wall Street may advertise for your investment dollar, but Main Street deserves your investment attention.

Main Street is your everyday mom-and-pop neighborhood store, where the Horatio Alger stories of hard work, sweat equity, gumption, ingenuity, and a little bit of being in the right place at the right time begin. Main Street is your local businessperson, your neighbor, your friend, your daughter, maybe even you. Main Street is value-based and long-term, maybe multigenerational, passed down from grandfather to daughter to granddaughter. When they say the Smith Brothers, they really are brothers. If it's Jones and Son, there really is a son. Main Street is in business for families, run and managed by families. Main Street is on the inside. It's about value.

Wall Street is the faceless world of transactions. It's the electronic blip on your screen representing thousands, maybe billions of dollars. It's the advertising, the self-interested advisors, the fine print, the contracts, and the quick deal. Wall Street is on the outside. It's about price.

INVEST IN COMPANIES CLOSE TO HOME

Warren was once asked how to get rich quick. He held his nose with one hand, and with the other he pointed to Wall Street. "Wall Street is the only place," according to Warren, "that people ride to in a Rolls Royce to get advice from those who take the subway."

It's all about Main Street, which in Warren's hometown of Omaha, Nebraska, is actually called Dodge Street. What Warren has learned from Dodge Street, you can, too. Warren has invested in companies that make bricks, paint, insulation, carpet, vacuums, jewelry, furniture, appliances, electronics, encyclopedias, shoes, ice cream, and candy, as well as electricity and America's second largest real estate brokerage firm. His companies operate under names like Acme Brick, Benjamin Moore Paint, Johns Manville, Shaw Carpet, Kirby Vacuum, Borsheim's Jewelry, Helzberg Diamond, Ben Bridge Jewelers, Nebraska Furniture Mart, R.C. Willey Home Furnishings, Star Furniture, Jordan's Furniture, Homemakers Furniture, Cort, World Book Encyclopedias, Dexter Shoes, H.H. Brown, Justin Boot, Dairy Queen, Sees Candy, Mid American Energy, and Home Services.

The Omaha influence on his Main Street approach is most telling in the story of the Nebraska Furniture Mart. A woman named Rose Blumkin launched this company when she was in her forties and a mother of four. She founded it without any money of her own, borrowing $500 from her brother so she could take the train to Chicago and line up suppliers. With one sale at a time, she built what is now the largest single-location retail enterprise in the world, selling $1 million a day of furniture, appliances, electronics, and floor coverings.

Warren was a customer of that business before he was an investor, because the store is just a few blocks from his home. In the 1980s, he walked in and asked Mrs. Blumkin (or Mrs. B as she was known) if she'd like to sell her business. She sold 80 percent of the business for $55 million. That location now enjoys more than $360 million a year in sales, which illustrates the success of investing in Mrs. Blumkin and looking at Dodge Street or Main Street, not Wall Street.

Warren asked Mrs. B. simple questions when he walked into the store with the intention of buying into the business. What are your sales? Will management stay on? What is your inventory and is it paid for? What are your earnings? (Sales were then $80 million.) Management, which consisted of her son and grandsons, would stay on. (Because they own 20 percent of the business, they have a natural incentive to grow the business and maximize profits). Mrs. B paid for everything in cash so she had no debt. And the business was earning then, as it is today, about 10 percent on sales, or $8 million.

Buffett bought the business without doing an audit, checking the figures, or even a complex business contract or noncompete agreement. The total closing costs were just $1,400, less than a typical residential real estate transaction.

The Nebraska Furniture Mart operates under the motto "Sell cheap and tell the truth." One of Buffett's management secrets is that Mrs. B, and now her grandsons, have forgotten that they sold the business to Warren Buffett, and Warren Buffett has forgotten that he bought it. Buying successful Main Street businesses with talented managers and leaving them alone is the true investment and management genius of Warren Buffett.

Borsheim's Jewelry, also on Dodge Street a few blocks from his home, is another example. He walked in one day and asked if the owners would sell the business. He was first a customer, then an owner, and he asked the original owners the same simple questions he had asked Mrs. B. What are your sales? What are your gross profits? What are your expenses? What's your inventory? Will the family managers stay on? There is no difference in buying a whole business, like these two on Main Street, or buying part of a business through the stock market.

You should ask the same questions. Remember Victor Kiam and his Remington Razor Company? "I liked the razor so much I bought the company." The Nebraska Furniture Mart and Borsheim's Jewelry are examples of being a customer first in your own hometown and then buying into the business. The next logical step is to begin looking elsewhere, but still following the practice of being a satisfied customer first and then investigating the company to see if it's worth buying into.

One of Warren's better investments may have been NetJets, which is literally based on Main Street in Woodbridge, New Jersey. NetJets started as the creation of Rich Santulli, who innovated the concept of time-sharing corporate jets. Instead of an individual or a company owning its own jet in its entirety, NetJets allows an individual or company to buy just the number of hours they need to fly each year. Customers receive all of the advantages of owning a fleet of corporate jets without any of the hassles and for substantially lower costs.

When Warren first tried the business, he called Rich Santulli and said, "If you ever want to sell the business, I would like to buy it." Santulli confided that "There's only one person I would sell my business to and that is Warren Buffett." He knew that Warren would bring him capital to expand, a AAA credit rating to order the largest fleet of airplanes, and a gold-plated customer list (including most of Berkshire's board members and CEOs). At the same time, Warren would leave him alone so that he could run the business.

In 1998, Berkshire paid $725 million for a business that will be as large or larger one day than Federal Express. In terms of quality of life, convenience, privacy, safety, and security, there probably isn't a better purchase for an individual or corporation with a net worth of $20 million or more. Net-Jets enjoys the best safety record (no fatalities since it started in 1986), flies at higher altitudes, uses less congested airports, and has the best trained pilots (trained by FlightSafety, a wholly owned Berkshire business).

You may recognize some of the owners of NetJets. Pete Sampras, Tiger Woods, and movie-megastar-turned-politican Arnold Schwarzenegger all enjoy the convenience of picking up the phone and, with just a four-hour notice, wherever they are, their jet will be delivered to take them and whoever else they would like to wherever they would like to go in the world.

NetJets operates more than 240,000 flights annually to over 140 countries (more than any of the major airlines). Based on the number of jets, it can be considered America's sixth largest airline. Warren Buffett knew about this business, used it as a customer, and then made his investment. Based on his background of investing in pieces of a business by owning shares, he instinctively knew that owning a share of an expensive plane made better economic sense than owning the whole thing.

Warren has shifted his wealth building from Wall Street to Main Street, or from partly owned and publicly traded businesses to wholly owned businesses often purchased from privately held families. Buffett began this shift almost immediately after acquiring Berkshire Hathaway textile mills. Buying control over a business is preferred so that the world's greatest capital allocator could take the earnings and redeploy them in the best possible use. Earnings were, and still are, then used to purchase more wholly owned enterprises at an excellent value to current assets and earn-ings. See Table 6.1 to understand the percentage breakdown between asset classes for the six-year period from 1997 to 2002.

Notice how stocks made up 73 percent of his asset mix in 1997, and by 2002 just 26 percent without selling any equities. Just as common stocks have been reduced as a percentage of assets, wholly owned subsidiaries have dramatically risen from 4 percent of assets in 1997 to 30 percent five years later. Not long ago, as an investor on Wall Street with common stock pur-chases, Buffett's asset mix was 90 percent Wall Street (stocks) and 10 per-cent Main Street (businesses).

Before, as a part owner, Buffett could look but not touch the earnings of the publicly traded companies. He called this "look-through earnings." Table 6.2 helps explain the simple concept of look-through earnings. For

---

Table 6.1 Buffett's Asset Allocation

Source: Berkshire-Hathaway annual reports.

	1997	1998	1999	2000	2001	2002
Cash	2%	18%	5%	5%	6%	10%
Bonds	21%	27%	39%	34%	39%	34%
Stocks	73%	51%	51%	39%	30%	26%
Businesses	4%	4%	5%	22%	25%	30%
	100%	100%	100%	100%	100%	100%

Table 6.2 Look-Through Earnings

Source: Company annual reports.

Company	Shares*	Earnings per Share	Look-Through Earnings (shares × eps)*
Coca-Cola	200	$1.65	$330
American Express	152	2.01	306
Gillette	96	1.15	110
Wells Fargo	53	3.40	180
Washington Post	2 .	22.61	45
Total Look Through Earnings			$971

*Shares and look-through earnings in millions

example, if you own two hundred shares of Coca-Cola, and the company earns $1.65 per share, you have $330 of look-through earnings. The company may choose to pay you 20 cents per quarterly dividend and therefore return part of those earnings and hopefully wisely use the rest of the earnings to grow the business, or even buy back its own stock in order to make the remaining shares more valuable.

This look-through earnings shown in Table 6.2 is actually the exact portfolio of stocks owned by Buffett. Just add one million to the second and fourth columns and you will see that his stocks earn nearly $1 billion per year, but he is unable to touch the earnings unless they are paid out as dividends.

U.S.-BASED INVESTING

When investors make that shift from Wall Street to Main Street, they invest not based on stock price, but based on what's going on in the business itself. They partner themselves with the CEO. They ask different questions when they're owners. What's the strategic plan of the business? Who are the competitors? What are the long-term prospects? They naturally begin to localize their investment choices.

The story of Coca-Cola offers another example of what Main Street taught Warren Buffett. The Buffett family was in the grocery store business for one hundred years. The family sold a lot of Coca-Cola, and Warren was able to make observations then and now by what's going on in his local market with the sale of Coca-Cola. The contents of each can are very easy to understand.

Warren can even monitor his investment in American Express. He can go into his local restaurant on Main Street and see just how American Express is doing based on the number of charges by the local customers. Even Gillette is all about what's happening on Main Street, not on Wall Street. The men's shaving market is global in scope but local in concept and easy to understand. Since Gillette owns 70 percent of the worldwide market, what is happening in your local community is probably happening each day around the world. As Buffett says, he likes the fact that 2.5 billion men go to sleep each evening and grow whiskers.

MAIN STREET INVESTING IS FOR THE LONG TERM

In the early 1970s, Warren bought Sees Candies, a boxed chocolate manufacturer and retailer based in California. The business was purchased for $25 million. Today, that business on Main Street, with locations throughout most California cities, enjoys earnings three times that original purchase price: $75 million in annual earnings. The business was not purchased to be sold, because all of the businesses Warren purchases are for life.

What would you think if your local businesses on Main Street kept changing owners? Yet that's exactly what happens on the NASDAQ with a new owner every six months, and on the New York Stock Exchange, with a new owner every twelve months. According to the *Wall Street Journal*, the NASDAQ has a 200 percent annual turnover and the NYSE has a 100 percent annual turnover, so the majority of Wall Street stock ownership shifts dramatically during a typical year. Wall Street invests in *stock*, whereas Main Street invests in *business*.

Another aspect of this turnover is that the typical CEO for a company with publicly traded stock is busy trying to attract new shareholders, spending on average fifty days per year outside the business. Because prospective owners are attracted to short-term price movements and because most managers are compensated with stock options based on price, the typical CEO spends a great deal of time and money talking about the stock price and its likely price in three months.

Main Street managers and Buffett CEOs, in contrast, are compensated on changes in the value of the business.

The Washington Post Company is an excellent example of a Wall Street–traded but Main Street–type investment. Purchased in part by Berkshire some thirty years ago, the daily newspaper is a local source for news in and around the Washington DC area that happens to include the president of the United States, so the *Post* is thought of as a national and international business. It isn't.

To keep its shareholders for the long term, the Washington Post stock price (as with Berkshire) is not split to encourage trading of its stock, and the Graham family controls most of the company with a separate class of stock. Washington Post managers concern themselves with the underlying value of their businesses, not the stock price.

WALL STREET VS. MAIN STREET

The real irony is that Wall Street looks to Warren Buffett. Just a rumor that his holding company is looking at an investment will send the stock up 5 to 10 percent. Wall Street investors show up by the thousands in Warren's hometown of Omaha to hear him answer unedited questions from shareholders each spring for six hours.

What works on Wall Street doesn't always work on Main Street. For example, one hundred ownership changes each minute on the stock exchanges would not work on Main Street. But what works on Main Street always works for an investor. Main Street is all about buying the ownership of a local business, not a stock. Wall Street is about buying and selling, and that's hard to do on Main Street. It would be ridiculous to imagine your Main Street businesses posting for-sale signs every day, and when one owner buys he or she immediately begins to think about selling. You would naturally question any one person owning several smaller portions of many businesses (Wall Street) instead of owning the majority of one business (Main Street).

The questions you ask when buying a business should be the same as if you were buying a stock. Do you understand the business? What about its management? What about the financials? *Then* you talk about the price. Conversely, Wall Street talks first about price.

Warren Buffett ironically is known as the "good guy on Wall Street." He participates in no unfriendly deals, and all of the employees are retained whenever he makes an acquisition. As Professor Benjamin Graham is known as the "Dean of Wall Street," Warren should be known as the "Dean of Main Street." You can skip reading the *Wall Street Journal* and instead read the *Main Street Journal* or your local hometown newspaper.

At the 2002 Annual General Meeting of Berkshire Hathaway shareholders, Warren was quoted as saying: "Wall Street loves the crook. Investment bankers don't care about investors. Stock-option-engorged CEOs are shameless and American business is teeming with fraud. Wall Street is the legal pickpocket of wealth."

Warren Buffett's methods differ from the prevailing wisdom on Wall Street. Main Street investing is about analyzing a business. It's about concentrating your ownership in one or just a few businesses. It's about management ethics, management values, management character. It's about loyalty—of customers, of employees, of managers, and of owners. In sharp contrast, Wall Street investing is different. It's about analyzing the market. It's about diversifying your portfolio among many industries, many companies, and other types of investment vehicles (which may include investing in international stock markets, the bond market, real estate, gold, etc.). It's about excessive trading. It's about activity for activity's sake. It's what everyone else is doing. It's about in today and out tomorrow. It's short-term in nature. It's not about value. It's all about price—the price of the stock at any given moment of any given day.

Warren is the antithesis of Wall Street. Traders make their money based on price movements of the stock. In contrast, Warren has built his wealth and makes his money based on the performance of the individual businesses in which he is invested. He focuses on and concentrates his investments in a few companies. He doesn't split his stock, and he doesn't believe that trading activity on Wall Street will ever build wealth. He is the only CEO to measure himself not on the price movement of his holding company, but rather on the annual changes in book value.

Moreover, a stock split does nothing for the economic value of a business. It does everything for Wall Street, though, because Wall Street has learned that if a stock is trading at $80 a share and the company splits it in two to sell the stock at $40 a share, stock brokers will sell twice as many shares and make twice the commission. But the split does nothing to the business on Main Street or the way that it runs or the way it makes money for its investors and partners.

Stock Splits and Pizza

A favorite Yogi-ism to help explain the benefit of stock splits:

When asked if he wanted his pizza split into four or eight slices, Yogi Berra replied: "Four. I don't think I can eat eight."

Warren Buffett's philosophy has always been to make wealth together, not at the expense of his partners. For every $1 of wealth he has created for himself, he has created $2 for his partners. When asked at a recent press conference what his greatest nightmare would be, many thought he would say some insurance calamity in a business that he owned or a major defection by CEOs, because he has more CEOs working for him than any other enterprise in the world. Instead, he said his greatest nightmare was attracting the wrong shareholder. He doesn't want to advertise for shareholders and say, "Opera inside," and for people to walk in and find a rock concert. He wants to attract loyal, long-term partners and owners who believe in and focus on what's going on inside the business, not what the stock price is doing on Wall Street. Loyal owners of businesses do best, and loyal owners treat employees like family.

Other Main Street investments of Warren's holding company include Jordan's Furniture of Boston and Star Furniture of Houston. Jordan's sells an estimated $200 million per year and is the largest furniture retailer in Massachusetts and New Hampshire. With over $100 million in sales, Star Furniture is the largest furniture retailer in Texas. When those businesses were purchased, the family managers and owners (Tatelman's of Jordan's and Wolff's of Star), with proceeds out of their own pockets, paid each employee $0.50 for every hour they had worked, or $1,000 a year. So if you had worked for either of these businesses when they were sold to Warren Buffett, you would have received a check—if you had worked ten years, your check was for $10,000, paid out of the proceeds of the managers of the business, the owners of the business, not from Warren Buffett. Those are the kinds of owner/managers and businesses that Warren looks for on Main Street, and those are exactly the kind of businesses to which he's attracted.

Since October 2002, Berkshire has transformed itself from an insurance company into a conglomerate with most of its revenue now coming from noninsurance businesses. Its employees now exceed 165,000 with the latest acquisitions of convenience store and wholesale food supplier McLane Company (14,500 employees) and manufactured home leader Clayton Homes (6,800 employees). Berkshire's employees will continue to grow, with three to four new acquisitions per year (see Figure 6.1).

Wall Street investing has little concern for the employee. In fact, many employees are made redundant to make the acquisition pay for itself. Main Street investors concern themselves with the managers and the employees, which is perhaps why Berkshire gets the first phone call when a business becomes available for sale.

Main Street concerns itself with selling goods and services at an attractive value to its customers. In contrast, Wall Street sells anything that investors will buy. The stock market is not your friend. To quote Warren, "Your broker is like a doctor who charges his patients on how often they

Figure 6.1 **Berkshire Employee Map**

Source: Fortune, Oct. 27, 2002; www.berkshirehathaway.com

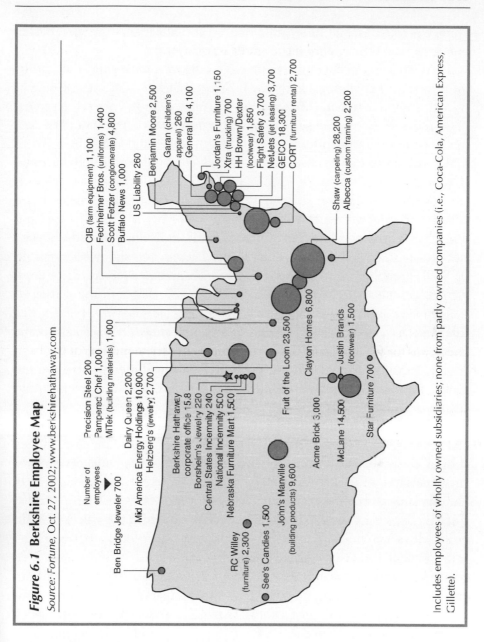

Includes employees of wholly owned subsidiaries; none from partly owned companies (i.e., Coca-Cola, American Express, Gillette).

change medicines, and he's paid more not for what will make you better, but rather from the stuff that the street is promoting."

And a word on buying on margin. To borrow against your stock to buy more stock is very profitable for Wall Street, but like Warren, you should not be in a hurry to build your wealth. In terms of debt, borrowing against your stocks, Warren would simply say, "Just don't do it." You should be debt free. The more transactions that Wall Street makes and encourages you to make, the more money Wall Street makes. Your money simply becomes their money.

Wall Street has even created its own jargon to intimidate the investor. Instead of empowering the individual investor, which Main Street has done, Wall Street has created jargon that the individual investor doesn't necessarily understand. If you can't understand it, you shouldn't invest in it. Wall Street has created terms like *inner day head and shoulders top, dead-cat bounce, buy on the rumor and sell on the news, going forward, consolidations, spread, value, indicator, overhead resistance, fade the market, put-to-call ratio, ask bid ratio, resistance level, the trend is your friend,* and *sell in May and go away.* They're all designed to instill insecurity in the individual investor. If you can't understand the terms and basic concepts of ownership, then maybe they are designed so you can't understand them. Don't ever do anything you don't understand.

Turn off the talking heads on your television and turn off the scrolling ticker tapes. Chances are the media personalities have made more money selling advice than following their own advice. Wall Street makes one hundred transactions per second. The ticker tape is merely a representation of the participants trading their dirty laundry for someone else's dirty laundry. Turn off the voices of Wall Street and instead tune into the voices of Main Street. It's your choice. Warren admires Main Street's local proprietors and entrepreneurs, and that's where he prefers to invest.

Unless you can watch your stock holdings decline 50 percent without panic, you shouldn't participate in the stock market. It's better if your mind-set is one of owning a business. Don't rent stocks. Become an owner, not a speculator. In Warren's 2000 letter to shareholders, he wrote as follows: "Leaving tax matters aside, the formula we use for evaluating stocks and businesses is the same, identical. Indeed the formula for valuing all assets that are purchased for financial gain has been unchanged since it was first laid out by a very smart man in 600 B.C." The ancient philosopher was

Aesop, maybe best known for the fable about the tortoise and the hare. But the fable Warren is referring to here is "A bird in the hand is worth two in the bush."

When Warren was asked, "When are you going to write the most definitive book on investing?" He replied, "Everything one needs to know about investing has already been written. Investors make it far more complicated than what it is." While others with the same investment education, character traits, and aptitude choose to study capital pricing models, beta and modern portfolio and efficient market theory, Mr. Buffett instead went against the Wall Street crowd and studied income statements, balance sheets, return on equity, capital requirements, debt, intrinsic value, management talent, ambition, and character.

Phil Fisher sought out management personnel and talked with them. Ben Graham believed in the contrary. He thought management would influence him to make an investment that wasn't the best. Lou Simpson (see Chapter 10) has the same philosophy as Phil Fisher. If management won't talk to him, he simply doesn't invest. Warren will research a company and understand its management without a visit. He can tell everything he needs to know about a company's management team by reading public information. The written word of the CEO reveals his or her true character traits.

Warren said that on his company's employment application, he would have one question: "Are you a fanatic?" He puts a premium on *management expertise*, whereas Wall Street's all-consuming focus is instead on *stock price*. In reference to Warren's managers, he jokingly says, "If they need me . . . if they need my help to manage the enterprise, we're probably both in trouble."

Aesop, some twenty-six hundred years ago, also told the story about the fox who had lost its tail. The fox tried to convince the other foxes that they didn't need their tail either. The moral of the story is that you should distrust interested advice. Wall Street is interested advice.

In the *New Republic* in 1992, Warren Buffett was quoted as saying, "To many on Wall Street, both companies and stocks are seen only as raw materials for trades," with little concern with what the company produces or even if the company is earning money.

An example of his attitude about Wall Street is revealed in his fantasy of stranding twenty-five brokers and option traders on a deserted island. With no chance for rescue and forced to develop their own economy, War-

ren jokes that twenty would be assigned to gathering food, making cloth-
ing, and building shelter, and the other five would trade options endlessly
on the future output of the other twenty.

Buffett has never met a man, including himself, who can forecast Wall
Street. He may know what will happen, but he will not know when. He
predicted the burst of the tech bubble, but he wasn't able to predict when it
would happen. He jokingly says that "God created economists to make as-
trologers look good."

Famed investor Peter Lynch said, "If an investor spends fifteen minutes studying economics, he has wasted ten minutes." When it comes to investing, Warren has written and said over and over again, "People will be
full of greed, foolishness, and fear, and it will be reflected on their investment behavior on Wall Street. The sequence isn't predictable. If the Federal Reserve chairman whispered in [my] ear about interest rates and
monetary policy, [I] wouldn't do anything different."

Citing an example, he said that when Sees Candy became available for
purchase in 1972, the economics of the business, the management team, and
the attractive purchase price interested him. The purchase had nothing to do
with what was going on in the stock market, interest rates, or the economy.

He goes on to say, "I never attempt to make money on the stock market. I buy on the assumption that they could close the market the next day
and not reopen it for five years. As far as you are concerned, the stock market does not exist. Ignore it. Much success can be attributed to inactivity.
Most investors cannot resist the temptation to constantly buy and sell."

COMPARING THE OLD MAIN STREET ECONOMY WITH THE NEW WALL STREET ECONOMY

Main Street investing is about the old-economy business, while all the
new-economy business can be found on Wall Street. Buffett is investing in
textiles, insurance, banks, shoes, candy, carpet, bricks, boots, jewelry, energy, furniture, electronics, appliances, encyclopedias, ice cream, steel,
kitchenware, uniforms, picture frames, children's apparel, underwear, paint,
and a daily newspaper.

Wall Street would have you invest in the latest and greatest but un-
proven offerings. They call them IPOs for Initial Public Offerings. Warren
would instead recommend OPOs for Old Public Offerings.

In 1971, the NASDAQ index—made up of mostly technology-based new-economy companies—was first launched at 100. By the end of the century it had zoomed to a record high of 5000 and ended at 2000. Meanwhile, old-economy Berkshire traded at $71 in 1971 and closed the century above $70,000.

Another oversold concept on Wall Street is the importance of getting in early before everyone else recognizes a major innovation. The average business purchased by Berkshire was started in 1909, almost sixty years before Warren took over the management and acquisition decisions for his holding company.

Notice in Figure 6.2 the impact on stock prices and earnings of major innovations during the Industrial Revolution. Those who sold the concept that the technology, dot-com, and Internet revolution would be different did a great disservice to Wall Street investors.

HOW TO EVALUATE BUSINESSES THE MAIN STREET WAY

Warren focuses on three areas of interest when he investigates a business on Main Street:

1. First, he looks at the business. Is it simple? Is it in an industry that he understands? Is it a high-profit-margin business? Any debt? What is its return on equity?
2. Then he looks at its managers. Are they candid? What are their expansion plans? Are they well financed? How much of the business do they own?
3. Then he looks at the marketplace. What is the business value? Can it be purchased at a discount to its market value?

In 1996, Buffett looked at FlightSafety International, the world's largest airplane pilot training organization. Even though it has over two hundred $20 million computer-intensive flight simulators, it was a publicly traded business that Warren understood. With 32 percent profit margins, little debt, and outstanding returns on equity, it was his kind of business.

FSI founder and CEO Al Ueltschi is the perfect manager: hands on, frugal, concerned, active, character driven, trustworthy, and with low employee turnover and substantial management ownership.

Last, Buffett considered the purchase price of $1.5 billion or 15 times current earnings to be very attractive.

Figure 6.2 **The Effect of Major Innovations on Stock Price and Earnings Source**

Source: Robert J. Shiller, Irrational Exuberance

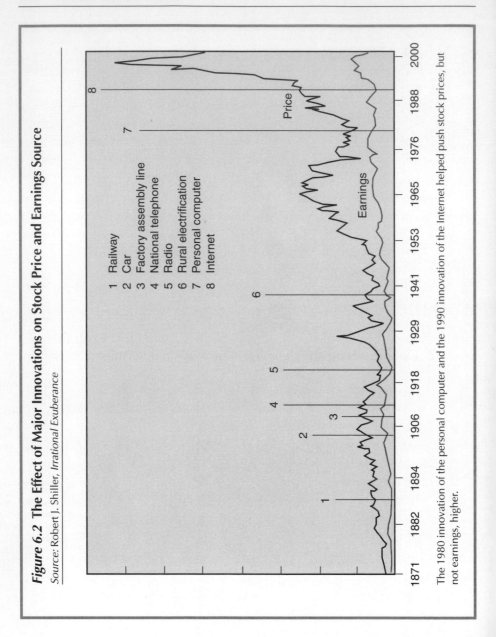

The 1980 innovation of the personal computer and the 1990 innovation of the Internet helped push stock prices, but not earnings, higher.

Buffett did his homework without inside information or without even requesting a meeting with Al Ueltschi. He simply read documents in the public domain.

If you want to emulate Warren Buffett's success, you should ask yourself about your best investments. Probably the answer is long-term investments in businesses that you understand and which are on Main Street. Again you should make fewer, better decisions.

QUESTIONS TO ASK WHEN YOU'RE CONSIDERING BUYING A BUSINESS

Phil Fisher asked fifteen questions when buying a business; note there is no mention of Wall Street:

1. Does the company have products or services with sufficient market potential to make possible a sizable increase in sales for at least several years?
2. Does the company's management have a determination to continue to develop products or processes that will still further increase total sales potential when growth potentials of current attractive product lines have largely been exploited?
3. How effective are the company's research and development efforts in relation to its size?
4. Does the company have an above-average sales organization?
5. Does the company have a worthwhile profit margin?
6. What is the company doing to maintain or improve profit margins?
7. Does the company have outstanding labor and personnel relations?
8. Does the company have outstanding executive relations?
9. Does the company have depth to its management?
10. How good are the company's cost analysis and accounting methods?
11. Are there other aspects of the business somewhat peculiar to the industry involved that will give the investor important clues as to how outstanding the company may be in relation to its competition?

12. Does the company have a short-range or a long-range outlook in regards to profits?
13. In the foreseeable future, will the growth of the company require sufficient equity financing so that the large number of shares then outstanding will largely cancel the existing benefit from this anticipated growth?
14. Does the company's management talk freely to investors about its affairs when things are going well, but clam up when troubles and disappointments occur?
15. Does the company have a management of unquestionable integrity?

Concern yourself with the company and its financials. Pay careful attention to management, what it says, what it doesn't say, what it does, and what it doesn't do. Successful active investors naturally focus on domestic companies found on Main Street and tune out the noise found on Wall Street. Table 6.3 lists Buffett's acquisition criteria.

Table 6.3 **Berkshire Hathaway Inc.'s Acquisition Criteria**
Source: www.berkshirehathaway.com

We are eager to hear *from principals or their representatives* about businesses that meet all of the following criteria:

1. Large purchases (at least $50 million of before-tax earnings),

2. Demonstrated consistent earning power (future projections are of no interest to us, nor are "turnaround" situations),

3. Businesses earning good returns on equity while employing little or no debt,

4. Management in place (we can't supply it),

5. Simple businesses (if there's lots of technology, we won't understand it),

6. An offering price (we don't want to waste our time or that of the seller by talking, even preliminarily, about a transaction when price is unknown).

The larger the company, the greater will be our interest: We would like to make an acquisition in the $5–20 billion range. *We are not interested, however, in receiving suggestions about purchases we might make in the general stock market.*

We will not engage in unfriendly takeovers. We can promise complete confidentiality and a very fast answer—customarily within five minutes—as to whether we're interested.

Table 6.3 *(continued)*

We prefer to buy for cash, but will consider issuing stock when we receive as much in intrinsic business value as we give.

　　Charlie and I frequently get approached about acquisitions that don't come close to meeting our tests: We've found that if you advertise an interest in buying collies, a lot of people will call hoping to sell you their cocker spaniels. A line from a country song expresses our feeling about new ventures, turnarounds, or auction-like sales: 'When the phone don't ring, you'll know it's me.'"

CONCLUSION

The takeaway exercises of this chapter are to:

- Turn off the stock market, forget about the economy, and buy a share of a business, not a stock.

- Choose a business that you know on your own Main Street and investigate it. Mentally, Buffett and company are always buying businesses on Main Street.

- Have a margin of safety and a circle of competence. They're both best acquired on Main Street.

- Look for and invest in businesses with a history of consistent earnings, little debt, and management that manages the business for the benefit of owners. Keep in mind that those businesses may be right up the corner on your own Main Street.

The next chapter talks about two concepts rarely heard on Wall Street: buying a lot of a few and buying to keep. Conventional wisdom says you reduce risk by purchasing many businesses. Try explaining that to your local Main Street proprietor. She would likely say that less is more. Buffett wisdom says *buy more of what you know*.

Chapter 7

Buy to Keep, and
Buy a Lot of a Few

"Concentration is my motto—first honesty, then industry, then concentration."

—Andrew Carnegie

Now that you know what kind of investor you are, have developed an investment philosophy, understand what you own, and are investing like a Main Street businessperson, you now are ready to buy for keeps. You need to buy a lot of a few.

To create vast wealth, you must buy concentrated amounts of stock and own it over a lifetime. This chapter covers buying a lot of only a handful of stocks and buying to keep. This philosophy is contrary to traditional investing wisdom, which preaches the benefits of diversification and advocates buying stock in order to sell it at a profit. In contrast to these ideas, Warren Buffett teaches us to buy a concentrated amount for life. His favorite holding period is *forever*, and all of the super-investors he knows, those who have beat the market over the long term, own a lot of a few.

Buffett's buy-and-hold approach has brought him more investment deals because sellers who stay on as business managers know that he is the best owner. Buffett ownership means business and job security, less CEO hassle dealing with fickle, short-term-oriented shareholders, and access to unlimited amounts of capital to expand their business.

INVESTING FOR THE LONG, LONG TERM

Warren will own his Berkshire stock, which represents 99 percent of his net worth, for his whole life without ever selling one single share and without giving himself any stock options. "Buy so well, you don't have to sell. Don't buy for ten minutes," he says, "if you don't intend to keep for ten years." Be a *decade* trader instead of a day trader and be like Warren; be a *century* trader. Be a long-term *investor*, not a short-term trader.

Warren says the best thing to do is to buy a stock that you don't ever want to sell, which is how he explains what Berkshire Hathaway does: "That's what we're trying to do, and that's true when we buy an entire business. We bought all of GEICO. We bought all of Sees Candies, the *Buffalo News*. We're not buying those to resell. What we're trying to do is buy a business we'll be happy with if we own it for the rest of our lives, and we expect to do that with those."

For example, Melvyn Wolff of Star Furniture tells the story that when he sold his business to Warren Buffett, he got an oversized telegram from Warren, four feet by six feet, that read: "Dear Melvyn: My enthusiasm for our marriage dwarfs the size of this telegram. Your partner for life, Warren."

Warren Buffett often compares investing, business management, and building wealth to marriage. He suggests carefully selecting a marriage partner as well as business associates so you don't have to worry about the expense of getting divorced. The secret to marriage, he suggests, as well as business partners and shareholders is to select those with low expectations.

If your focus is to own for life, you consider different things during your research. You look at the franchise value and how big a moat (or durable competitive advantage) surrounds the business. You look at management and employee loyalty and happiness. You look at the customers. Are they satisfied, and do they return on a regular basis? Speculators and traders don't concern themselves with those factors. It's kind of like a restaurant where you can take the risk out of it if you go for the known. Buy a lot and buy for life means no hurry; in fact, it requires you to do your homework and to take your time.

For example, Coca-Cola was in business for more than one hundred years before Warren purchased it. Warren's investment in the *Washington Post* was purchased thirty-five years after Warren delivered the paper as a teenager. There's no difference between buying pieces of a business or the whole business. What's most important is that you buy a lot and leave it alone.

In the *Omaha World Herald*, in 1986, Warren is reported as saying, "We like to buy businesses; we don't like to sell them." When Susan Jacques, CEO of Borsheim's Jewelry, was asked the difference between her and Warren Buffett, she said, "Well, Warren and I really like to buy; but unlike Warren, I really like to sell." That's a good thing, because she's in the retail business; if she didn't like selling, her store would not be the nation's largest-volume jewelry store with a single location.

Earlier writings of Warren Buffett pointed out the benefits of holding an investment for the long haul. Besides eliminating potential for emotion and ongoing mistakes to decide when to sell and what to buy next, you can also save tax and transaction costs. Buffett's example is to start with a dollar investment and double it every year. In option one, you sell the investment at the end of the year, pay tax and reinvest, and you do the same thing every year. At the end of twenty years, you would have made $25,000. In option two, if you had simply sold after twenty years, your gain would have been nearly $700,000. Option one requires forty times more work for nearly thirty times less profit.

CREATE YOUR CIRCLES OF COMPETENCE

To build wealth like Warren Buffett, you first need to draw a circle around the businesses you know or are capable of knowing. The size of the circle you draw isn't important, but rather how well you know the companies in your circle. With more than nine thousand publicly traded stocks just in the United States, you may want to limit your circle to seventy or fewer companies. Define your borders carefully, and be leery of having too large a circle.

Next draw a smaller circle (inside your circle of competence) of those companies whose businesses have strong economics, durable competitive advantages, little debt, and an excellent return on equity. Next draw a smaller interlocking circle of those companies that have managers you admire, who run the business for the benefit of shareholders, have strong ethics and character. This third circle should overlap with some of the businesses in the second smaller circle of outstanding businesses. Now draw a fourth interlocking circle of businesses with an attractive market price in relation to its intrinsic value (Figure 7.1).

Wayne Peters of Peters MacGregor Capital Management located in Sydney, Australia, uses a similar chart. In *Identifying Great Investments*, Peters first searches and draws a circle around outstanding businesses that:

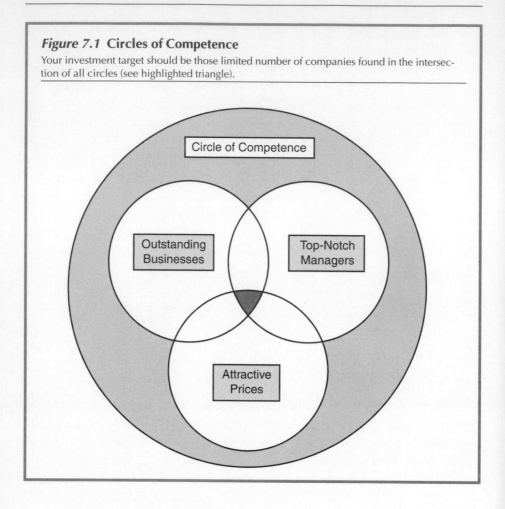

Figure 7.1 Circles of Competence
Your investment target should be those limited number of companies found in the intersection of all circles (see highlighted triangle).

- Are understandable
- Have a strong balance sheet
- Have good economics (i.e., free cash flow that will grow, pricing power, high return on equity, and bright prospects)
- Have competitive advantages

Next Peters's competent management interlocking circle identifies:

- Capable management
- Rational capital allocators
- Appropriate incentives

- A shareholder orientation
- Share ownership by management

Lastly, Peters's great price interlocking circle is defined by focus on:

- Companies that trade at 75 percent or less of economic value
- Competitor analysis
- Multiple comparisons
- Present value of future owner earnings

What you are trying to identify are those handful of companies that interconnect (see highlighted triangle), as shown in Figure 7.1: four or six that are in your circle of competence, that are outstanding businesses, and that have top-notch managers and attractive prices. This approach encompasses the quantitative (measurable) and qualitative (nonmeasurable) aspects of investing.

BASEBALL'S GREATEST HITTER

Drawing comparisons to Ted Williams, known as baseball's greatest hitter and the last player to bat .400, Buffett likens selecting pitches to hit with stock selection, requiring the same kind of discipline. (For you baseball nonfans, a .400 hitting percentage means getting a base hit four out of every ten official at bats. Baseball players who hit "only" .300 are considered in the elite of the game, making Williams's feat that much more impressive.)

In 1997, Buffett examined Williams's book *The Science of Hitting* for his explanation of his hitting success. In it Ted writes about carving the strike zone into seventy-seven circles of competence or cells, each the size of a baseball. Williams labeled each cell based on his percentage of a likely hit. "Swinging only at balls in his 'best' cell," Warren observed, "would allow him to bat .400; reaching for balls in his "worst" spot, the low outside corner of the strike zone, would reduce him to .230. In other words, waiting for the fat pitch would mean a trip to the Hall of Fame; swinging indiscriminately would mean a ticket to the minors."

Figure 7.2 represents the baseball strike zone (the height roughly from the chest to the knees; the width defined by the width of home plate). The three-and-a-half dark circles represent Williams's sweet spot. Waiting for

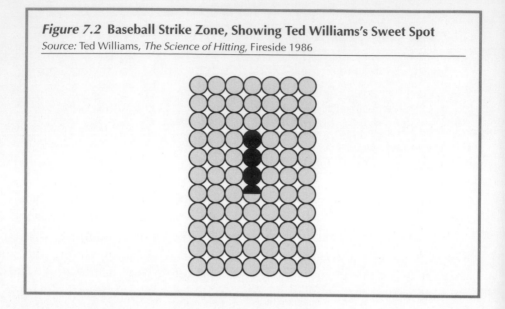

Figure 7.2 Baseball Strike Zone, Showing Ted Williams's Sweet Spot
Source: Ted Williams, *The Science of Hitting*, Fireside 1986

pitches in that sweet spot and ignoring the other seventy-three-and-a-half strikes and hundreds of balls (pitches outside the strike zone) made Williams baseball's greatest hitter.

Citing more comparisons between baseball and investing, Buffett suggests that with investing you need to wait for the fat pitch within your circles of competence. Unlike baseball, investors are never called out for not swinging, because there are no called strikes. All you need to do is figure out which opportunities are in your circles of competence and wait.

To become baseball's best hitter, Ted Williams patiently waited for those three-and-a-half pitches, letting seventy-three-and-a-half strikes go by, until he was forced to select within the circles so he wouldn't be called out. He preferred to let balls go by that were strikes, in order to wait for the strike zone pitches that would give him a higher percentage for a hit. Buffett's investing philosophy takes a similar approach.

INVEST IN A COMPANY'S MANAGEMENT

CEOs collectively breathe a sigh of relief when they find out that Warren Buffett is investing in their stock and their business. As Chapter 6 pointed out, he engages in no takeovers that are unfriendly or that lay off employees. There are no management changes, because to buy a business without managers, Warren says, "is like buying the Eiffel Tower without the eleva-tor." He never buys a business to resell it, and therefore his focus is never on short-term trading profit. The loyalty and trust throughout his organization is evident in most of his 165,000 employees as well as his managers, cus-tomers, and particularly shareholders.

The manager often keeps a minority interest in the business, and his or her compensation is based solely on the profits of the enterprise, not on what the stock price is doing or the performance or lack of performance from another subsidiary. Possibly the real secret and magic of Buffett Wealth is, as one manager described it: "I don't feel as though I sold my business to Warren Buffett. I just traded *my* publicly traded stock for *his* publicly traded stock."

Berkshire's CEO manages his subsidiaries just like they were a small portfolio of stocks. Just because you purchase an interest in a company does not give you the right to phone and require meetings, budgets, and per-formance guidelines from the CEO. Subsidiaries send monthly financial statements, are required to request all major capital expenditures, and CEO compensation changes need his approval. But other than those three things, Buffett makes no other demands.

FOCUS YOUR INVESTMENTS: QUALITY, NOT QUANTITY, IS IMPORTANT

Thousands of years ago, Aesop told the fable of a lioness, which relates to this idea of investing in quality instead of focusing on quantity. A contro-versy arose among the beasts of the field as to which animal produced the greatest number of offspring at a birth. They rushed clamorously to the li-oness and demanded she settle their dispute. "You," they said, "how many sons have you at a birth?" The lioness laughed at them and said, "Why, I have only one, but that one is altogether a thoroughbred lion." The moral of the story is that the value is in the worth. Neither the number nor the quantity matter, but rather the quality.

Wall Street wants you to believe that a concentrated portfolio carries too much risk and thus wants you to buy and sell a quantity of stock. Instead, Warren believes in making fewer, but better, decisions. Most stock market participants truly subscribe to a philosophy of "buy and hold and sometimes sell" or "buy and hold until the market trend changes." But if you follow War-ren's way of building wealth, you will buy so well that you don't need to sell, or you sell only if something fundamental changes within the business or if a better-quality investment presents itself. Obviously, if you are an active investor, very few companies would meet all of your investment criteria.

The rewards of lifetime ownership and concentrating your wealth are detailed in the biographies of just about every successful investor. Rarely will you read about anyone who became wealthy without being loyal to a business and owning stock in just one or a few companies, at the most. It's rare to read about wealth from someone who didn't concentrate his or her holdings in a few world-class companies. You never read about super wealth by somebody who just put a little bit into a business and bought and sold many businesses every six to twelve months.

It's better to buy a wonderful business at a fair price than to buy a fair business at a wonderful price. Note that "wonderful" business can also be pronounced 'one'derful business. Or as Mae West said, "Too much of a wonderful thing is wonderful."

If you invest in turnarounds, beware: Warren says that turnarounds seldom turn, and that "restructuring" is just another word for "mistakes."

Remember that Warren's hero and mentor was Benjamin Graham. One of Graham's investment strategies was the "twenty punch-card strategy": Every time you make a buy or a sell investment decision, you take a punch out of your twenty-punch card. When you've made twenty decisions, you're all done for the rest of your life. Buffett's extraordinary success can be attributed to just fifteen decisions. There is no wealth with quantity of trades and constant turnover.

When you sell something, you need to then make another decision as to what to buy. Warren has purchased only one home, and he plans to live in that home and to own it for the rest of his life. He also owns only one holding company—Berkshire Hathaway—and the same philosophy regarding his home applies to the ownership of his stock. His philosophy is one body, one mind, one home, and one holding company. Think of your own investing as buying a wonderful home and living in it.

If you invest like Noah, buying two of everything, you will end up having a zoo for a portfolio. Contrary to popular wisdom, which advocates diversification, Warren follows Andrew Carnegie's advice: "Put all your eggs in one basket and then watch that basket." Traditional investment counsel says, in essence, "scatter your money and your attention." Seventy percent of Berkshire's common stocks, representing more than $30 billion, are concentrated in just four stocks. Table 7.1 shows Berkshire's common stock holdings.

Table 7.1 **Berkshire's Common Stock Holdings, December 31, 2002**
Source: Berkshire-Hathaway 2002 Annual Report

Company	BUY A LOT OF A FEW		
	Cost*	Market*	Portfolio Percentage
Coca-Cola	$1,299	$8,768	31
American Express	1,470	5,359	19
Gillette	600	2,915	10
Wells Fargo	306	2,497	9
Washington Post	11	1,275	5
Other	5,478	7,549	27
Total Common Stocks	$9,164	$28,363	

*dollars in millions, 12/31/2002

Buffett's Fifteen Most Important Investment Decisions

1. Read *The Intelligent Investor*
2. Graduate study under Ben Graham at Columbia University
3. GEICO research and initial purchase
4. Launching Buffett Partnership
5. Berkshire Hathaway (worth less than $20 million in 1965; now worth over $100 billion; textile mills closed in 1985, but name continues as conglomerate and holding company)
6. National Indemnity (purchased for $8.6 million in 1967; now worth over $13 billion)
7. Washington Post (purchased for $11 million in 1973; now worth over $1 billion)
8. Sees Candy (worth $25 million in 1973; now earns three times purchase price)
9. *Buffalo News* (purchased for $32.5 million in 1977; earned over $1 billion over last twenty years)
10. Nebraska Furniture Mart (led to purchase of the largest home furniture retailers in Iowa, Texas, Utah, Idaho, Nevada, Massachusetts, and New Hampshire)
11. Scott Fetzer (purchased for $230 million in 1986; returned over $1.3 billion in earnings)
12. Coca-Cola (purchased for $1.3 billion in 1989; now worth $9 billion)

13. FlightSafety and NetJets (purchased for a total of $2.23 billion in 1996 and 1998, respectively; Berkshire's flight services will one day be as large or larger than Federal Express)
14. GenRe ($22 billion purchase in 1998; now the world's only AAA-rated reinsurance company)
15. MidAmerican Energy (purchased for $1.6 billion in 2000; energy is second-largest earnings contributor after insurance)

All of these are own-for-a-lifetime investments.

If Berkshire were a mutual fund, the Securities and Exchange Commission (SEC) would prevent it from following Buffett's basic investment principle. The SEC requires all equity mutual funds to have no more than 25 percent in one stock and then all other stocks in the portfolio must not exceed 5 percent of its holdings. In other words, all stock mutual funds need to have a minimum of sixteen stocks; while four stocks make up 70 percent of Buffett's portfolio, the best a mutual fund can do is ten stocks to make up 70 percent. Table 7.2 lists how long Warren has held some of his stock, and Figure 7.3 compares that with the average holding period of stocks traded on the New York Stock Exchange and the NASDAQ.

Warren said at the 1996 annual meeting,

Great personal fortunes in this country, weren't built on a portfolio of fifty companies. They were built by someone who identified one wonderful business. We think diversification, as practiced generally, makes very little sense for anyone who

---

Table 7.2 Buffett Buys to Keep

Source: Berkshire Hathaway Annual Reports

Stock	Years of Ownership
Washington Post	30 years
Coca-Cola	14 years
Gillette	14 years
Wells Fargo	13 years
American Express	12 years
Average Holding Period	17 years

Figure 7.3 Average Annual Turnover for NASDAQ, NYSE, and Berkshire
Source: *Business Week*, February 17, 2003; www.nasdaqnews.com; www.nyse.com; www.berkshirehathaway.com

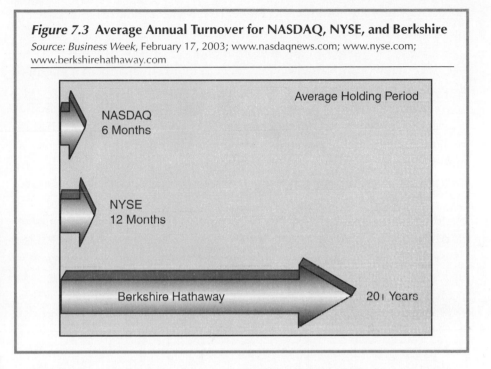

knows what they are doing. Diversification serves as protection against ignorance. If you want to make sure that nothing bad happens to you relative to the market, you should own everything. There's nothing wrong with that. It's a perfectly sound approach for someone who doesn't know how to analyze businesses. But if you know how to value businesses, it's crazy to own fifty stocks or forty stocks or thirty stocks, probably because there aren't that many wonderful businesses understandable to a single human being, in all likelihood. To forego buying more of some super, wonderful business and instead put your money into number 30 or number 35 on your list of attractiveness just strikes me as madness.

Warren also teaches the power of compounding, and it works when you concentrate your investments and you buy to keep. Remember the joys of compounding and the examples of the Mona Lisa, Christopher Columbus's voyage, and the purchase of Manhattan from the Indians?

In the *Financial Review* in 1989, Warren said, "We don't get into things we don't understand. We buy very few things, but we buy very big positions." Know what you own, own a few, and buy a lot.

Like a portfolio of a typical mutual fund, a portfolio of many stocks is like what flamboyant Broadway producer Billy Rose said about a harem of seventy girls. "You don't get to know any of them very well." Instead, own a stock, don't rent it. Knowing what you own—which was discussed at length in Chapter 5—automatically restricts you to owning a few things, because it's virtually impossible to know everything about a lot of companies; you need to focus your research and attention. Spreading your capital into many companies is a recipe to receive an average or below-average return on your investments. Instead, take your time to own a few. Even the world's most successful investor finds comfort in having four stocks make up 70 percent of his company's $30 billion portfolio (see Tables 7.1 and 7.3).

The fewer stocks you own, the more of an expert you can become in each and in all. Always invest for the long term. Do not take quarterly or annual investment results too seriously. Instead, focus on the four- to five-year returns.

Why would a corporate CEO sell a subsidiary that was a star performer and keep a poor performer? Yet that is the conventional wisdom on Wall Street. Have you ever heard, "You'll never go broke taking a profit"? Well, a CEO would get fired if he or she kept selling profitable businesses and keeping less profitable ones.

Traditional wisdom on Wall Street says, "Risk can be reduced by owning many stocks." Ask yourself, what has been your best investment? Chances are it is something you have invested in for the long term and something you probably wish you bought more of. "It is not necessary to do extraordinary things to get extraordinary results," says Warren.

Table 7.3 Buffett Buys a Lot of a Few
Source: Berkshire Hathaway 2002 Annual Report

Stock	Percentage Ownership
Washington Post	18 percent
American Express	11 percent
Gillette	9 percent
Coca-Cola	8 percent
Average Percentage Ownership	12 percent

If you want an average return, you should own the S&P 500 Index of the largest domestic companies representing 70 percent of the market. Figure 7.4 illustrates that owning 250 stocks will statistically give you a 3 percent chance of outperforming or underperforming the market. However, if you own fifteen stocks, you have a 25 percent chance of outperformance or underperformance. Robert Hagstrom's research and chart below prove the merit of a concentrated portfolio.

At a recent annual meeting for his shareholders, Warren offered this question: If a genie were to appear and told you that you could have any car that you wanted, what car would you choose? But before you could answer, suppose the genie said, "There's one caveat. You would have to own this car for the rest of your life." Well, the criteria in your selection might change, if you knew you were looking for a car that is more durable: low operating costs, simple repairs, and requiring less maintenance. The same thing should be true of the stocks in which you choose to invest.

Warren used this example because the same principle applies when it comes to your mind, your brain, and your body. You're given one of them for life, and you should act as if you only have one. Why not the same for your investments? It's kind of a one-punch investment theory. To have too

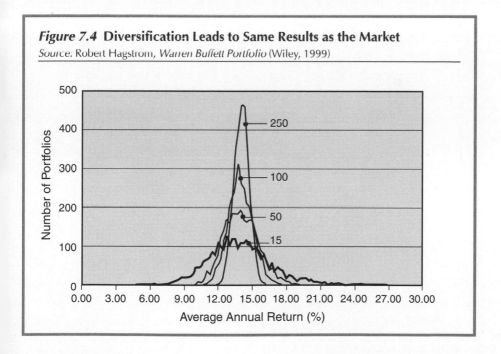

Figure 7.4 **Diversification Leads to Same Results as the Market**
Source: Robert Hagstrom, *Warren Buffett Portfolio* (Wiley, 1999)

many stocks is to be like the market. To beat the market, you must look differently and act differently. Think of yourself as an investment juggler—the more balls (stocks) you have in the air, the more difficult it is. Have fewer stocks and know more about them.

At the age of thirty-six and writing to his partners, Warren suggested that the overwhelming majority of investment managers fail to beat the general market averages because they diversify. They suffer from five built-in structural disadvantages:

1. Group decisions
2. Conformity
3. Emphasis on safe behavior with no personal reward for independent action
4. Irrational diversification model
5. Inertia

Buffett would not be afraid to invest up to 40 percent of his investment portfolio in one company. In fact, he invested 100 percent of his portfolio in one company when he was twenty-one years old (GEICO).

In the chairman's letter in 1978, Warren wrote: "Our policy is to concentrate holdings. We try to avoid buying little of this or that when we are only lukewarm about the business or its price. When we are convinced as to its attractiveness, we believe in buying worthwhile amounts."

In his 1996 letter to shareholders, Warren wrote: "Intelligent investing is not complex, though it is far from saying that it is easy. What an investor needs is the ability to correctly evaluate selected businesses. Note the word 'selected': You don't have to be an expert on every company, or even many. You only have to be able to evaluate companies within your circle of competence. The size of that circle is not very important: knowing its boundaries, however, is vital."

Better to be exactly right a few times than almost right or wrong a hundred times is another way to look at your portfolio. Get the business economics and probabilities right, and keep emotions from overriding good judgment. Otherwise, a concentrated portfolio simply offers no benefit.

Famed economist John Maynard Keynes once observed, "One's

knowledge and experience are definitely limited and there are seldom more than two or three enterprises, at any given time, in which I personally feel myself entitled to put full confidence."

Warren's partner and vice chairman Charlie Munger said this rather profoundly at the annual meeting in 2001: "In the United States, a person or institution with almost all wealth invested long term in just three fine domestic corporations is securely rich." In Chapter 10, Warren's backup stock picker (who, by the way, has a better stock-selection record than Warren) invests some $2.5 billion, and he owns just seven stocks.

Coke is an example in which Warren knows what he owns, has made a substantial purchase, and plans on owning for a lifetime. In fact, he put 25 percent of Berkshire's assets into the world's largest soft-drink seller. If he had the money at the time, he would have purchased all of Coca-Cola for $16 billion (now it's worth ten times that). Concentrate your investments and focus on your goals. Warren said, "If we get on the mainline, New York to Chicago, we don't get off at Altoona and make side trips. We like to buy businesses. We don't like to sell, and we expect the relationships to last a lifetime." He goes on to say, "Stocks are simple. All you do is buy shares in a great business for less than what the business is intrinsically worth, with managers of the highest integrity and ability, then you can own those shares forever."

PHIL FISHER'S INVESTING PHILOSOPHY: "NEVER SELL"

Phil Fisher, in his book *Common Stocks for Uncommon Profits*, wrote about the basic principles of owning a lot and owning for a long time. He says, "As long as the company behind the common stock maintains the characteristics of an unusually successful enterprise, never sell it." Fisher points out that many fortunes have been made when investors have refused to sell their position in a rapidly appreciating equity. "If the company is of a high quality, then selling it is rather foolish," he points out, "at almost any price, because of the scarcity of high-quality investments. What will you do," he asks, "with the proceeds from the sale of a world-class company?" Even if the stock seems at or near a temporary peak and that a sizable decline may strike in the near future, Fisher would not sell, provided the long-term future was sufficiently attractive.

For example, consider Warren Buffett's investment in The Washington Post Company: he is the largest outside shareholder. During the bear markets of 1973–74 (during the oil shortage crisis), he bought 15 percent of

Washington Post for $11 million. The Post today earns some $250 million a year, which Berkshire's interest would represent about $45 million. *His original $11 million investment annually earns four-and-a-half times its original purchase price and now pays Berkshire back $9 million a year in dividends.* This wonderful business today has a market price of over $1 billion. An $11 million investment turns into $1 billion some thirty years later, because he bought a lot and planned (and still plans) to own it for a long time.

"Your goal as an investor," Warren writes, "should simply be to purchase at a rational price, a part interest in an easily understandable business, whose earnings are virtually certain to be materially higher 5, 10 and 20 years from now," he wrote in 1996. He goes on to say:

> [Over] time, you will find only a few companies that meet these standards. So when you see one that qualifies, you should buy a meaningful amount of stock. You must also resist the temptation to stray from your guidelines. If you aren't willing to own a stock for ten years, don't even think about owning it for ten minutes. Put together a portfolio of companies whose aggregate earnings march upward over the years and so also will the portfolio's market value.

If you read and review Buffett's owner-related business principles at www.berkshirehathaway.com, you will find that nearly half of his fourteen principles speak to owning for life and owning a lot. For example, consider these:

- In number one, Warren talks about the relationship between himself and the shareholders as being a long-term partnership.
- In the second principle, he states that 99 percent of his net worth is in one stock, Berkshire Hathaway.
- In principle four, he writes that his first choice is to completely acquire outstanding businesses. His second choice is to acquire pieces of outstanding public companies.
- In principle six, he explains the concept of look-through earnings, where if he owns 8 percent of Coca-Cola, which his holding company does, and Coca-Cola earns $4 billion, he can look through and capture 8 percent of Coke's annual earnings and say that his investment that year earned $320 million.

- In principle eight, he reveals how acquisitions are made only to boost the long-term performance of his company.
- In principle number eleven, he discusses the importance of loyalty. As long as a business that he's acquired generates some cash, Berkshire won't sell it.

Phil Fisher writes, "Taking small profits in good investments and letting losses grow in bad ones is a sign of abominable investment judgment. A profit should never be taken just for the satisfaction of taking it, which is contrary to the standard dogma." He goes on to say, "There are a relatively small number of truly outstanding businesses."

While some investors think that Berkshire should sell stocks that have appreciated, Table 7.4 demonstrates the return on its per-share cost with a median return of 25 percent per annum. Rather amazingly, the Washington Post is now earning almost four times its purchase price each year.

CONCLUSION

The takeaway exercises of this chapter are to:

- Concentrate your investments in world-class companies managed by top-notch managers.

- Limit yourself to companies you truly understand. Five to ten companies is a good number. More than twenty is asking for trouble. If

---

Table 7.4 Return on Cost

Source: Berkshire Hathaway, Coca-Cola, American Express, Gillette, Wells Fargo, and Washington Post Annual Reports.

Company	Cost	2002 Earnings Per Share	Return
Coca-Cola	$6.50	$1.65	25%
American Express	9.70	2.01	21%
Gillette	6.25	1.15	19%
Wells Fargo	5.75	3.40	59%
Washington Post	6.37	22.61	355%
Median return			25%

you own more than twenty, you may want to review the stocks in your portfolio.

■ Select the very best and concentrate your investments. Remember the opposite of concentration is distraction; when it comes to wealth building, the last thing you want to do is lose your focus. As Warren says, "With each investment you make, you should have the courage and the conviction to place at least 10 percent of your net worth in that stock." So you should evaluate your portfolio to look at the number of stocks that you currently own and to make sure they fit Buffett's criteria of owning a lot and owning for a lifetime.

The next chapter discusses some of the mistakes Warren has made and how you can learn from them. You may have made many blunders in your investment lifetime, and it may make you feel better to learn that even the world's best investor made a $2 billion mistake that keeps growing each year. He made another mistake by not purchasing a lot of a wonderful company—an $8 billion mistake that is also growing. The good news is that even multibillionaires make mistakes—billion-dollar ones. The better news is that you can learn from them without it costing you more than the price of this book and the time to read it.

Chapter 8

How You Can Learn from Buffett's Investment Mistakes

"A man only learns in two ways, one by reading, and the other by association with smarter people."

—Will Rogers

Even if you buy a few quality businesses managed by honest and able people, you too can make mistakes. Just as you increase the probability to outperform the market by 25 percent with a concentrated portfolio, you also should not ignore the equal chance of underperforming by the same probability. Buying a lot of a few can dramatically increase your mistakes, which is why conventional investment wisdom oversells the merit of diversification.

Even the greatest investor has made mistakes on his journey to create the world's largest source of liquid wealth. This chapter describes Warren Buffett's investment mistakes and how you can learn from them: why you shouldn't be afraid to admit them, how to avoid them, why a certain amount of them are inevitable, and why it is okay to make them (although making too big or too many mistakes can prove hazardous to your financial health and has prevented many from building any meaningful amount of wealth).

Yogi Berra said about mistakes, "I don't want to make the wrong mistake." Understanding Buffett's mistakes and studying the common mistakes of the average investor can help you from making the wrong mistake. The study of mistakes should not leave you less confident in your wealth-building journey and should not take away any enthusiasm for beginning, no matter your age or starting point.

MISTAKE #1: WARREN'S BIGGEST INVESTING MISTAKE: NO LONG-TERM DURABLE COMPETITIVE ADVANTAGE

Warren likes to say his biggest mistake was the purchase of Berkshire Hathaway Textile Mills in New Bedford, Massachusetts. He took control of the company in 1965 and closed it some twenty years later because he was unable to sustain the textile business against cheaper foreign competition. So the original business exists now in name only and acts as a reminder as to what can happen with investments that do not have a durable competitive advantage. Buffett considers it a failure to close American manufacturing plants, as he was forced to do. He feels personally responsible to the employees and their families. However, his ultimate responsibility is to his shareholders.

Unfortunately, New Bedford, once a leading center of the American textile industry, has become a ghost town of empty factory buildings and a declining population. This town has been through tough problems before, and will no doubt rebuild itself, as it once was the leading center for the whaling industry, only to see whale oil, used principally in lamps, be replaced by cheaper kerosene oil.

Although Berkshire's chairman was forced to shut down the textile business, his feat of redeploying the underused assets of the parent company into a variety of businesses, most notably the insurance and banking industries, will go down in history as one of the most remarkable business stories of all time. Taking a less than $20 million investment in Berkshire and managing it over four decades into more than $100 billion in market value and one of the largest corporations in the world is the very reason Warren Buffett is considered the world's greatest investor.

Choosing an American textile business and having to close it is a very small investment mistake. It was an old-economy business (Charlie Munger would later call this a cigar-butt investment, something that you buy cheap and that has one or two puffs of earnings left in them). Warren knew what he owned, and he bought it at a discount to its real value. He bought a significant amount of it so he didn't make the mistake of not buying enough. His mistake was buying in the wrong industry. So if Berkshire Hathaway is Buffett's biggest investment mistake, wouldn't it be fascinating if all investors had to name their investment portfolios or personal holding companies after their biggest mistakes? What would be the name of your company?

Asked recently to name his top three investment mistakes, Warren listed these purchases:

1. Berkshire Hathaway textile mills (closed)
2. Baltimore-based department store Hochschild, Kohn & Co. (sold; first business purchased in its entirety)
3. Blue Chip Stamps, in 1968, with sales then of $120 million and now with just $50,000 (still owned)

One could argue that the textile manufacturer investment was not Buffett's biggest mistake, because he bought it cheap and converted its assets and earnings into one of the world's foremost conglomerates.

Table 8.1 compares Berkshire's 1967 balance sheet to year 2002. Table 8.2 compares Berkshire's 1967 and 2002 income statements. With a beginning purchase price of $7 per share, Berkshire was earning four hundred times that by 2002. Hardly a big mistake.

Table 8.1 Berkshire's Balance Sheet
Source: Berkshire Hathaway 1967 and 2002 Annual Reports

	1967	2002
Cash	$835,301	$10.3 billion
Stocks	$3,825,077	$28.4 billion
Total Assets	$39,940,590	$169.5 billion
Debt	$641,300	$4.5 billion
Total Liabilities	$8,397,655	$104 billion
Shareholder Equity	$31,542,935	$64 billion
Book Value per Share	$31	$41,727

Table 8.2 **Berkshire Hathaway 1967 and 2002 Income Statements**
Source: Berkshire Hathaway 1967 and 2002 Annual Reports

	1967	2002
Textile Revenue	$39,055,671	$0
Insurance Revenue	$791,938	$19 billion
Interest, Dividends,		
Investment Income	$295,687	$3 billion
Investment Gains	$100,147	$637 million
Total Revenue	$40,243,443	$43 billion
Total Expenses	$39,135,984	$35 billion
Net Earnings	$1,107,459	$4.3 billion
Earnings Per Share	$1.12	$2,795

MISTAKE #2: INVESTING IN ANOTHER TROUBLED INDUSTRY

Remember the old joke, "How do you become a millionaire?" The punch line is "Start as a billionaire and buy an airline." That's what Warren did in 1989, when he invested $358 million into U.S. Air's preferred stock. It was a short-term mistake, because six years later, in 1995, Warren wrote off most of that investment. U.S. Air had good management, but like textiles, the airline industry was the wrong industry to invest in.

The preferred stock paid Berkshire a 9¼ percent dividend each year, but U.S. Air suspended its dividend in 1994, and Warren tried to find a buyer for his preferred stock. A student once asked Warren why he invested in an airline. Warren said the airline industry would have been better off if a capitalist had known about the Wright brothers and their Kitty Hawk flight and shot them down, because there hasn't been any value added to the capital invested in the whole airline industry. He said, "The Wright brothers' flight was one small step forward for mankind and one huge step backwards for capitalism."

He called his investment in the airlines temporary insanity. He jokingly says that he "now carries an 800 number for Airlines Anonymous," and whenever he gets the urge to invest in an airline, he calls it and says, "Hi. My name is Warren and I'm an airaholic." And he says the guy at the other end talks him down. At the time of this mistake, an investment banker said, "Buffett still walks on water. He just splashes a bit."

In 1996, the best year ever for U.S. Air, Buffett was eventually paid back some $660 million, nearly twice the original purchase price. The mistake was buying in the wrong industry without favorable long-term prospects. But even that mistake, like Berkshire itself, turned out pretty well.

The problem with the airline industry is that it is capital-, labor-, fuel-, weather-, economy-, and competition-sensitive. The only winner has been the low-cost provider Southwest Airlines.

As a brilliant stroke of genius, Buffett ignored his 800 number and purchased two flight-services businesses with dominant market share and wide business moats. Both FlightSafety International, the world's largest simulated airplane pilot trainer, and NetJets, the world's largest corporate aircraft fleet, own more than 70 percent of their respective markets, have high barriers to entry, and durable and sustainable advantages. Both businesses are still being managed by their founders.

Perhaps in 1993, Buffett made his biggest investment mistake. Not learning the lessons of textiles and airlines, he once again invested in the wrong industry. This time it was shoes, Dexter Shoes, named for a small town in Maine. Cornering the market on bowling and golf shoes, Dexter proudly advertised that it was made in the USA. They even got a U.S. president to wear and advertise them.

Bragging that Dexter Shoes was the largest U.S.-based shoe manufacturer was a mistake when, like textiles, other manufacturers were able to outsource production to Asia for one thirtieth the cost.

MISTAKE #3: INVESTING WITH STOCK, INSTEAD OF CASH

Compounding his mistake by investing in the largest U.S.-based shoe manufacturer, which was saddled with the highest production costs, was paying for the purchase with stock. Berkshire paid $420 million in 1993 for all of Dexter, but instead of paying cash, Buffett offered 2 percent of the stock in his emerging conglomerate.

His mistake now is ever escalating, because 2 percent of his stock is now worth $2 billion. So his $420 million investment in Dexter cost him

$2 billion, and he wrote off the entire purchase price of this investment mistake in Dexter Shoes in 2001.

It's important to analyze this mistake. Dexter was not a mistake in management, because the company was well managed by Harold Alfond and his nephew Peter Lunder. The business was a leader in the footwear industry, generating $250 million in annual sales while making 7.5 million shoes. With 1.3 billion pairs of shoes sold annually in the United States alone, the shoe market is huge, but 96 percent of those shoes are now manufactured overseas.

MISTAKE #4: SELLING TOO SOON

GEICO auto insurance is another example of an investment mistake Warren made. In 1951, at the age of twenty-one, Warren invested nearly all the money he had, which was roughly $10,000, into GEICO stock, and he sold it a year later for roughly $15,000. Now you might think—as Warren did at the time—that a 50 percent return on his investment in only one year was a huge success. But this was a short-term win and a long-term mistake, because he sold too soon. Now he did place the proceeds from the GEICO sale into a security selling for just one times earnings (meaning he would be paid back his investment in its entirety within one year), and he didn't know at the time he would eventually buy back his interest and more in GEICO.

Buffett waited until he had the money and bought a third of the company beginning in 1976 for $46 million and the balance of the company in 1996 for $2.4 billion. Today the company is worth in excess of $10 billion, with more than $400 million in annual contribution to earnings and a substantial share of the $2 billion in annual investment income. GEICO is the largest advertiser on cable television with an annual budget approaching $300 million. Additionally the auto insurer gives its parent company nearly $5 billion in annual float to invest, usually free of costs.

After a major scandal and a subsequent share price drop, Warren purchased 5 percent of American Express for $13 million in 1964 on behalf of his investment partnership. It should be noted that $13 million represented 50 percent of his partnership holdings, so he didn't make the mistake of not buying concentrated amounts when the right opportunity came along. He sold that interest for a cool $20 million profit, but had he held on, a 5 percent interest would be worth $3 billion today and he would have over ten times the purchase price as annual look-through earnings.

In 1966, after meeting with Walt Disney himself, Buffett purchased 5 percent of Disney for $4 million. Remarkably at that time, had he the money, he could have purchased all of Disney for $80 million, which is now the cost of a single roller-coaster. Today that same investment and ownership interest would have a value of $2 billion. The mistake of GEICO, American Express, and Disney is that he sold too soon and would later buy back all three stocks at substantially greater prices.

MISTAKE #5: NOT BUYING WHEN HE SEES VALUE

Warren puts mistakes into two categories: mistakes of commission, which are mistakes he's actively made, and mistakes of omission, or mistakes he made by not acting. All of the previous mistakes are of commission. Very few, if any, CEOs will admit to errors that go unreported or mistakes that shareholders would never know about unless they are admitted. As an example of a mistake of omission, Warren describes his lack of investment in Wal-Mart. He understood the retail business, was capable of investing a substantial amount, but didn't act. That mistake of omission has cost his shareholders some $8 billion and more each passing year.

He can't be faulted for not buying all of GEICO, American Express, or even Disney because he didn't have the money. Back then, he says, he had more ideas than money. Even when asked why it took him so long to buy the rest of GEICO auto insurance, he said, "It takes money, you know."

Today the reverse is true. He has more money than ideas: more than $150 million per week flows into Berkshire that needs to be allocated among a few attractively priced, publicly traded stocks and an average of four privately negotiated acquisitions per year.

MISTAKE #6: TOO MUCH CASH

All of Buffett's mistakes have come at a time that he had too much cash. Like most investors, the overwhelming need to allocate excess cash can interfere with disciplined thoughts and proper application of well-defined principles. Even the best capital allocator has fallen victim to this mistake.

The way to overcome this mistake is to wait until you have an excellent business, with management you admire and trust, and available at a discount to its intrinsic value and buy a substantial part of it. Recognize that patience is an important virtue of every outstanding investor. Very few big ideas come along, and when they do you need to act decisively.

Currently Berkshire is sitting on liquid net worth with $24 billion in cash and an equal amount in junk bonds, all waiting to be allocated mistake-free.

THE MISTAKE THAT WASN'T

Some Buffett watchers and Berkshire shareholders, including vice chairman Charlie Munger, initially thought Berkshire's purchase of the *Buffalo News* to be a mistake. Making its acquisition in 1977 for $32.5 million because of strong competition, the *News* sustained six more years of million-dollar annual losses. This drove the actual investment up to $44.5 million and looked very much like another investment mistake. Instead, over the past twenty years, the *News* has earned on average $50 million per year, more than its purchase price and subsequent losses, and has given Berkshire $1 billion in cumulative earnings, earnings that its CEO has used to acquire more companies in their entirety.

Similarly, Berkshire's investment in General Re, America's largest reinsurer (an insurance company that insures other insurance companies), has met with its share of critics, both inside and outside the company. Reinsurance is a business that Buffett understands, and he was able to purchase it at a substantial discount to its real value. At the end of 1998, Berkshire acquired GenRe for $16 billion in stock. In exchange, Berkshire received $19 billion in bonds, $5 billion in stocks, $16 billion in float, and a company earning $1 billion per year.

Critics point to the subsequent accumulated losses (the biggest—$2.8 billion in 2001—as the result of the September 11, 2001, terrorists attacks) adding an additional $8 billion to the purchase price. Keen observers instead see this deal as adding 65 percent to Berkshire's assets, while only increasing its shares by 23 percent. GenRe losses are offset, in part, by the earnings from the $24 billion in assets it brought along with it. Furthermore, GenRe float (premiums paid and available for investment before insurance claims are made against it) has continued to rise to over $22 billion. Currently, as the only AAA-rated reinsurer in the world, GenRe has passed on unprofitable business and no longer has to write business to keep market share, and as a result will likely become the most profitable reinsurer in the world.

If there is a mistake with GenRe, it was buying at the wrong time, but naysayers could also say the same thing about the *Buffalo News*.

DON'T BE AFRAID TO ADMIT YOUR MISTAKES

Admitting mistakes is a sign of maturity and is good for the soul. A critical quality for management to have in a trust business like financial management is the ability to admit mistakes. It's also the highest form of self-respect. Admit and learn from mistakes and make amends. To make a mistake is only an error in judgment, but to keep making mistakes with full knowledge that they are mistakes shows weakness in character.

For example, it wasn't a mistake when Warren invested $700 million in 1987 in Salomon Brothers; it was a mistake of Salomon's management to allow a rogue trader to trade illicitly in government bonds. Four years after Berkshire bought its preferred stock, Salomon admitted that it had attempted to control more than 35 percent of a government bond auction, which threatened the collapse of the fixed-income markets of the United States. Salomon's management put itself on the brink of bankruptcy, and Berkshire's investment was in jeopardy.

Warren Buffett's sterling reputation saved Salomon Brothers. He immediately replaced management with new people capable of working within the rules and he appealed to investors, clients, and Congress to not hold the eight thousand employees of Salomon responsible for short-sighted, unethical management decisions. He declared, under oath, before a congressional hearing, that he instructed all of Salomon Brothers' employees "that if they lose money for the firm," he would understand; "but if they lose a shred of reputation," he will be ruthless.

In early 1992, Salomon agreed to pay $290 million in fines to the government. It should be noted that Buffett saved Salomon for a salary of $1. Berkshire sold its interest in Salomon to Travelers in 1997.

Never Make the Mistake of Losing Your Reputation

"We can afford to lose money," Warren writes his managers every other year, "even a lot of money. We cannot afford to lose reputation—even a shred of reputation. Let's be sure that everything we do in business can be reported on the front page of a national newspaper in an article written by an unfriendly but intelligent reporter. In many areas, including acquisitions, Berkshire's results have benefited from its reputation, and we don't want to do anything that in any way can tarnish it."

Never make the mistake of losing your reputation. "It takes twenty years to build a reputation and only five minutes to destroy it," he once said to his son. "If you think about that, you might do things differently."

Berkshire's CEO's admission of his mistakes, whether they be mistakes of commission or omission, is less than typical. Most CEOs are too busy trumpeting their own management accomplishments to ever take the time to explain where they may have gone wrong. It would prove too costly for most publicly traded companies, whose CEOs spend as much as 20 percent of their time trying to attract and keep shareholders. Because most CEO compensation plans are tied to stock price and not active operating results, management is forced to meet with analysts, issue quarterly earnings guidance numbers, and talk up their "mistake-free" enterprises in the media.

Too many CEOs bury their mistakes with accounting shenanigans, like filing pro-forma reports with the most favorable light on their operations, only to file amended, actual, less favorable reports weeks later that are unlikely to be revisited by shareholders. Other ways to flush away mistakes are to bury them in "one-time" restructuring charges or hide them during the transition between acquisitions.

Mistakes are acceptable and sometimes difficult to overcome, but in a business that has a reputation for great management and poor economics, unfortunately poor economics will win out. To further explain this concept, Buffett used the analogy of a business with bad economics to be a boat with a leak. Instead of great managers trying to fix the leak and spend all of their time bailing water, they may be better advised to find another boat.

Look to his annual reports for admission of his mistakes. It's guaranteed that Warren will admit at least one a year. In 2001, his annual report mentions several mistakes. From Page 3:

> Though our corporate performance last year was satisfactory, my performance was anything but. I manage most of Berkshire's equity portfolio, and my results were poor, just as they have been

for several years. Of even more importance, I allowed General Re to take on business without a safeguard I knew was important, and on September 11th, this error caught up with us. I'll tell you more about my mistake later and what we are doing to correct it.

From Page 11:

This is what happened at General Re in 2001: a staggering $800 million of loss costs that actually occurred in earlier years, but that were not then recorded, were belatedly recognized last year and charged against current earnings. The mistake was an honest one, I can assure you of that.

From Page 13:

I've made three decisions relating to Dexter that have hurt you in a major way: (1) buying it in the first place, (2) paying for it with stock and (3) procrastinating when the need for changes in its operations was obvious. I would like to lay these mistakes on Charlie (or anyone else, for that matter) but they were mine. Dexter, prior to our purchase, and indeed for a few years after, prospered despite low-cost foreign competition that was brutal. I concluded that Dexter could continue to cope with that problem, and I was wrong.

In his 2000 letter to shareholders Buffett reported more of his mistakes. From Page 8:

At Berkshire, we strive to be both consistent and conservative in our reserving. But we will make mistakes. And we warn you that there is nothing symmetrical about surprises in the insurance business: They almost always are unpleasant.

From Page 10:

Agonizing over errors is a mistake. But acknowledging and analyzing them can be useful, though that practice is rare in corporate boardrooms. There, Charlie and I have almost never witnessed a candid post-mortem of a failed decision, *particularly one involving an acquisition*. A notable exception to this never-look-back approach is that of The Washington Post Company, which unfailingly and objectively reviews its acquisitions three years after they are made. Elsewhere, triumphs are trumpeted, but dumb decisions either get no follow-up or are rationalized.

From Page 14:

[W]e make many mistakes: I'm the fellow, remember, who thought he understood the future economics of trading stamps, textiles, shoes and second-tier department stores.

In 1989, Buffett's letter to his partners included a section on his mistakes from his first twenty-five years of investing (see Figure 8.1).

Mistake admission lowers the expectations of his shareholders and partners, and discourages short-term ownership. Berkshire's CEO uses his communications as well as its corporate culture to attract the owners it deserves.

Most annual reports are written as marketing documents for the CEO and his or her company. Many CEOs gloss over any mistake they may have made, thereby losing credibility. Therefore, you should look for the CEO, like Warren, who will admit mistakes, and then you'll know you're dealing with somebody who you can trust.

It's kind of like going to a restaurant. You want the waiter or waitress to tell you if there is something on the menu that they don't recommend and point out the mistakes of the restaurant in order to gain credibility.

You want to be the first to hear bad news when you're an investor, and you want it without delay. Leaders do just that.

NINE COMMON INVESTMENT MISTAKES PREVENTING WEALTH CREATION

1. *Purchasing stocks you do not understand.* If you can't explain it to a ten-year-old, just don't invest in it.

2. *Overdiversifying.* This is the most oversold, overused, logic-defying concept among stockbrokers and registered investment advisors.

Figure 8.1 **Excerpt from Buffett's Letter to Shareholders, 1989**

Mistakes of the First Twenty-Five Years (A Condensed Version)

To quote Robert Benchley, "Having a dog teaches a boy fidelity, perseverance, and to turn around three times before lying down." Such are the shortcomings of experience. Nevertheless, it's a good idea to review past mistakes before committing new ones. So let's take a quick look at the last 25 years.

• My first mistake, of course, was in buying control of Berkshire. Though I knew its business—textile manufacturing—to be unpromising, I was enticed to buy because the price looked cheap. Stock purchases of that kind had proved reasonably rewarding in my early years, though by the time Berkshire came along in 1965 I was becoming aware that the strategy was not ideal.

If you buy a stock at a sufficiently low price, there will usually be some hiccup in the fortunes of the business that gives you a chance to unload at a decent profit, even though the long-term performance of the business may be terrible. I call this the "cigar butt" approach to investing. A cigar butt found on the street that has only one puff left in it may not offer much of a smoke, but the "bargain purchase" will make that puff all profit.

Unless you are a liquidator, that kind of approach to buying businesses is foolish. First, the original "bargain" price probably will not turn out to be such a steal after all. In a difficult business, no sooner is one problem solved than another surfaces—never is there just one cockroach in the kitchen. Second, any initial advantage you secure will be quickly eroded by the low return that the business earns. For example, if you buy a business for $8 million that can be sold or liquidated for $10 million and promptly take either course, you can realize a high return. But the investment will disappoint if the business is sold for $10 million in ten years and in the interim has annually earned and distributed only a few percent on cost. Time is the friend of the wonderful business, the enemy of the mediocre.

You might think this principle is obvious, but I had to learn it the hard way—in fact, I had to learn it several times over. Shortly after purchasing Berkshire, I acquired a Baltimore department store, Hochschild Kohn, buying through a company called Diversified Retailing that later merged with

(continued)

Figure 8.1　(continued)

Berkshire. I bought at a substantial discount from book value, the people were first-class, and the deal included some extras—unrecorded real estate values and a significant LIFO inventory cushion. How could I miss? So-o-o— three years later I was lucky to sell the business for about what I had paid. After ending our corporate marriage to Hochschild Kohn, I had memories like those of the husband in the country song, "My Wife Ran Away With My Best Friend and I Still Miss Him a Lot."

I could give you other personal examples of "bargain-purchase" folly but I'm sure you get the picture: It's far better to buy a wonderful company at a fair price than a fair company at a wonderful price. Charlie understood this early; I was a slow learner. But now, when buying companies or common stocks, we look for first-class businesses accompanied by first-class managements.

• That leads right into a related lesson: Good jockeys will do well on good horses, but not on broken-down nags. Both Berkshire's textile business and Hochschild Kohn had able and honest people running them. The same managers employed in a business with good economic characteristics would have achieved fine records. But they were never going to make any progress while running in quicksand.

I've said many times that when a management with a reputation for brilliance tackles a business with a reputation for bad economics, it is the reputation of the business that remains intact. I just wish I hadn't been so energetic in creating examples. My behavior has matched that admitted by Mae West: "I was Snow White, but I drifted."

• A further related lesson: Easy does it. After 25 years of buying and supervising a great variety of businesses, Charlie and I have *not* learned how to solve difficult business problems. What we have learned is to avoid them. To the extent we have been successful, it is because we concentrated on identifying one-foot hurdles that we could step over rather than because we acquired any ability to clear seven-footers.

The finding may seem unfair, but in both business and investments it is usually far more profitable to simply stick with the easy and obvious than it is to resolve the difficult. On occasion, tough problems *must* be tackled as was the case when we started our Sunday paper in Buffalo. In other instances, a great investment opportunity occurs when a marvelous business encounters a one-time huge, but solvable, problem as was the case many

Figure 8.1 (continued)

years back at both American Express and GEICO. Overall, however, we've done better by avoiding dragons than by slaying them.

• My most surprising discovery: the overwhelming importance in business of an unseen force that we might call "the institutional imperative." In business school, I was given no hint of the imperative's existence and I did not intuitively understand it when I entered the business world. I thought then that decent, intelligent, and experienced managers would automatically make rational business decisions. But I learned over time that isn't so. Instead, rationality frequently wilts when the institutional imperative comes into play.

For example: (1) As if governed by Newton's First Law of Motion, an institution will resist any change in its current direction; (2) Just as work expands to fill available time, corporate projects or acquisitions will materialize to soak up available funds; (3) Any business craving of the leader, however foolish, will be quickly supported by detailed rate-of-return and strategic studies prepared by his troops; and (4) The behavior of peer companies, whether they are expanding, acquiring, setting executive compensation or whatever, will be mindlessly imitated.

Institutional dynamics, not venality or stupidity, set businesses on these courses, which are too often misguided. After making some expensive mistakes because I ignored the power of the imperative, I have tried to organize and manage Berkshire in ways that minimize its influence. Furthermore, Charlie and I have attempted to concentrate our investments in companies that appear alert to the problem.

• After some other mistakes, I learned to go into business only with people whom I like, trust, and admire. As I noted before, this policy of itself will not ensure success: A second-class textile or department-store company won't prosper simply because its managers are men that you would be pleased to see your daughter marry. However, an owner—or investor—can accomplish wonders if he manages to associate himself with such people in businesses that possess decent economic characteristics. Conversely, we do not wish to join with managers who lack admirable qualities, no matter how attractive the prospects of their business. We've never succeeded in making a good deal with a bad person.

(continued)

Figure 8.1 (continued)

• Some of my worst mistakes were not publicly visible. These were stock and business purchases whose virtues I understood and yet didn't make. It's no sin to miss a great opportunity outside one's area of competence. But I have passed on a couple of really big purchases that were served up to me on a platter and that I was fully capable of understanding. For Berkshire's shareholders, myself included, the cost of this thumb-sucking has been huge.

• Our consistently conservative financial policies may appear to have been a mistake, but in my view were not. In retrospect, it is clear that significantly higher, though still conventional, leverage ratios at Berkshire would have produced considerably better returns on equity than the 23.8% we have actually averaged. Even in 1965, perhaps we could have judged there to be a 99% probability that higher leverage would lead to nothing but good. Correspondingly, we might have seen only a 1% chance that some shock factor, external or internal, would cause a conventional debt ratio to produce a result falling somewhere between temporary anguish and default.

   We wouldn't have liked those 99:1 odds—and never will. A small chance of distress or disgrace cannot, in our view, be offset by a large chance of extra returns. If your actions are sensible, you are certain to get good results; in most such cases, leverage just moves things along faster. Charlie and I have never been in a big hurry: We enjoy the process far more than the proceeds—though we have learned to live with those also.

* * *

We hope in another 25 years to report on the mistakes of the first 50. If we are around in 2015 to do that, you can count on this section occupying many more pages than it does here.

3. *Not recognizing difference between value and price.* This goes along with the failure to compute the intrinsic value of a stock, which is simply the discounted future earnings of the business enterprise.

4. *Failure to understand Mr. Market.* Just because the market has put a price on a business does not mean it is worth it. Only an individual can determine the value of an investment and then determine if the market price is rational.

5. *Failure to understand the impact of taxes*. Also known as the sorrows of compounding. Just as compounding works to the investor's long-term advantage, the burden of taxes because of excessive trading works against building wealth.

6. *Too much focus on the market*. Whether or not an individual investment has merit and value has nothing to do with what the overall market is doing.

7. *Inertia*. Investors, both private and professional, tend to keep doing what they have *always done*.

8. *Not enough attention given to evaluating management*. Also known as the qualitative aspect of investing. Most investors stick to what is measurable, understandable, and stated in accounting reports, instead of taking a careful look at the managers of the enterprise.

9. *Agonizing over errors*. Mistakes will happen. Even the greatest baseball hitter of all time, Ted Williams, was not successful 60 percent of the time.

LEARN FROM YOUR MISTAKES

Study failures to learn. James Joyce said, "A man of genius makes no mistakes. His errors are the portals of discovery." Mistakes are your true teachers, not just about wealth building. A father teaching his son to ice skate told him he needed to fall down one thousand times. So his son promptly went out onto the ice and started falling down to get his thousand falls out of the way. Well, unfortunately, investing and wealth building do not give us the opportunity to make many mistakes. Unfortunately, two or three critical mistakes can prevent any serious attempt at wealth building.

Mistakes are important, because if you can't make a mistake, you can't make anything. Remember there are two kinds of people to stay away from: people who don't make mistakes and those who make the same mistake twice. You're going to make mistakes, and you need to take calculated risk in order to build wealth.

Famed management guru Peter Drucker said, "People who don't take risk generally make about two big mistakes a year. And people who do take risk generally make about two big mistakes a year." Legendary architect Frank Lloyd Wright once noted, "The doctor can bury his mistakes, but an architect can only advise his client to plant vines." It's easy to cover up your private portfolio mistakes, but it's difficult in a business that is so measurable for public investment managers to hide their mistakes.

"The higher you go up, the more mistakes you are allowed. Right at the top, if you make enough of them, it's considered to be your style," noted dancer extraordinaire Fred Astaire. Albert Einstein may have said it best: "Anyone who has never made a mistake has never tried anything new."

Remember the inspiration and persistence of Abe Lincoln's political pursuit: He lost six elections before becoming president of the United States. Mistakes and misfortunes build character. It is a good thing that Warren Buffett did not stop after purchasing his first stock—City Services Preferred—or his first wholly owned business—Hochschild, Kohn & Co. Neither were great successes.

The mistake Warren Buffett made was to strike out on his own while still a teenager and make all the typical investment mistakes. He made the usual errors of following the madness of crowds, emotion-based investing, being trader oriented instead of owner oriented, and investing based on price instead of value. On the other hand, the brilliance and genius of Warren was to learn at the foot of Benjamin Graham how to properly value businesses, how to think about market prices, to buy businesses when they're cheap, and to learn about the mistakes of others early enough in his investing career. He became a journalist investigating other people's mistakes, but we too can learn from the mistakes of Buffett. The collection of them is what you would call experience.

One of our most valuable assets is self-evaluation. Admit your mistakes, like Warren does each year in his "Mea Culpa" annual letter. Don't show weakness with self-righteousness. Don't make the mistake of arrogance. Mistakes are learning experiences and the jewels of wisdom, as long as you don't make them twice. Ridicule is simply ignorance. In order to see the rainbow, you need to get past the storm. Turn past failures and mistakes into assets.

Mistakes and adversity just teach you self-discovery and help you recognize that your emotions are your greatest handicap of accurate thinking. Every bull market, where the prices of stocks continue to rise each year, has seemingly created many investment and wealth-building geniuses, but remember when the tide goes out, you can learn who's been swimming naked.

Bear markets, when prices continue to decline, reveal all investor mistakes. It naturally uncovers those who have failed to define what kind of investor they are, who is operating without a written set of investment philosophies, those investing based on price, not value, in equities they know little about and have purchased in small quantities.

"An investor needs to do very few things right as long as he or she avoids big mistakes," writes Warren. He goes on to say, "It is more important to say no to an opportunity than to say yes. A good management record is far more a function of what business boat you get into than it is how effectively you row. There's no extra credit for a degree of difficulty. . . . I don't try to jump over seven-foot bars; I just look around for one-foot bars that I can step over." Lower your degree of difficulty.

HOW TO AVOID BIG INVESTING MISTAKES

Even the world's greatest investor tried other methods until he realized he was mistaken. He writes, "I went the whole gamut. I collected charts and I read all the technical stuff, I listened to tips and then I picked up Graham's *The Intelligent Investor*, and that was like seeing the light." He goes on to say, "One of an investor's biggest mistakes is to focus on a stock price instead of its value." According to Warren, "you make a huge mistake if you invest in that which you don't understand or because it worked for someone else last week. The dumbest reason in the world to buy a stock is because it's going up." How many of us have made those mistakes?

The following paragraphs offer a quick refresher course to help you avoid the biggest investing mistakes:

Figure out if you are an active or passive investor. There is nothing wrong with buying a low-cost index fund that represents the broad market and doing other more enjoyable things with your life if you do not savor the day-to-day reading required of active investors.

Develop a philosophy. You must have some principles and guidelines to select investments.

Stick to what you know and understand. Remember to read and research to minimize your risk. You should be able to understand what you're reading; don't invest in a company if you can't understand the information they provide about its products, services, or financials. When Warren reads a financial report and cannot understand what he is reading, he assumes that the writer or the CEO purposely didn't want him to understand, and therefore, he won't invest.

Focus on Main Street. It's the everyday, old-economy businesses that you drive by every day that should be your focus. Avoid the complex deals offered by Wall Street that are difficult to understand and that carry high returns to the salesman selling them to you.

Concentrate. Pay attention both to what you are investing in and your percentage of assets. Remember Warren put 50 percent of his partnership's assets in American Express, 25 percent of Berkshire's net worth in Coca-Cola, and 99 percent of his personal net worth in Berkshire Hathaway.

Don't sell too soon. Some of Buffett's investors wondered why he reinvested in Capital Cities, which later merged with ABC, which then later merged with Disney. When he reinvested in 1985, he bought Capital Cities at $172.50 per share, and his shareholders were confused, because he had previously sold his stock, earlier in 1978 through 1980, for $43 per share. To answer that, he simply said, "I need more time [to explain that mistake] please." Phil Fisher said, "The only reason to sell is upon realizing you made a mistake." Even then Fisher would give his investee a minimum of three years before he sold.

Don't make the mistake of following the crowd. All progress and greatness come from the uncommon man. You are neither right nor wrong because the crowd agrees with you. All great builders of wealth are independent thinkers and get no pleasure from crowd approval. Ignore the madness of crowds. Look at the business before you invest. Make sure you understand it, evaluate management, review the financials, and then look at the price and determine if there is sufficient discount in its market price to its intrinsic value or margin of safety. Remember that you only need a very few good investment ideas for a lifetime. The hard work is looking at hundreds, if not thousands, before you select the one meeting your strict criteria.

Finally, avoid these typical mistakes:

- **No discipline.** Remember how much discipline Ted Williams had in baseball, which made him the last player to hit .400 and who is now considered the best hitter ever. Baseball is an apt analogy for understanding Warren Buffett's wealth-building strategies, because baseball is one of Warren's favorite sports. Almost 30 years ago, in *Forbes* magazine, Warren was quoted as saying, "Investing is the greatest business in the world, because you never have to swing. You stand at the plate, the pitcher throws you General Motors at

47, US Steel at 39 and nobody calls a strike on you. There's no penalty except opportunity. All day, you wait for the pitch you like. Then when the fielders are asleep, you step up and hit it."

- *Complexity.* For some strange reason, many investors think the more complex the investment scheme, the better. Warren points out that wealth building is simple, but it certainly is not easy. Genius is often noted in its simplicity.

- *Ego and arrogance.* Many an investor has an inflated sense of self and thinks he or she has what it takes to be a super-investor without assessing the degree of difficulty of beating the combined talents of the market.

- *Perfection.* To be perfect is not achievable and is setting yourself up for disappointment. It would be like Ted Williams thinking he would make a hit every time he went up to bat. The investment business is so measured and defined that perfectionists have great difficulty entering and staying in the business.

- *Too much information.* Also known as "analysis paralysis," information overload can prevent an investor from making a decision because of too much information.

CONCLUSION

The takeaway exercise for this chapter is very straightforward:

- Analyze your investment mistakes
- Admit them
- Do postmortems
- Learn from them

Can you admit your biggest investment mistakes? What did you learn from them? Have you ever repeated any of them?

The next chapter talks about common myths about investments, wealth building, and Buffett. Surrounding every cultural icon and legend are myths and untruths. Let's take a look at a few and dispel them.

Chapter 9

Common Myths about Investing, Wealth, and Buffett

"The most dangerous untruths are truths moderately distorted."
—Georg C. Lichtenberg

Earlier chapters outlined just how extraordinary Warren Buffett's accomplishments are, and the last chapter highlighted the fact that he is indeed human and is capable of making errors. Having the title of being the world's greatest generally spawns myths and the stuff of legends: some untruths and some embellishments.

Greatness is always surrounded by myth. This chapter discusses and debunks various myths about investing, wealth building, and of course, Buffett's investing in particular. Earlier chapters have already dispelled many myths, but this chapter explores more. When it comes to building wealth, don't fall for the obvious. If it's too good to be true, it probably is, and there is no quick wealth in taking immediate action. Buffett Wealth has taken a lifetime to create.

COMMON INVESTMENT MYTHS

Myth #1: Anyone can make a killing just by investing in the stock market. First let's address the most common investment myth. Trading for a living is a contradiction in terms, because most traders don't have much of a life. They're always staring at a computer screen trying to figure out if it's a green or a red day. In the short term, it's possible and easy, but no member of the *Forbes* 400 Richest got there by trading for a living. Traders do not generally sleep very well because their opportunity for profit comes by the action or inaction of other market participants. Conservative investors sleep well because they have looked inside the business and have a margin of safety. It's difficult to develop a wonderful business. Selecting a variety of stocks consisting of wonderful businesses and trading them in and out is even more difficult.

Myth #2: Initial public offerings, also known as IPOs, are great investments. If you can't get in on the actual IPO, it's best to buy a new issue as early as possible. Well, the reality is that new stock issues come out at the most favorable time for the promoters of the stock. So instead of buying early, do what Buffett and company does. Buy an "OPO," otherwise known as "old public offerings," like Coke. Great wealth does not flow to those who were in early in an investment, but rather to those who saw the *long-term value* of their investment.

Myth #3: Your age should predict your amount of fixed-income investments. For example, this myth says that a forty-two-year-old investor should have 42 percent of his assets in fixed-income investments. However, the danger of fixed-income investments, like bonds, is that when interest rates rise, the value of the bonds fall. A 1 percent rise in interest rates lowers the value of a long-term bond by 10 percent. The simple truth is that wealth has been created and enjoyed by those who own a business, either directly or indirectly, in whole or in part, through the stock market. A value investor looks for value wherever he or she can find it and follows no predetermined asset allocation mix.

Myth #4: Investing is complicated. Investing is simple, but it's not easy. How can it be easy? Read and research public documents. No newsletters or subscriptions are necessary. You may want to consult Valueline at your local library to get the data or quantitative information on a company of interest. Read corporate annual reports and listen to quarterly management conference calls to gauge the qualitative aspects of a potential investment. Phone investor relation departments of companies that you are considering. There wasn't anything terribly complicated about investing in Dairy Queen or World Book Encyclopedia. Buffett recognized the value, thought they had competent and honest managers, and bought the businesses at a discount.

Myth #5: There's no point to investing if you don't have any money. Well, the story of Warren Buffett shows that a kid with $100 can create billions by applying his principles and practical methods. Many great fortunes have been created by individuals who started with very little money. Often times, the lack of money provides the desire and passion to create and to recognize opportunity. The abundance of wealth often takes away the desire and drive to create more. Figure 9.1 shows the growth of $100 per month invested at 10 percent per year for 20 years.

The value at the end of twenty years would be $76,000, with a total of $24,000 invested and $52,000 in compound gains. Note that whatever amount you invest per month for seven years at 10 percent is the same amount you can withdraw per month forever without touching the principal. So if you set aside $500 per month for seven years, you can take $500 per month—forever (as long as you are able to get 10 percent annual returns).

Myth #6: Bank accounts are excellent investments. This isn't true, if you consider taxes and inflation. Like Warren, you need to save before you can invest, but there just isn't anyone who created great fortunes by relying on savings accounts. Banks are great for short-term emergencies, but not for building long-term wealth.

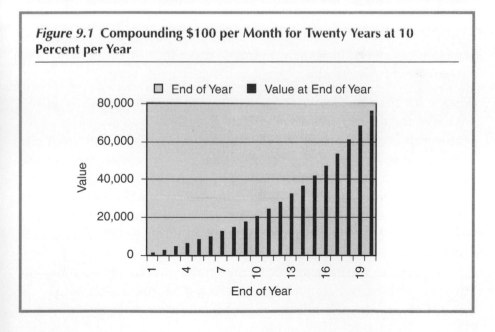

Figure 9.1 **Compounding $100 per Month for Twenty Years at 10 Percent per Year**

Myth #7: You should follow your investments daily. This action will get you into trouble, and it labels you as an emotional investor. It's kind of like getting on the scale every hour when you're trying to lose weight. All investments take time to realize their full potential. Just ask people what their greatest investment was, and they will tell you it's something they have done for a long time. You're not going to get a great education in a few days or months or even years. Education takes decades; so does the development of your wealth.

Myth #8: Mutual funds beat the market. Unfortunately, mutual funds are far too diversified, carry extra costs of active management, and are far too actively traded without regard to taxes to outperform the stock market. Low-cost index funds are a better way to go, if you don't know how to value businesses and understand market prices like Warren Buffett.

The old axiom that the best mutual funds this year will usually become next year's average performer is true. Unfortunately, money flows to successful funds from underperforming funds and then becomes a handicap to future superior returns. Rapid inflows of cash handicap outstanding investment managers.

Myth #9: Market timing works. You can determine the top of the market and sell and wait for the bottom and buy. This isn't possible. People who get in and out of business ownership so quickly don't understand business ownership. Instead, buy businesses that you can understand with honest management and at an attractive price—determined by the present value of a stream of future earnings.

Myth #10: Rich people and large institutions have an enormous advantage over average investors. Although Warren has the advantage of seeing many deals first and can use the cash from his ever-expanding empire to purchase more businesses, smaller investors have the advantage of size, or the lack of size. You see, the greater the wealth, the greater the anchor against superior returns. The small investor armed with the proper training and principles can move into a wide variety of investments without notice or disruption. A small investment portfolio can attain greater returns than the same smart investment of a large portfolio.

Remember Warren put 100 percent of his portfolio, or $10,000 at the time, into GEICO when he was twenty-one years old. He captured a 50 percent gain in one year, but he couldn't do the same thing today, because his portfolio is too big. He now has more money than ideas.

Myth #11: Any kid with a computer can buy stocks. Yes, in rising bull markets, just about anyone can know absolutely nothing about how to value a business and can nevertheless profit in the stock market. But those who know how to calculate business valuations and patiently wait for the right price to buy achieve long-term wealth.

Myth #12: Investing in stocks is like gambling. It can be if you are a speculator. You are gambling if you don't know what you own. Betting on a stock requires little skill but investing ever-increasing sums of money (all successful investors become rich) wisely takes skill, knowledge, patience, and hard work. Buffett Wealth is the result of applied knowledge over many decades and has nothing to do with luck or gambling.

Myth #13: The stock market is an exclusive club for brokers and the rich to make money. This simply isn't true. Profits go to those who do the work. For every investment super-investors make, they have looked at hundreds if not thousands of investment ideas but took a pass. Every significant investment idea that Buffett decided on came after careful study, not by someone dropping by his office and whispering in his ear. The small investor has the same advantage as the professional full-time financier as long as he or she does the homework.

Myth #14: When stocks decline, they will always go back up. Some people think a declining stock will eventually return to its previous high, and that's why people invest in those stocks. But why not buy stocks that have increased in value and which have *not* come back down?

Myth #15: A little knowledge of Wall Street is better than none. In fact, sometimes a little knowledge can cause you more trouble. Some people rely on the myth that stocks will return 20 percent on the original investment. If you believe this, you're setting yourself up for great disappointment. Long-term stocks have returned, on average, 11 percent. Unfortunately, some think returns twice that are the norm. It's just not so.

Myth #16: New-economy stocks generate better returns than so-called "old-economy" stocks. In *The Millionaire Next Door*, the authors proved this myth wrong. They showed that most millionaires are owners of businesses like gas stations and dry cleaning establishments—that is, old-economy businesses. Success comes from business ownership over long periods of time, regardless of whether or not it's a new-economy or old-economy business. Warren has had great success in boring, old-economy enterprises because the earnings are more predictable and therefore the value calculation is easier.

Myth #17: *Buying and holding your investments always works.* If you don't know what you own, or if you simply buy according to your neighbor's hot tips, no amount of time will overcome these classic mistakes.

Myth #18: *Business success is a function of a rising stock price.* Absolutely not. Eventually, the stock price will reflect what is going on in the business, but some unethical business managers manipulate the stock price, because they are given incentives based on short-term changes in the stock price. Therefore, you should invest in businesses that focus on the long-term prospects of the business, not the stock price. Look how Warren Buffett evaluates himself each year: not by the annual changes of his stock price, but rather according to the annual changes in his company's book value.

Myth #19: *Unethical CEOs are to blame for the tech market collapse.* This claim is partly true, but unfortunately, many speculators and traders got caught owning things they didn't understand. Rather than taking personal responsibility for their losses, they have attempted to blame others.

Myth #20: *Stocks are risky*. They are if you purchase without figuring out their true valuation or if you trade stocks. Equities have been excellent investments for Warren Buffett because he has trained himself to recognize when they are at excellent values.

Myth #21: *You need a broker.* Online brokers have reduced the cost of owning stocks. Do it yourselfers can ignore interested advice. Some registered investment advisors and stockbrokers do encourage financial education; careful stock selection and long-term ownership should be considered excellent teammates to your wealth creation.

Myth #22: *Buy the biggest house possible.* You should buy whatever home you would enjoy living in that is way below your means. Saddling yourself with a hefty mortgage, annual real estate taxes, and working to pay for it is not necessarily the fastest way to wealth.

Myth #23: *Life insurance is a good investment.* It can be for those parents needing to insure the financial future of their dependent children. Thinking that investors without dependents need life insurance is a mistake.

Myth #24: The market is always efficient. Some mistakenly believe, and even teach at major universities, that everything that is known about a stock is already reflected in its stock price. This assertion flies against everything that Warren Buffett believes. This myth is, in essence, saying that thinking does not pay. Value investors know that if they do their homework and think for themselves, they can indeed find excellent investments in any market.

Now on to some myths about wealth.

COMMON MYTHS ABOUT WEALTH

People who create wealth have a certain mind-set that allows them to attract what they need to know and do to accomplish financial freedom. They would never allow the following wealth myths to influence them.

Myth #1: Hard work will turn into greater earnings. Although industrious people have created most, if not all, wealth, they do not necessarily work harder than a day laborer. They have created wealth by hard work combined with business ownership over long periods with a lifestyle below their income. Generally, they love their work, and their businesses are a personal extension and expression of them.

Myth #2: Doing work you don't enjoy creates wealth. This statement would mean that the only reason people work is for the money, and once you have acquired financial freedom for you and your family you would stop working. Not so for the Buffett CEOs. Managers of the Berkshire subsidiaries are worth, on average, $100 million. They all love what they are doing. Otherwise, they would retire, since they are no longer working for money.

Myth #3: Fortunes are created by those with the most education. Keep in mind that the current richest man in the world, Microsoft's Bill Gates, undoubtedly a brilliant thinker, did not graduate from college. Don't let lack of education be a deterrent. Wealth creation knows no prejudices and is blind to race, religion, age, gender, geography, and educational level. Earned wealth is merit based. Pursue knowledge. Learn from others' mistakes and remember the journey of a thousand miles (or a thousand dollars) begins with the first step.

Myth #4: Creating wealth used to be easier. With more millionaires and billionaires every passing decade the "I remember when" stories are more fiction than fact. The best time to create financial independence is now, with more opportunity than ever. Some people say they are too old to become wealthy. Fortunately, Colonel Sanders, the founder of Kentucky Fried Chicken, didn't hear that or consider it. In the investment business, a few gray hairs and worldly experience is an advantage.

Do You Have What It Takes to Be a Millionaire?

If you have the time and the discipline to live below your means, becoming a millionaire is relatively easy. Simply set aside $158 month (less than $2,000 per year) for forty years at 10 percent. See Table 9.1 for the amount of money you would have to invest each month at 10 percent to accumulate $1 million. Who wants to be a millionaire?

Myth #5: Successful wealth-builders aren't young; they have experience. In addition to people who believe they're too old to be rich are people who believe they're too young. Fortunately, the pioneers at Microsoft didn't think that. Fortunately, Buffett started at the age of eleven and wishes that he had started earlier. Look at Warren as your model: he, without compromising his ethics, turned thousands into billions.

Myth #6: You need to learn and know everything before you can create wealth. Well, you'll be waiting a long time. It's impossible to know everything. Besides, things change, opportunities present themselves along your

---

Table 9.1 Years and Amounts to Accumulate $1 million at 10 percent

Years to Invest	Investment Needed per Month
40	$158
30	$442
20	$1,317

journey, and people and resources appear when you are ready for them. Charlie Munger did not become Warren's partner at the beginning of their journeys, but along the way after both started independently to create wealth.

Myth #7: *The size of your home is the measure of your wealth.* Warren Buffett paid less for his home than any other billionaire. Possessions are not the true or sole indicator of a person's wealth. For example, when *Forbes* calculates wealth for its *Forbes 400* list of wealthiest people, it doesn't count the number of cars, jet airplanes, or square footage of your home. Instead, it counts the value of your business holdings. (Unfortunately they also don't count other measures of true wealth: the number of friends, sense of humor, people who love you, knowledge, ethics, and principles.)

Myth #8: *Wealthier people are happier.* This myth is perhaps the biggest regarding wealth. Unfortunately, wealthy people have all the same problems as those less fortunate. Comedian Robin Williams observed, "A cocaine addiction is God's way of saying you have too much money." Still, as Pearl Bailey once said, "I have been poor and I have been rich, and I prefer rich."

Myth #9: *New technological innovations create the most wealth.* Actually the boring, old-economy businesses managed by the regular guy next door have created the most wealth. Trying to find and capitalize on the latest and greatest invention or technological breakthrough is a much higher probability game, fraught with more disasters than winners.

Myth #10: *You need a lot of money to get started.* If Buffett Wealth has proved anything, you need sound investment and practical methods more than you need money. Take away all of Buffett's wealth and he will recreate it. Take away his foundation of investment philosophies and principles and guiding mentors, and no amount of money will create or re-create wealth. Wealth is in the *principle*, not the *principal*.

Myth #11: *Wealth means shrewdness and unethical schemes.* A foundation of wealth must be based on sound ethics in order to be duplicated, preserved, and passed to future generations. The risk of employing deceitful methods is that the rule of law will eventually even the score and recover illicit gains. Character and reputation matter.

MYTHS ABOUT WARREN BUFFETT

Now onto some myths about Warren Buffett. Many try to put words into his mouth, or twist and reinterpt what he means. Therefore it is best if you go online to his website at www.berkshirehathaway.com and read for yourself his own words. You will probably find his writing to be impactful, easy to understand, commonsensical, down home, humorous, and very entertaining. Read his owner's manual, which is probably the best way to dispel commonly held myths about him.

Myth #1: The buy-and-hold strategy that Warren Buffett practices doesn't work. Some people even say that Warren Buffett trades stocks short term and therefore doesn't follow his own advice. But if you skip the research, follow the crowd, purchase without knowing the intrinsic value of what you're buying, pay too much, invest in a rapidly changing industry, or buy a wonderful business with lousy management, then it's true: no amount of time will cure your investment mistakes.

Besides, "buy-and-hold" are the wrong three words to describe the incredible wealth creation of Warren Buffett and his partners. Instead, consider any of these three-word phrases—any one of which better describes Buffett's investment style:

- "cheap and keep"
- "margin of safety"
- "circle of competence"
- "Graham and Dodd"
- "timeless value investing"
- "calculate intrinsic value"
- "purchase superior management"
- "know your stocks"
- "concentrate your ownership"
- "partner for life"
- "value always matters"
- "twenty investment moves"
- "read, then own"
- "investor, not speculator"
- "wise, intelligent investor"
- "owner, not trader"

Myth #2: Warren has just been lucky. Creating more than $100 billion in value from scratch is hardly lucky. Moreover, besting the market by more than two times its average, over five decades of professional management, is nothing short of remarkable. Berkshire's chairman disregards all games of chance and is a great admirer of skill and discipline in all areas.

Myth #3: Warren Buffett doesn't do as well in bear markets or down markets. In fact, his best performance comes when the market is declining over time instead of rising. Actually, all of his best-performing years over the past five decades have come during market declines, and conversely, he has not been able to add value to his partners' investments when the market has reached its highest level. All value investors do better in declining markets and find more opportunities.

Myth #4: The average investor can't do what Warren has done and continues to do. Although it's true that most people can't buy whole companies and are unable to create a cash flow machine that now generates more than $150 million per week, the real advantage of the small individual who knows how to value companies is to buy a meaningful amount of stock without causing any disruption to the capital markets. The average stock market participant has the whole universe of stocks and investment opportunities. Buffett is limited more and more each year to attractively priced and competently managed companies that are now earning in excess of $50 million per year. You—the *hoi polloi*—can add rabbits to your portfolio, whereas Warren can add only elephants to his.

Myth #5: Change means risk. Because investors believe this myth, many attempt to get in and out of the market in order to reduce their risk. But it's a myth to associate change with risk. Invest in what is most stable. For example, Coca-Cola is the same business today as it was a hundred years ago, just larger. Traders fail to realize that rapid movements in and out of a stock or mutual fund are actually increasing risk. It would have been very risky for Buffett to buy Coca-Cola for a short time period, because it very likely would have declined further. Owning old-economy stocks, purchased at a discount to their intrinsic value, for the long term is not risky.

Myth #6: The company you bought today may not be the same tomorrow. Notice that Warren has built wealth in companies that are stable and enduring—bricks, footwear, paint, insurance, candy, newspapers, jewelry, furniture, underwear, children's apparel, beverages, and (everyone's favorite) Dairy Queen. He is invested in a wide, diverse group of businesses—at last count, more than one hundred, many managed by families for the benefit of families.

Myth #7: Because people are no longer loyal in business and in general, we shouldn't invest for a lifetime, as Warren does. One of the secrets and the magic of Buffett is his ability to choose loyal managers. With an underlying philosophy of never laying off employees or selling a business that he has bought in its entirety brings him more business and the right kind of investments. Most CEOs and employees who care about their business and their jobs welcome the opportunity to become part of the Berkshire family. They know their loyalty will be returned.

Myth #8: Warren can't maintain his CEO talent pool. With more than fifty CEOs and adding, on average, four more each year, some people think it is impossible for the world's best investor to also be the world's best manager. Yet on average, the CEO of a top-fifty company will last only six years, in contrast to a Buffett CEO, who has been managing for the past twenty-three years and counting, because there isn't a Berkshire-mandated retirement age. Warren manages his businesses as though he is acquiring a small portfolio of businesses. The original managers forget that they sold their business to him, and Warren forgets he bought it.

He has never lost a CEO to a competing enterprise. He's only lost a CEO to either retirement or death.

Myth #9: Warren invests differently today than when he first started. This is a myth, because he's still interested in simple businesses with quality management with little debt at a favorable price. Still today, he's attempting to invest or buy a dollar of assets for 50 cents, to find a quality and predictable investment selling at a fair price.

Myth #10: Warren can analyze the market for you, so you can buy what he's buying and you will have the same returns. Well, unfortunately, Berkshire Hathaway is no longer a quasi-mutual fund; instead, more and more of its net worth is now in wholly owned companies that are not for sale for any price. Warren is a *business* analyst, not a *market* analyst, so he can't help you much in interpreting the market.

Even those who think they can buy the same stocks that Warren has purchased miss the most important lesson—the principles employed to value and purchase stocks, not the specific stocks. Unfortunately, many people think if they buy the same stocks as Warren Buffett, they will get the same returns. Yet this is a myth, because he purchased these stocks many years ago, and to buy them now would be buying them with a different valuation.

Moreover, Warren buys things that you can't buy. He'll buy a preferred stock that pays a dividend and can be converted later into a common stock. He buys businesses that can pay him in the form of earnings from his investments, with which he can then use to buy even more businesses. The ordinary investor can't replicate that, but what you can do is invest in value companies and attempt to do what he does—buy a dollar in assets for 50 cents, buy companies with stable and predictable earnings, and buy for a low multiple of earnings.

Myth #11: Warren measures his success based on the changes in the price of Berkshire Hathaway stock. Indeed, he did originally pay $7 a share for his stock and it's now currently selling in excess of $80,000. But even if it were selling for $700,000 per share, it would not affect him one way or the other, because he never intends to sell a share of his stock. He measures himself with what is going on inside the business and what he has control over. Annual changes in book value (assets minus liabilities) and CEO retention are his simple measurements.

Warren does want his partners to do well over the time period they have been invested and therefore he does want the long-term stock price to eventually reflect the changes in Berkshire's intrinsic value.

Myth #12: Buffett doesn't invest in technology because he doesn't understand it and has failed to change his investment style. Actually, he knows a lot about technology and most days plays bridge online, often with technological guru Bill Gates. He regularly does research on the Internet to find out as much as he can about potential investments. He routinely reads the next day's *Washington Post* after 9 pm the night before. He buys his books on Amazon and agreed to have lunch with the winner of a charity auction on eBay. Berkshire owns one of the world's most sophisticated flight services companies in the world loaded with the most advanced technologies. Technology or not, Warren doesn't invest in any company that doesn't have any earnings because he can't value them.

Myth #13: Buffett doesn't split his stock because he doesn't want to make it available to the average investor. Not true. He created and offered the B class of shares at the end of 1995 that trade on the NYSE for one-thirtieth the price and economic value of A class shares. With A shares then trading for $30,000 each, Berkshire offered B class shares for $1,000 each. Splitting his stock would attract traders, instead of owners. Attracting owners is part of the corporate culture that will last beyond Warren's death.

Myth #14: Dividends are an excellent way to return capital to investors. On the contrary, Warren thinks dividends are a poor way to return capital to his partners—that dividends are taxed twice, once at the corporate level and again at the individual level. Why take capital out of the hands of the world's greatest capital allocator? He believes it would be better to reinvest that capital back into acquiring more businesses than it would be to subject them to double taxation. Certainly some businesses that do not have the Berkshire business model should consider buying back their own stock, if it is attractively priced, or returning the capital and earnings to its shareholders if it is in a mature cycle and further investment will not grow the underlying enterprise.

Myth #15: Buffett's holding company will diminish after his death. With a horizontal organizational structure, without a large headquarters staff, without vice presidents, without divisions, without meetings or budgets, Buffett's successors will have the simple task of keeping the culture alive for many succeeding generations of shareholders, employees and customers. Upon his death, his job will be divided into three: one CEO will be in charge of operations (the other CEOs), another CEO will be in charge of capital operations, and a third, most likely a Buffett family member, will become chairman of the board to ensure the corporate culture stays in place.

Decisions and the corporate culture are cumulative in nature and are not easily changed or reset back to zero when the architect of them passes the baton to succeeding managers. In the next chapter, we discuss the designated backup to Warren on the investment side of Berkshire.

CONCLUSION

The takeaway exercise of this chapter is to:

- Be aware of the typical myths about investing, wealth building, and Warren Buffett.

- Look at your own myths of your investment life:
  - Do you believe that investing is complicated?
  - Do you think that you need money to start your wealth-building journey?
  - Have you realized that Warren Buffett has laid a successful road map to wealth that should be studied?

- Read more of Buffett, invest like Warren, own for life, and be encouraged that a man with thousands grew it into a multibillion-dollar fortune, and it's possible that someone else just might do the same.

The next chapter identifies the five investment principles from the *next* Warren Buffett. Perhaps the biggest Buffett myth is that nobody can do what Warren has done and continues to do. Let's meet someone who has been hand-picked to succeed Warren, if necessary, on the investment side of the business—someone who has an even better investment record at investing in stocks than his boss.

Chapter 10

Five Investment Principles from the Next Warren Buffett

"In science the successors stand upon the shoulders of their predecessors; where one man of supreme genius has invented a method, a thousand lesser men can apply it."

—Bertrand Russell

Many investors, private and professional, have applied the same principles and practical methods as Warren Buffett and achieved similar results. Lou Simpson proves that everyone can successfully apply the wealth methods of Warren Buffett, some even to a better result. This chapter discusses five investment principles from the next Warren Buffett: Lou Simpson, CEO of Capital Operations for GEICO Auto Insurance, a wholly owned Berkshire subsidiary. He's also the hand-selected, back-up investor to Warren Buffett.

In Buffett's 1995 letter to shareholders he wrote this about Simpson:

Lou runs investments just as ably. Between 1980 and 1995, the equities under Lou's management returned an average of 22.8% annually vs. 15.7% for the S&P. Lou takes the same conservative, concentrated approach to investments that we do at Berkshire, and it is an enormous plus for us to have him on board. One point that goes beyond Lou's GEICO work: His presence on the scene assures us that Berkshire would have an extraordinary professional immediately available to handle its investments if something were to happen to Charlie [Munger] and me.

The following year, Buffett wrote that his back-up successor beat the S&P 500 index by 6.2 percent for a total for 1996 of 29.2 percent. "Our marketable securities outperformed most indices," wrote Warren in his letter to shareholders in 2002. "For Lou Simpson, who manages equities at GEICO, this was old stuff. But, for me, it was a welcome change from the last few years, during which my investment record was dismal."

You can learn more about Warren's methods of wealth building by studying his successor because Warren's selection defines him.

WHAT LOU SIMPSON AND WARREN BUFFETT HAVE IN COMMON—AND HOW THEY DIFFER

Lou is more like the common and professional investor, because he buys pieces of businesses or stocks, rather than whole businesses, as Warren prefers and does. Furthermore, Lou Simpson has a better record at picking stocks than his boss, Warren Buffett.

Understanding how insurance works is important to understanding how Simpson fits into the picture. When you pay premiums to insurance companies, those premiums can be, and often ar,e invested, and before they're paid back to you in the form of a claim, an insurance company gets to enjoy those earnings. So every dollar can be an interest-free loan to an insurance company. This "float" explains why Warren has built a conglomerate that is mainly an insurance company. Lou Simpson manages $2.5 billion in equities for GEICO Auto Insurance, which is more than half of GEICO's $4.7 billion float.

Many investors want to be like Warren, and many say they are the next Warren. But Lou Simpson is not Warren Buffett, he's different. Unlike his boss, Simpson holds outside directorships, including being a director of AT&T. He has selected a different set of value stocks than Warren, and he buys *pieces* of companies or stocks rather than the *whole* business; therefore, he is unable to access the earnings of subsidiaries to reinvest in other businesses. His methods, though, are the same as Warren's. However, whereas Warren has a whole menu of available investment options, Lou is a buyer of stocks and only stocks. Simpson is 100 percent in stocks, in contrast to his boss, who is 30 percent stocks now and 70 percent wholly owned businesses. What's more, Warren is striving to own 90 percent wholly owned businesses and only 10 percent stocks.

When Buffett announced in late 1999 that Berkshire was purchasing Cort Business Services, an office furniture rental company, Simpson had to notify his boss that he had personally purchased an interest in Cort and would tender his stock. This example shows how much in sync these two superinvestors are: They recognize the same value in the same investment, even though they hadn't discussed this specific company.

Lou Simpson makes much smaller purchases, in the half-billion-dollar range versus Warren's desire to make purchases in the $5 billion range.

Lou, like his boss, works quietly alone with a very small staff. However, his boss receives more than three thousand letters per year and is host to the world's largest annual meeting, the first Saturday in May. In contrast, Lou Simpson seeks no celebrity or fame. He has no reason to do media interviews to talk up his investments or to tout his performance. He reads everything, but he doesn't write or publish like his boss does. He makes more salary and bonuses than Warren Buffett. Buffett pays himself $100,000 in salary and increases his wealth, along with his shareholders, when the book value, intrinsic value, and stock value of Berkshire go up.

Lou, on the other hand, is paid salary and a performance bonus based on a rolling three-year average of adding value to GEICO's portfolio over and above the S&P 500 index. Unlike his investment management peers, Simpson is not compensated by how much money he has under management, but on how well he invests. He meets with management before he makes an investment. He's living a reclusive life in the mountains. He declines all interviews, thinks independently of his boss, and ignores all typical investment noise. As Warren says, "a public opinion poll is no substitute for thought." That, in essence, is Lou Simpson.

So what are their similarities? They're both voracious readers, and they think independently. They each choose to live away from Wall Street and live within a few blocks of their offices. They're value investors looking to buy a dollar's worth of assets for 50 cents. Both have master's degrees in economics from Ivy League schools. They invest without emotion. They're naturally long-term investors. They focus on the business, management, and finances of a company, and then its stock price. Most importantly, they both have a source for new capital arriving each day, available for investment in the form of insurance float. Neither has to sell investment gains to access capital and, it should be noted, neither has to advertise or promote his performance to attract more capital. If they see extraordinary stock values, Simpson and Buffett can raise capital by simply lowering insurance rates to attract more customers.

IV League Education

Because both Buffett and Simpson are graduates of Ivy League schools, it is interesting to note how the league got its name. Over a century ago, an interscholastic athletic league was formed by the prestigious northeastern universities of Harvard, Yale, Columbia, and Princeton. It was officially known as the "Four League." The Roman numeral "IV" was often used instead of the word "four," and the term "IV League" came into use.

When spoken, the IV was spelled out and sounded like "Ivy League." Brown, Dartmouth, Cornell, and Pennsylvania were the major opponents of the IV league, and were invited to join in the early 1900s.

The more you understand investing like Warren Buffett and Lou Simpson, the more likely you are to talk about intrinsic value (IV) first and market price second. Buffett received his master's degree in economics from Columbia, where he studied under his mentor, IV League professor Ben Graham. Simpson not only received his master's degree in economics from an IV League school (Princeton), he also stayed on to teach. Most who follow the principles of Graham, Buffett, and Simpson have their own IV League degree.

From the 1998 annual report, Warren writes, intrinsic value can be defined simply as the discounted value of the cash that can be taken out of a business during its remaining life. While a company's book value (assets minus liabilities) is a static number and reported each quarter, intrinsic value is constantly changing. On September 10, 2001, Berkshire had an intrinsic value much higher than on September 12, 2001. Warren has pointed out that Berkshire's intrinsic-value-change could swing from $20,000 per share to $100,000 per share during the course of one day depending on what is going on inside the business.

Lou will make a modest investment in a company and then meet with its management. If management doesn't meet with him, he doesn't invest any more. Both he and Warren are inquisitive and have investigative minds. They ask questions and explore what they own.

Lou's office sits in the mountains outside of San Diego, surrounded by fresh air, large estates, horse trails, and golf courses. There is no typical California traffic congestion, and it's about thirty minutes from the international airport. It's a quaint village of real estate brokers, banks, investment advisors, and stock brokerage firms. There's one school, one library, one fire department, and just a couple of stop signs.

He works in a small but appealing freestanding office building with an office right out of *Architectural Digest*. Picture, if you will, a very clean, wood-floored, modern library with custom file cabinets full of annual reports and filings. Wood magazine racks are full of every business and investment publication currently published.

Tom Bancroft, his assistant, said it was a great place to think. Self-help author Napoleon Hill once wrote *Think and Grow Rich*, and as you will learn, Lou Simpson thinks and has grown rich. Ayn Rand said, "Wealth is the product of man's capacity to think." Lou and his office are very wealthy.

On a typical day, Simpson arrives early and stays late, often working twelve-hour days and weekends. There are few super-investors in the world. But you, too, can be a super-investor if you have the same discipline, principles, and methods as Lou Simpson. "An ideal day," he says, "would be a day when I'm here in the office, the market is closed, there are no telephone calls, and I can read all day." In fact, reading is the way he spends the majority of his time. "I say I try to read at least five to eight hours per day. I read a lot of different things including a wide variety of filings, annual reports, industry reports, and business magazines." During the springtime annual report season, he is known to read fifteen to twenty annual reports per day.

In 1979, when Jack Byrne, GEICO Auto Insurance chairman, was looking for a new chief investment officer, he interviewed Simpson along with four other job candidates. In deference to Warren Buffett, who at that point owned about 30 percent of the insurance company, Byrne had agreed to have all four men go to Omaha to see Buffett. "But," John Byrne said, "he called me as Lou was leaving his office and said, 'Stop the search. That's the guy.'"

The investment world became very aware of Lou Simpson because of Warren's famed annual letters to shareholders. "Why would he even consider following in the footsteps of the legend?" he was asked. "I would do it at the invitation of the board of directors for all those that have been kind to me," Simpson replied.

But Warren Buffett's actual successor may be somebody else besides Lou Simpson, because there's only six years' age difference separating Warren and Lou. And as Warren has said on more than one occasion, he intends on retiring five years after his death.

HOW LOU SIMPSON BECAME A GREAT INVESTOR

Born in a Chicago suburb of Highland Park in 1936, Lou graduated from high school in 1954 and enrolled at Northwestern University to study engineering. As he later told a reporter, though, "I was a misfit in engineering." After only a year at Northwestern, he transferred to Ohio Wesleyan University where he majored in accounting and economics, earning a bachelor's degree in 1958. Two years later, he received a master's degree in economics from Princeton and, contemplating a career in academia, he remained to teach at the university, but he wasn't satisfied with the financial rewards of teaching. In 1962, he joined a Chicago investment firm.

He learned his investment craft at Stein, Roe & Farnham and left after seven years, thinking that the firm was too conservative. He then jumped head first into an aggressive and questionable mutual fund based in Los Angeles, known as Shareholders Management. Lasting less than one year, Simpson learned the perils of a shoot-for-the-moon investment philosophy. Moving on to the asset management division of Western Bancorporation, Simpson applied more conservative value-oriented strategies and rose to president and CEO. He left Western Asset Management in 1979 to head up investments for GEICO.

When he took over the investments for GEICO, its portfolio was invested 20 percent in stocks and the rest in fixed-income investments—conservative and very typical for an insurance company. So Lou increased GEICO's investments in stocks substantially. The value grew from $280 million to $1.1 billion. There were thirty-three stocks in GEICO's portfolio; he reduced them to ten. Now he has $2.5 billion under management, in just seven stocks. Contrast that with the average mutual fund, which owns more than one hundred stocks. Lou believes, as Warren does, in a concentrated portfolio. Buffett has long followed a concentrated approach, with more than 70 percent of Berkshire's common-stock holdings in just four stocks. Warren wrote, "Lou takes the same conservative concentrated approach to investments that we do at Berkshire."

Here's where Simpson turns passionate about one of his five investment principles (described in detail in the next section of this chapter): Do not diversify excessively. He couldn't have spoken more frankly when he said, "If we could find fifteen positions that we really had confidence in, we'd be in fifteen positions. We'll never be in one hundred positions because we're never going to know one hundred companies that well. I think the merits of a concentrated portfolio are you live by the sword, you die by the sword. If you're right, you're going to add value. If you're going to add value, you're going to have to look different from the market. That means either being concentrated, or if you're not concentrated in a number of issues, you're concentrated in types of businesses or industries."

Beginning in 1976, Berkshire purchased one third of GEICO for $46 million. In part, because of Lou's incredible investment success and talent, GEICO Auto Insurance was able to buy back its own shares, and without further investment on Warren Buffett's part, Berkshire's one-third ownership grew to more than one half—all because of Lou Simpson's talent of investing in value stocks and using those proceeds to buy back GEICO's shares.

By 1995, Berkshire agreed to buy for $2.3 billion the 49 percent it didn't already own. That means Buffett's $46 million eventually represented 51 percent of the company and was now worth $2.4 billion, earning Berkshire a cool 22 percent annual return over twenty years. No wonder Buffett authored "The Security I Like Best: GEICO" in 1951 when he was twenty-one years old.

Where does Lou Simpson get his investment ideas? Well, as mentioned, he regularly works twelve-hour days and reads every annual report and every financial publication. He also spends time talking with managers, customers, suppliers, and competitors before making a significant investment. He works with a small team that excels in filtering out the noise, asking the right questions, and examining every bottom line. After his reading and research, on average lasting three months, Lou believes in visiting a company's management. Without a visit to management, he makes no substantial investment.

In terms of value investing, Simpson has stated, "When you ask whether someone is a value or growth investor, they're really joined at the hip. A value investor can be a growth investor because you're buying something that has above-average growth prospects, and you're buying it at a discount to the economic value of the business."

Warren Buffett admires three qualities about Lou Simpson: his intellect, his character, and his temperament. Here's what Buffett said about Simpson: "Temperament is what causes smart people not to function well. His temperament probably isn't different than mine. We both tend to do rational things. Our emotions don't get in the way of our intellect." Lou and Warren are not people intensive, but very thought intensive. They're not like the average investor, who is trading intensive; instead, they're IV league–trained and reading intensive.

LOU SIMPSON'S INVESTMENT PRINCIPLES

Now on to the five timeless investment principles of Lou Simpson. He first wrote down and published his classic timeless investment philosophies in GEICO's 1986 annual report to shareholders. These are the same principles to use if you are buying a piece of the business through the stock market or the whole business.

1. Think independently. "We try to be skeptical of conventional wisdom and try to avoid the waves of irrational behavior and emotion that periodically engulf Wall Street. We don't ignore unpopular companies; on the contrary, such situations often present the greatest opportunities."

2. Invest in high-return businesses that are run for the shareholders. "Over the long run," Simpson writes, "appreciation in share prices is most directly related to the return the company earns on its shareholders' investment. Cash flow, which is more difficult to manipulate than reported earnings, is a useful additional yardstick. "We ask the following questions when evaluating a company's management:

- Does management have a substantial stake in the stock of the company?
- Is management straightforward in dealing with the owners?
- Is management willing to divest unprofitable operations?
- Does management use excess cash to repurchase shares? This last question may be the most important. Managers who run a profitable business often use excess cash to expand into less profitable endeavors; repurchase of shares is in many cases a much more advantageous use of surplus resources."

3. Pay only a reasonable price, even for an excellent business. "We try to be disciplined in the price we pay for ownership even in a demonstrably superior business. Even the world's greatest business is not a good investment," he concludes, "if the price is too high. The ratio of price to earnings and its inverse, the earnings yield, are useful gauges in valuing a company, as is the ratio of price to free cash flow. A helpful comparison is the earnings yield of a company versus the return on a risk-free long-term United States government obligation."

4. Invest for the long term. "Attempting to guess short-term swings in individual stocks, the stock market, or the economy," he argues, "is not likely to produce consistently good results. Short-term developments are too unpredictable. On the other hand, owning shares of quality companies run for the shareholders stands an excellent chance of providing above-average returns to investors over the long term. "Furthermore, moving in and out of stocks frequently has two major disadvantages that will substantially diminish the results: transaction costs and taxes. Capital will grow more rapidly if earnings compound with as few interruptions for commission and tax bites as possible," he concludes.

5. Do not diversify excessively. "An investor is not likely to obtain superior results by buying a broad cross section of the market," he believes. "The more diversification, the more performance is likely to be average, at best. We concentrate our holdings in a few companies that meet our investment criteria. Good investment ideas—that is, companies that meet our criteria—are difficult to find. When we think we have found one, we make a large commitment. The five largest holdings of GEICO amount to more than 50% of the stock portfolio."

SIMPSON'S TERRIFIC RETURNS ON GEICO'S INVESTMENTS

Warren Buffett reprinted Simpson's investment results in his company's 1986 annual report. So one assumes he is at the very least impressed with them, which in turn helps explain why he thinks Simpson would be more than able to replace him as head of investments for Berkshire. In fact, not only are their investing approaches very similar, the results of their efforts have also been extremely close. Simpson's average of 24.7 percent return between 1980 and 1996 is slightly less than Buffett's 26.8 percent during the same period. But both handily beat the S&P index of 16.9 percent over the same period.

What makes Simpson's record even more outstanding is his returns are based solely on equities, whereas Buffett's annual return is calculated on changes in Berkshire's book value, which is enhanced by float and other factors, including the earnings of wholly owned businesses. Therefore, comparing only the return on their equity selections of Simpson and Buffett, Simpson might actually win as the superior stock picker.

Again, though, keep in mind that investing for Simpson is a little different from investing like Buffett. It's the difference between buying *part* of a company versus buying the *whole* company, similar to the difference between an individual investor and a conglomerate. Small portfolios have more investment alternatives, or as Lou says, "a much bigger pond to fish in." Despite the size of the portfolios, the analysis is the same, but the economics of buying the whole business can ultimately create more value and can be more attractive from a control, tax, and cash-flow perspective.

Even though the percentages are the same, Simpson can more easily compound $2.5 billion into $25 billion than Buffett can compound $30 billion into $300 billion. The law of large numbers and a shrinking pool of available investment options work together to create an ever-increasing challenge for Berkshire's huge equity portfolio. So the advantage swings to Simpson and even more to the smallest of investors using the same value investing principles and methods.

As of year-end 2003, 70 percent of Berkshire's equity portfolio is in Coca-Cola, American Express, Gillette, and Wells Fargo. Lou is currently invested in stocks like Gap, HCA, Nike, and Outback Steakhouse. So you can see that their underlying principles are the same, but their equity selection is different.

In fact, the stocks in GEICO's portfolio point out another distinction between Simpson and his boss. They have both beaten the widely held market, represented by the S&P 500 index, with a different lineup of stocks, further proving Buffett's theory of super-investors all originating from the small town of Graham and Doddsville.

This was Warren's way of saying that the value investors like Simpson, who follow the value methods taught by Graham and Dodd, can succeed even by investing in different stocks, using the same value principles. Simpson personally invested in Cort Furniture Rental before his boss recognized the same value and bought the whole company.

SIMPSON'S INVESTMENT MISTAKES AND INVESTING STRENGTHS

Simpson's biggest investment mistake wasn't selling too soon, investing in technology, excessive trading, or blindly following a stock tip; instead, his biggest mistake was listening to inside information on a company in which he had an ownership position. This, in effect, froze his position because he became an insider. Lou recounts how he lost some money, and he could neither buy nor sell because he had the information. He said he'll never do that again. He doesn't want any insider information. He wants to be as flexible as possible. Again this narrows the playing field for the small investor who might think if he were a big investor he would have access to inside information and be able to take advantage of it.

When asked about his greatest strength, Simpson said, "If we have any strength, it's really an understanding of businesses and hopefully management. To be able to get the conviction, assuming that you're buying a business at a fair price, maybe a cheap price to go in and take very concentrated bets."

As for the one piece of advice he would give individual investors, he repeats the same advice that he heard from Warren Buffett. "When I first met him," Simpson says, "one of the things he suggested to me was to think of investing as a situation in which you are given a fare card with twenty punches. You can only make twenty investment moves, and at the end of those twenty moves, you have to stay with what you have. Thinking of it that way really helps, because it focuses you on being very careful and having a lot of conviction about whatever changes you want to make.

"In general," he continued, "people are just churning their portfolios. Ben Graham once told me that the way a lot of individuals and institutional investors invest reminded him of people who traded their dirty laundry with each other. They were just trading for the sake of trading, and they didn't really 'own' businesses. Investors are going to make out a whole lot better if their whole emphasis is on owning businesses and having a reasonable time horizon."

CONCLUSION

With the kind of wealth that Lou Simpson has created for GEICO Auto Insurance, for Warren Buffett, and for the Berkshire Hathaway shareholders,

Lou has also created substantial wealth for himself following his five investment principles. Financially independent, he doesn't have to work; he does it for the love of it. It's his passion; it's what he's been born to do.

What Lou Simpson teaches all of us, and could teach you, is that if you have the same passion of investing that he does, you too could enjoy the same success that he has enjoyed. Who knows? Maybe you could be the next Warren Buffett.

The takeaway exercise for this chapter is to:

- Read and research any company extensively before you make a purchase.

- Don't overpay for your stocks.

- Think independently.

- Invest for the long term.

- Hold only a few stocks.

- Invest in shareholder-friendly companies.

- Review your own investment principles to see how they compare to Lou Simpson and Warren Buffett's investment principles.

The next chapter discusses lessons about money, wealth, success, children, power, giving back, and life in general. The circle of wealth is to create it, preserve it, make it grow, and to pass it on for the benefit of future generations.

Chapter 11

Warren Buffett's Lessons on Having a Rich Life

"We make a living by what we get, but we make a life by what we give."

—Winston Churchill

Wealth is about more than money, riches, stocks, and Warren Buffett. This chapter offers some lessons about life: ethics, integrity, health, reputation, character, partnerships, discipline, and good habits. Although this book is primarily about building wealth and understanding and using Warren's principles and practical methods, Warren would be one of the first to point out that life is more than the accumulation of money and amassing great fortune. This chapter hopefully can serve as a reminder that *how* you amass your riches also contributes to the overall richness and satisfaction of your life.

Buffett Wealth is in the *principle*, not the *principal*.

If you learn to forsake gratification and live below your wealth, you can leave this world a better place by returning wealth back to society, as Warren intends to do with his good fortune. You may be interested to learn that the majority, if not all, of Buffett Wealth will be for the benefit of the world and generations yet to be born. In this manner, genius becomes wealth and wealth becomes a foundation for the betterment of humankind. Call it the Circle of Wealth.

MONEY CAN'T BUY HAPPINESS

There is a Yiddish proverb that says, "With money in your pocket, you are wise and you are handsome and you sing well, too." Someone once observed, "No matter how rich you become, how famous or powerful, when you die, the size of your funeral will still pretty much depend on the weather." Someone always reminds you that wealth will not buy you happiness. To counter that, comedian Henny Youngman once said, "What's the use of happiness, if it can't buy you money?"

Nevertheless, most people agree that if you have created wealth at the expense of your relationships, health, or ethics, then you have nothing. Most people would agree that you would be bankrupt as a person. Life is more than money and more than wealth. What would you be worth if you lost all of your money? Rather profoundly, Franklin D. Roosevelt observed, "Happiness is not the mere possession of money; it lies in the joy of achievement, in the thrill of creative effort."

Buffett Wealth teaches that true happiness is doing what you were born to do, also known as self-actualization or following your bliss. Warren has more wealth than many countries, yet he chooses to live a simple life and work every day, often on Saturdays. He tap dances to work and although he is paid a modest salary, he would pay to have his job. It's his canvas, how he expresses himself, and how he manifests unique talents that he was born with and has developed.

Each person is born with a different genetic code. The challenge for each of us, in order to find our happiness, is to figure out what our passion is, what our talents are, and how best to express them.

Many people have found the attainment of wealth is without happiness if you fail to:

- Give credit to others
- Live with moderation
- Select the right heroes and mentors
- Give back and mentor others
- Look after your health
- Earn the respect you deserve
- Stay well within the laws (including paying taxes)
- Be industrious

- Be socially connected and have friends
- Have the love of those you want to love you

How has Warren achieved bliss? He has always given credit to those managers who make up his family of companies. With the ability to buy most things, he chooses to enjoy few possessions and to keep the things he does have for a lifetime. He wisely selected his father and Ben Graham as his heroes and mentors. "Tell me who your heroes are," he explains to college students, "and I'll tell you what kind of person you will become."

Warren finds happiness not in his vast fortune, but instead in delivering newspapers with his grandson and taking his family to the Dairy Queen on Sunday, talking with and mentoring college students, explaining that he lives no better than they do, he just travels better.

Although wealthy people tend to live longer (probably because of less stress and better access to health care), Warren looks after his health with daily treadmill exercise in the morning. He naturally walks at a pretty fast clip. His mind is exercised each day with enormous amounts of reading and several hours a day of online bridge.

Buffett is respected because he respects, taking the time to answer as many as three hundred pieces of correspondence per day. He respects his managers, employees, and shareholders as partners. His compensation is the lowest of the Fortune 500 CEOs. "Good managers," he said recently, "never take credit for more than they do."

He admires patriotism and is patriotic, stepping in to give the markets confidence after the terrorist attacks and putting the American flag on his annual report later that year. While others create wealth by setting up corporations and insurance companies outside the United States, Berkshire's chairman brags about the amount of taxes his corporation pays.

The nation's second richest man doesn't do any heavy lifting, but he works hard. He personally pays for the use of his company's corporate jet service but uses it exclusively for business. He's always working. It's how he has fun.

Most want to be his friend, and the most powerful man in business can get anyone he wants on the telephone, but he carefully chooses those friends who, when they are around, bring out the best in him. Hang out with people who are bigger than you, bring out the best, and inspire you, and you will have a network of giants.

In the end, happiness does not come from Buffett Wealth, but rather from the number of people who love you. The most important thing is not how many or how large his assets are, but how his children feel about him. Warren considers parenthood vital to happiness, and unfortunately there is no rewind button on child development.

The more love you give, the more you get, and you can never give too much of it away. It is inexhaustible.

GOOD CHARACTER, STRONG ETHICS

True wealth, in the broadest sense of the word, is about character. If there's one takeaway from this book, let it be that business success and wealth creation can be achieved with the highest ethical standards and without shady, questionable practices.

As you have seen in the chapters in this book, Warren's success in building wealth also derives from his character. For example, he put his own character on the line to save partly owned Salomon Brothers and its employees from destruction, and he only accepted $1 in salary to do it. He does his own tax return. He never issued himself or anyone else management stock options. He never sold a share of his own company's stock. He never even recommends the purchase of his stock. (He does recommend buying it upon his death and will be miffed if the shares of his holding company go up on that news.)

He talks almost exclusively to groups of college students. He has never taken a fee to speak; in fact, he pays his own way to every college presentation. He has never taken a fee from any author who has written about him or used copyrighted material owned by him.

He never comments on his stock price. He doesn't have a building with his or his company's name on it. He doesn't have an investor relations or public relations department, let alone a staff member in either. He treats his shareholders like partners and has created wealth with them, not at their expense. He doesn't advertise for acquisitions. He doesn't comment on the market or stocks he may be buying or selling. He generally declines all interviews.

Character is tested most in defeat or when you have great power or great wealth. As the most powerful man in business, Buffett's character has stood the test of time and power.

The real measure of your wealth is how much you would be worth if you lost all your money. Before he was known as the world's greatest investor; before he was able to attract three times more shareholders to an annual meeting than any other enterprise, both private and public; before his endorsement was sought by political candidates and business associates alike, Buffett lived the same simple life then that he does today. Nothing has changed, except for trading in his Volkswagen Bug for a Lincoln Town Car and flying more efficiently, safely, and securely by corporate jet. He is the only corporate chief that pays for the use of a corporate jet, for his and his family's travel, out of his own pocket, and he expects his managers and directors to do the same.

Mr. Buffett enjoys challenging college students to pick out someone in their class who they would like to buy 10 percent of their future earnings. Most would probably not select the best-looking student, the best athlete, the tallest, the fastest, or even the most intelligent. In the end, the student chosen is the one with the best character because that is the student who everyone instinctively knows will earn the most.

Conversely, he challenges them to pick which student they would short or expect the least amount from. Most likely, again, it is not the student with the poorest grades, or perennial sports bench warmer, or even the lowest IQ, but rather the student known to cut corners, tell untruths, take false credit—someone who is undependable, egotistical, arrogant, self-righteous, and untrustworthy.

The difference between these two people is the difference between success and failure in life.

One of the most powerful messages Buffett delivers with his down-home humorous style is this: Make a list of all the traits you admire and respect in others. Think of people close to you or even those who have passed away, like Ben Graham or Benjamin Franklin. His point is that whatever character traits you put on your list, you can adopt those same qualities and be that person.

Just as the characters in the Wizard of Oz sought the wizard for help in acquiring intelligence, heart, and courage, they found out they had them all along and didn't need anyone else to validate them.

The world's greatest business manager also suggests to his student audiences to make another list of the character traits that they don't admire or respect in others. If you think about it and put some effort to it, you too can avoid all of the negative characteristics of the person you don't want to be.

Character cannot be hidden or faked. For Warren, the character of managers he will invest in shines through their writings, and he can tell from thousands of miles away if someone is the type of person with whom he wants to associate.

What good is being a *value investor* if you are not also a *values* manager?

Country singer Garth Brooks wisely said, "You aren't wealthy until you have something money can't buy," because fame, popularity, and money may be temporary, and they often are. Get this: If Buffett lost all of his money, the only thing he would give up is the use of a private jet.

Ultimately, what matters most is character and the relationship between wealth, the mind, and the character of its possessor.

A German motto says this, "When wealth is lost, nothing is lost; when health is lost, something is lost; when character is lost, all is lost."

THE IMPORTANCE OF INTEGRITY

Whenever anyone associated with Warren Buffett is interviewed—author, manager, supplier, shareholder, seller of a business—one of the first things they mention is his integrity. In fact, Warren looks at three character traits in the people who surround him: integrity, energy, and intelligence. He says, if you don't have the first, the last two will kill you. In fact, if they don't have integrity, he would rather his managers be lazy and dumb. One CEO once said, "Integrity is like oxygen. If you don't have it, nothing else matters." Testifying before Congress, Buffett said the same thing about trust. "Like the air we breathe, you don't notice it until it's gone."

"Be honest," he says. "Never lie under any circumstances. Don't pay attention to the lawyers. Just basically lay it out as you see it." Berkshire's chief is amazed at all the CEOs who utter public comments crafted by public relations personnel instead of simply speaking openly and frankly, as he does.

Speaking of integrity and forthrightness, he once said, "If anything is wrong with my health I would post it immediately on my website," in order to treat his shareholders as partners, assuming they would be very concerned if he fell seriously ill. Integrity is also about principles, full disclosure, and openness.

Integrity is a choice, and the lack of it most often leads to self-destruction.

THE VALUE OF A GOOD REPUTATION

Given that Berkshire Hathaway is one of only a handful of companies with an AAA credit rating, its reputation brings many deals to its door. Buffett and Company often receive the first phone call and the first opportunity. CEOs collectively breathe a sigh of relief when they learn that Warren Buffett is interested in their enterprise—because they know his reputation.

Local, statewide, and gubernatorial candidates even from other states, as well as presidential hopefuls, make a visit to Omaha to seek advice and an endorsement from Buffett, because of his sterling reputation. Even CEOs from major corporations phone and visit for his wise counsel and in some cases to ask him to purchase shares in their enterprises. Corporate chiefs in trouble with federal, state, and local regulators stop in for sagely suggestions and reputation repair.

Those corporations lucky enough to have him on their board of directors ask his review and approval before any major acquisition.

Berkshire's managers report that they are often advised to follow the advice of banking pioneer J. P. Morgan: "At all times the idea of doing only first-class business, and that in a first-class way, has been before our minds." "Conduct all business way inside the lines," Buffett tells his team of CEOs (and he has more than any other enterprise), "and if it is near the line or on the line don't do it"—advice that would keep not just his managers, but also all corporate leaders, out of trouble.

An internal memo he once wrote to his managers suggested that they guard their reputation and, "never do anything in business that you wouldn't want printed on the front page of your local newspaper written by an intelligent but critical reporter."

Managers are reminded that "they can lose money, even a lot of it, but they cannot lose their reputation, not even a shred of it. Berkshire has benefited in many areas because of its reputation, including many acquisitions. Always be on the lookout for managers and business with excellent reputations as possible acquisitions."

Probably his most powerful message about reputation is when he put his own reputation on the line to save Salomon Brothers during the government bond trading scandal. Before Congress he said, "Lose money for the firm [Salomon] and I will be understanding. Lose a shred of reputation for the firm and I will be ruthless." He went on to say to the Congressional hearing that all of the employees of Salomon would work to restore the reputation temporarily ruined by a handful of now former managers. Buffett replaced all the top executives and instilled a new code of ethics.

"It takes twenty years," he once said to his son, "to build a reputation and only five minutes to ruin it. If you'd think about that, you'll do things differently."

Benjamin Franklin said it this way, "He that is of the opinion that money will do everything may well be suspected of doing everything for money." Warren would probably advise that you follow the reputation guidelines laid down by Mark Twain: "Let us so live that when we come to die even the undertaker will be sorry."

THE BENEFIT OF DISCIPLINE

Despite receiving as many as three hundred letters a day, Warren Buffett answers his personal correspondence the same day. He is known to read a four-hundred-page book in one sitting, and with a photographic memory, be able to recall specifics years later. He often works on Saturday, and he is always on the lookout for wonderful businesses.

Carefully chronicling each and every trade he has ever made, he proudly displays on his office wall the framed handwritten transaction of his first purchase of Berkshire Hathaway in 1962 for 30,952 shares at 7\frac{9}{16}$ and jokes about paying too much in commission. (Those same shares purchased for $234,014.50 are now worth over $2.5 billion.)

He still has his hand-written general ledger and stock portfolio from when he was twenty years old, and tax returns from when he was fourteen years old. Living in Washington DC as his father served in Congress, the teenager reported $364 from his newspaper route plus $228.50 in dividends and interest for a total of $592.50 and a federal tax liability of $7.

His newspaper route business was carefully handwritten and listed by month, by number of papers delivered (both the *Post* and the *Herald*), income as well as expenses ($10 for watch repair and $35 for bicycle repair). Any fourteen-year-old with this kind of money consciousness and eye for detail would no doubt become a very wealthy person even if he didn't learn about Graham's approach to stock selection. Warren has never given up on his diligence, tracking, still today, most if not all of Berkshire's investments for many years before making a purchase. Table 11.1 shows the portfolio of a billionaire in the making at age twenty. Notice that starting at a very early

Table 11.1 Warren Buffett's Portfolio at Age Twenty

Source: Andy Kilpatrick, *Of Permanent Value* (AKPE, 2002)

Shares	Stock	Value	% of Portfolio
1200	Selected Industries	$3,750	38%
700	US & International	$2,887.50	30%
200	Parkersburg Rig & Reel	$2,600	27%
	Total Net Worth	$9,803.70	

age, Warren demonstrated extraordinary discipline, kept meticulous records, and had a very concentrated portfolio.

Table 11.2 shows the same thing as a twenty-one-year-old, but even more amazing is the return he achieved. This twenty-one-year-old would-be billionaire added $2,500 in capital contributions and enjoyed $7,433.93 in investment gains for a 75.8 percent annual gain, which was 54.5 percent value added over the Dow Jones Industrial Average in 1951.

The SEC would forbid a young Buffett from having this concentrated of a portfolio today if he were managing a mutual fund, restricting the largest holding to 25 percent of the portfolio and the other stocks to a maximum of 5 percent each.

Table 11.2 Buffett's Portfolio at Age Twenty-One

Source: Andy Kilpatrick, *Of Permanent Value* (AKPE, 2002)

Shares	Stock	Type of Business	Value	% of Portfolio*
350	GEICO	Auto insurance	$13,125	67%
200	Timely Clothes	Men's suits	$2,600	13%
100	Baldwin	Musical instruments	$2,200	11%
200	Greif Brothers	Shipping containers	$3650	19%
2000	Des Moines Railway	Railroad	$330	2%
200	Thor Corp	Hand power tools	$2,550	13%
	Total Net Worth		$19,737.63	

*Includes $5000 bank loan

RESPECT YOURSELF AND OTHERS

Common courtesy and political politeness are rules that Mr. Buffett closely follows. All photo and autograph requests are always honored. As mentioned earlier, all letters (except the marriage proposals, money requests, stock tips, unsolicited advice, and investment offers that do not meet his criteria) are promptly answered—often with a lighthearted one-paragraph reply.

The majority of his and his wife's Berkshire stock will go to the Buffett Foundation after both of their deaths (more on the Buffett Foundation later in this chapter). Warren once offered his wallet—including a stock tip—to be auctioned for charity. It sold for $210,000. Another winning bid of $250,000 received lunch with Warren, and a bid of $650,000 won a round of golf with Tiger Woods and included Warren Buffett as the caddy. All bids were more than double his annual salary and 100 percent were given to charity.

Warren would undoubtedly be the highest-paid speaker but has never charged for his town hall–style meetings, usually before college audiences and sometimes broadcast on public television.

He proves Plato's theory wrong that it is impossible to be exceedingly wealthy and good. "Of the billionaires I have known," Warren said, "money just brings out the basic traits in them. If they were jerks before they had money, they are simply jerks with a billion dollars."

MAINTAINING GOOD HABITS—AND A SENSE OF HUMOR

In terms of habits, Warren says, "The chains of habit are too light to be felt until they are too heavy to be broken." Read and learn every day. Keep an active mind by reading, playing what-if games, and engaging in mathematical games of probability and skill, like bridge. Communicate both orally and in writing. Respect others. Associate with people you admire and trust. Ask probing and intelligent questions. Listen. Prioritize. Follow your principles first, and then the principal will follow.

Warren is certainly working as hard as when he was first starting out— maybe harder, because of more demands on his time and fewer options available to invest with such a large pool of liquid capital.

In terms of humility and self-deprecating humor, he says, "I buy expensive suits, they just look cheap on me." Groucho Marx said, "Money frees you from doing things you dislike. Since I dislike doing nearly everything, money is handy." Each year, as we noted in Chapter 8, Berkshire's chief writes about his mistakes, and he frequently quotes Mae West, Woody Allen, and Yogi Berra for comic relief. Once when attempting to explain why he repurchased a stock (Capital Cities, now ABC Broadcasting), he admitted it was a mistake to sell it in the first place and asked for more time to explain it. He has gone as far as labeling his annual list of errors as "mistakes du jour."

Anyone who has built wealth has denied or delayed gratification. Of all the four ways to gain wealth—inheritance, marriage, lottery, or the long-term ownership of a business—all must also include living below your income or assets. "A man is rich," said Henry David Thoreau, "in proportion to the number of things he can afford to let alone."

Although he doesn't believe in leaving his children a great deal of wealth, Buffett did say once, "Someone is sitting in the shade today because someone planted a tree a long time ago."

THE REWARD IS IN THE DOING

Ask any successful craftsman, artist, athlete, poet, or entrepreneur, and they will say they lose themselves in their craft. Actually the phenomenon of losing a sense of time and place is the definition of finding your passion, your purpose in life. That's why the idea of retirement is hard for an accomplished and talented person to accept.

To those so gifted, the concept of retirement is undesirable and unattainable. One of Buffett's many secrets is his ability to select and surround himself with those managers who love what they are doing and choose not to do anything else. With wealth already assured to the average Buffett CEO, even at an average age of sixty-four, few have any desire to retire to the beach or golf course. If they do, they know they will be back. With an average net worth of $100 million, one worth over $1 billion, they're working for passion—to create, to contribute, and to satisfy customers.

"We enjoy the process far more than the rewards, although we have learned to live with those as well," Warren has said. "You cannot motivate the best people in the world in any field with money. They are motivated by passion."

Consider this, from Warren's 2002 letter to shareholders:

We continue to be blessed with an extraordinary group of managers, many of whom haven't the slightest financial need to work. They stick around, though: In 38 years, we've never had a single CEO of a subsidiary elect to leave Berkshire to work elsewhere. Counting Charlie, we now have six managers over 75, and I hope that in four years that number increases by at least two (Bob Shaw and I are both 72). Our rationale: "It's hard to teach a new dog old tricks."

Berkshire's operating CEOs are masters of their crafts and run their businesses as if they were their own. My job is to stay out of their way and allocate whatever excess capital their businesses generate. It's easy work.

My managerial model is Eddie Bennett, who was a batboy. In 1919, at age 19, Eddie began his work with the Chicago White Sox, who that year went to the World Series. The next year, Eddie switched to the Brooklyn Dodgers, and they, too, won their league title. Our hero, however, smelled trouble. Changing boroughs, he joined the Yankees in 1921, and they promptly won their first pennant in history. Now Eddie settled in, shrewdly seeing what was coming. In the next seven years, the Yankees won five American League titles.

What does this have to do with management? It's simple—to be a winner, work with winners. In 1927, for example, Eddie received $700 for the 1/8th World Series share voted him by the legendary Yankee team of Ruth and Gehrig. This sum, which Eddie earned by working only four days (because New York swept the Series) was roughly equal to the full-year pay then earned by batboys who worked with ordinary associates.

Eddie understood that how he lugged bats was unimportant; what counted instead was hooking up with the cream of those on the playing field. I've learned from Eddie. At Berkshire, I regularly hand bats to many of the heaviest hitters in American business.

Actress Bette Davis may have said it best: "To fulfill a dream, to be allowed to sweat over lonely labor, to be given a chance to create is the meat and potatoes of life. The money is the gravy." Aspire for knowledge, experience, and ability. They all are long lasting and full of just rewards. Money is fleeting. Follow your passion.

A PENNY SAVED . . .

In terms of frugality, Charles Dickens in the 1800s wrote in *David Copperfield*, "Annual income, 20 pounds. Annual expenditure, 19.6. Result, happiness. Annual income 20 pounds. Annual expenditure 20.6. Result, misery." Ben Franklin said, "The way to wealth is as plain as the road to market. It depends on two words, industry and frugality." Warren certainly personifies both. When his shareholders presented him with a pinball machine on his seventieth birthday to remind him of one of his first teenage business ventures, he smiled and said he still has the first two nickels he has ever earned. Later, he produced, more than five decades after the business was sold, detailed records showing the income and expense of the Wilson Coin Operated Machine Company. His personal auto license plate reads, "THRIFTY."

He lives no better than the average college student: he sleeps on a $600 mattress purchased from Nebraska Furniture Mart, watches college football on a big-screen TV (available at most local pubs), plays card games on a home computer, and reads financial reports available as public information at most libraries.

Buffett is not paid as chairman of the board of Berkshire Hathaway because he is also an employee of the company. Outside directors are given $900 to attend the annual meeting. Berkshire does not pay for the use by directors or managers of any of its five-hundred-plus corporate jets under management. Most of Berkshire's directors and many of its managers have purchased air flight time in Berkshire's NetJets subsidiary. Directors may choose to travel to Omaha by NetJets, but they are only reimbursed the cost of first-class commercial air travel.

The ultimate value to Berkshire's shareholders is that Warren Buffett is paid more to be a director of Coca-Cola than he is to manage Berkshire, a more than $100 billion enterprise. He is even offered more at charitable auctions to have lunch ($250,000) than his combined Berkshire salary ($100,000) and Coca-Cola director's fee ($125,000).

Julius Wayland, an American author, wrote, "Wealth is not acquired, as many people suppose, by fortunate speculations and splendid enterprises, but by the daily practice of industry, frugality, and economy. He who relies upon these means will be rarely found destitute, and he who relies upon any other will generally become bankrupt."

CHOOSE THE RIGHT PARTNERS—IN BUSINESS AND IN LIFE

After wisely picking the right heroes and mentors, Buffett's success must also be attributed to carefully selecting his partners—first the family and friends of his Buffett Partnership, then the partners joining as shareholders of his holding company, and finally the hand-selection of his operating managers.

He has never successfully done a good deal with a bad person, so Warren has been gifted with the unique ability to size up a person often thousands of miles away by reading what they have written, by reading what others have said, and by interpreting the financial results over time. Occasionally, he has been fooled by the merits of an industry and a business, but a manager has rarely fooled him. Also he has never fooled his managers, as demonstrated by his record in attracting and keeping competent CEOs.

The secret is to find managers who love their business more than the money. Most all are already wealthy, so doing a deal with Warren is not going to change their lifestyle. If an owner puts their business up for sale by the auction method, they telegraph that they are more interested in the monetary rewards and less concerned about the future well-being of the company and its employees. Berkshire prefers managers who care who the parent company will be and how their corporate culture will be affected. Buffett reassures them of many things:

- The business will continue with the same culture, managers, and employees under Berkshire as before Berkshire. In fact, if management does not come along, Berkshire is not interested in the deal.
- No employees will be laid off.
- No parent company interference. No meetings, no budgets, no divisions, no vice presidents, no synergy, no bother.
- Unlimited amounts of AAA capital and credit to expand the business.
- No more short-term irrational shareholders or probing analysts and media to answer to (this fact alone saves the CEO fifty days per year).
- They will be able to immediately replace high-cost debt and bank loans with Berkshire's deep pockets.
- Management will be respected.
- Buffett will always return their phone calls promptly, even while

traveling, and be available (only when asked) to strategize and improve their business.

- Owner managers can access capital held inside their businesses without compromising control and the business's culture.
- Management cash compensation will be simple and based on the performance of the individual subsidiary, not on the whole conglomerate or stock price.

Many investors understand the importance of the quantitative aspects of investing or the measurable numbers behind an enterprise. What they often fail to recognize is the importance of the qualitative or hard-to-measure managers behind an investment. For this reason, one of the best CEOs, Jack Welch, retired CEO of the world's largest business, GE, commented that "everyone knows that Warren is the greatest investor of our time," but his true genius is as a manager. What makes him a great manager is the partners he has carefully chosen.

LUCK PLAYS A ROLE, TOO

Although the world's greatest investor does not enter into any games of chance, he does acknowledge his own luck in the world of investing. He admires all games of skill, particularly those based on probability and applied reasoning, like bridge and chess.

In terms of luck, Warren likes to point out that he won the ovarian lottery: the probability of him being born a white, American male in the 1930s was 2 percent. Had he been born female, he would have naturally taken on the role of women in his era and become a housewife or teacher, like his older and younger sisters, or nurse, secretary, or maybe a flight attendant.

The unique and financially rewarding skill of allocating capital, determining the most optimal spot for it and a fair price to pay, would have been little regarded had he been born one hundred or more years earlier.

He was lucky to be born in the United States, the center of the free world and capital markets with a skill set that perfectly matches his environment. There is no greater gift to someone wired to instinctively know how best to invest and manage than to also be born in the United States, representing just 4 percent of the world's population but 50 percent of the world's capital, with an economic system favoring the capitalist and a political system guaranteeing certain freedoms, all based on meritocracy. Buffett was born in a time period when capital markets enjoyed their greatest advance in history, with the Dow Jones Industrial Average rising from 165 in 1930 to close the century seventy years later at 11,000.

Said differently, had Berkshire's architect been born two hundred years ago in Bangladesh, without the skills to hear very well or run fast, he would, according to his good friend Bill Gates, have been some wild animal's lunch.

Not to downplay his investment and management skills, but Buffett was blessed with the right genetic code and the right time, place, and gender to apply them.

In terms of health and having no debt, "a person who has health is young, so the person who owes nothing is rich," as read in Proverbs. When he found out that good health had a lot to do with the luck of good genetics, he bought his mother a treadmill. He would then go out and eat hamburgers, hash browns, Dairy Queen for dessert and a snack from Sees candy, and then come home and phone his mother to make sure she was using her treadmill.

Actually Warren does use a home treadmill in the morning before he leaves for his office and has annual physical checkups. With very little to no stress, he doesn't need or enjoy alcohol or tobacco products and has the ultimate choice in those with whom he chooses to work and associate with.

He has never been a fan of debt, particularly credit card debt. Regularly he advises college students to shun credit cards that often charge as much as 18 percent, saying that even he could never get ahead having to pay such a load of interest. Buffett's holding company has a net worth of $72 billion with only $4 billion in debt.

TALENT AND PASSION LEAD TO SUCCESS

One of the great advantages of wealth is that you can surround yourself with managers of your own choice. You cannot motivate the best people in any field by money. They are motivated by passion. It's not money and fame, but rather talent and passion that lead to success.

Disregard old age. Love what you are doing so much you don't need or want to retire from it. Work for the fun of it. "I have a blank canvas," says Warren, "and a lot of paint. And I get to do what I want. Now there is more money and more things are on a bigger scale, but I had just as much fun ten to twenty years ago when it was on a smaller scale."

Warren Buffett also said, "My guess is if Ted Williams was getting the highest salary in baseball and he was hitting .220, he would be unhappy. And if he were getting the lowest salary in baseball and batting .400, he'd be very happy. That's the way I feel about doing this job. Money is a byproduct of doing something I like extremely well.

"We find it hard to teach a new dog old tricks. But we haven't had a lot of problems with people who hit the ball out of the park year after year. Even though they're rich, they love what they do and nothing ever happens to our managers. We offer them immortality."

KEEP WORK IN PERSPECTIVE AND LIVE A BALANCED LIFE

In Janet Lowe's book *Warren Buffett Speaks*, she discusses the relationship between money, friends, family, and work. Warren believes one should "live where you're happiest. Have a hobby." Warren's hobby, of course, is bridge; he enjoys it so much that he has said, "Any young person who doesn't take up bridge is making a mistake." Warren's greatest indulgence is playing bridge online—about twelve hours per week. He doesn't have a computer in his office, but he has one at his home where he researches companies and reads the newspaper, but he also loves playing online bridge with a two-time world champion, Sharon Osberg, and he often plays with his pal Bill Gates.

Don't think that doing everything that Warren does—like living in Omaha and playing bridge as a hobby—will lead to wealth. Aim high but don't overreach. Warren says, "I don't try to jump over seven-foot bars. I look around for one-foot bars I can step over." Keep life in perspective. When he purchased The Washington Post Company, it was trading at one-fifth its value—that's a one-foot bar. Attempting to value Internet companies and dot-coms and trading in and out of the market—that's a seven-foot bar.

Money, to some extent, sometimes lets you be in more interesting environments. But it can't change how many people love you or how healthy you are, said Warren. Warren's wife said, "Soon a fool and his money will be invited everywhere." She framed that statement and he hangs it in the lobby of his small office.

In terms of children (he has three), he says, "Don't spoil them. Give them enough so that they can do whatever they want, but not too much where they do nothing."

Go to bat for your friends and develop lifelong friendships. Work with good people. Warren says, "I choose to work with every single person that I work with. That ends up being the most important factor. I don't interact with people I don't like or admire. That's the key." "I don't work with anyone who causes my stomach to churn," he often tells college students. "I don't do it. I say that working with people you don't like or that you don't respect is a lot like marrying for money. It's probably a bad idea under any circumstances, but it's crazy if you're already rich."

Shared by college professors, religious and motivational speakers, and even told at university commencement addresses is the story about time management and life priorities. One version is told like this:

A philosophy professor stood before his class and had some items in front of him. When the class began, wordlessly, he picked up a very large and empty mayonnaise jar and proceeded to fill it with rocks. Rocks about two inches in diameter. He then asked the students if the jar was full. They agreed that it was.

So the professor then picked up a box of pebbles and poured them into the jar. He shook the jar lightly. The pebbles of course rolled into the open areas between the rocks. He then asked the students again if the jar was full. They agreed it was.

Next, the professor picked up a box of sand and poured it into the jar. Of course, the sand filled up everything else. He then asked one more time if the jar was full. The students responded with a spirited and unanimous yes.

The professor then produced two cans of beer from under the table and proceeded to pour their entire contents into the jar, effectively filling the empty space between the sand. The students laughed. "Now," said the professor as the laughs subsided, "I want you to recognize that this jar represents your life. The rocks are the important things: your family, your partner, your health, and your children. Things that if everything else was lost and only they remained, your life would still be full. The pebbles are the other things that matter like your job, your house, and your car. The sand is everything else, the small stuff.

"If you put the sand into the jar first," he continued, "there is no room for the pebbles or the rocks. The same goes for your life. If you spend all of your time and energy on the small stuff, you will never have room for the things that are important to you.

"Pay attention to the things that are critical to your happiness. Play with your children. Take time to get medical checkups. Take your partner out dancing. There will always be time to go to work, clean the house, give a dinner party, and fix the disposal. Take care of the rocks first, the things that really matter. Set your priorities. The rest is just sand."

One of the students raised her hand and inquired what the beer represented. The professor smiled. "I'm glad you asked. It just goes to show you that no matter how full your life may seem, there's always room for a couple of beers."

College students can relate to this story, and the professor doesn't suggest you literally pour beer over your life to make it full. You can pour your favorite beverage. Warren would undoubtedly pour a cherry Coke. The point of the story is to focus on what really matters.

Although building wealth is desirable and following ethical methods and the principles of Buffett are honorable, ultimately, if you build wealth at the cost of your rocks (i.e., your relationships, your health, your family) and pebbles, you have paid too great a price. If you focus too much on the little things that do not matter, then in the end you have paid too great a price. Keep your eye on the bigger picture.

THE CIRCLE OF WEALTH

Aesop, twenty-six hundred years ago, told the story of the miser who sold all that he had and bought a lump of gold, which he buried in the ground. He went to look at it every day. One day the lump of gold was stolen and the miser was distraught. A neighbor, learning of his grief, suggested that he find a stone and bury it in the hole and imagine that the gold is still lying there. "It will do you the same service, for when the gold was there you didn't really have it because you didn't make the slightest use of it." The moral of the story is that the true value of wealth is not in its possession but in its use. Wealth unused might as well not exist.

The burdens of wealth are in the act of creating, the fear of keeping, the temptation of using, the guilt of abusing, the sorrow in losing, and the responsibility of handing it over to a succeeding generation. Just like building a business, with wealth you need to create, build, sustain, and pass the baton.

Most of the $100 billion in Buffett Wealth will be returned back to society, to hospitals, universities, education, health, and religious and political causes, some of it from the Buffett Foundation, but most of it from individual shareholders. Remember Don and Mid Othmer circled their $800 million of Buffett Wealth back to education and health-related issues. Certainly a percentage of it will pass to the next generation of family, but the world at large has been and will continue to benefit from the Buffett Wealth creation and transfer.

Unlike many who have made or inherited substantial fortunes, Buffett does not believe in setting his children and heirs up to be nonproductive citizens and recipients of wealth welfare or instead of claim checks on the government, claim checks on your family's fortune. So he is eager and ready to pay his taxes and looks unfavorably at those individuals and corporations that enjoy the benefits of the United States but choose to domicile themselves off-shore to avoid paying taxes.

Warren Buffett believes that he won the ovarian lottery by being born a white male in the United States with certain unique talents—mainly being able to value businesses and allocate capital.

The Buffett children, he believes, along with many others, have been born on second base. To give them a greater advantage and inheritance strikes him as unfair—kind of like giving the firstborn son of this year's starting Super Bowl quarterback an automatic starting position on a Super Bowl team twenty years from today.

Buffett admires and believes in merit and thinks the wholesale transfer of wealth based on birthright is rewarding a monarchy, not a meritocracy.

Unlike other rich people, Warren is in favor of an estate tax where wealth is taxed and given back to the society that fostered an environment to help create it in the first place, or to do as he has done and create a foundation to fund major world problems that do not have a natural funding source—like population control, women's rights, nuclear containment, world health, hospitals, universities, need-based college scholarships, and rewards for outstanding teaching.

Warren and his wife's share of the Buffett Wealth after both of their deaths will pour into the world's largest foundation and it will all be given back to society. Currently, if both of them passed away, a nearly $40 billion foundation would pay out $2 billion per year. With a combined life expectancy of twenty more years the Buffett Foundation could easily reach a staggering $200 billion. With a 5 percent annual payout, the Buffett Foundation one day may pay out $10 billion per year, equivalent to the annual earnings of just a few major corporations. Warren hopes the foundation will concentrate its funding in no more than ten major world issues which may receive $1 billion each annually.

The Buffett Foundation was founded in 1964 and is run by Warren's former son-in-law, Allen Greenberg, from a small second-floor office in the same high rise that houses Berkshire Hathaway's small headquarters in Omaha, Nebraska. "If they (the trustees) do something big and they fail, it won't really bother me at all," he has said. "What will bother me is if they do a whole bunch of little things—a half million or a million to this hospital or school and keep handing out money with an eyedropper."

Actually the skill set necessary to create a fortune is the opposite of the skills to prudently give it away, and maybe that is why Warren has decided to keep his focus on the creation part and leave the distribution to the foundation's board. In creating wealth, you need to focus on the simple, easy things, businesses that are understandable and simple. Staying with what you know on Main Street creates wealth. With philanthropy, the opposite is true: you need to place large amounts of money in the hands of people capable of attacking big global problems with uncertain solutions, like weapons of mass destruction and the earth not having enough natural resources to care for an ever-increasing world population.

Board members include himself as vice president, his wife as president, his daughter, his son Peter, a media executive, a business magazine editor and his former son-in-law. A majority of women directors and a female president may mean that the foundation has favored and will favor women's global issues.

Further violating his investment principles that created the wealth, the Buffett Foundation currently has most of its $25 million in U.S. treasuries (66 percent) and just $4.3 million in a very unconcentrated portfolio of over two hundred different stocks (although 37 percent is concentrated in Costco, as of June 30, 2002). The foundation owns one hundred shares of most stocks in its equity portfolio, including one hundred shares of Microsoft. Having a few shares of so many stocks gives Warren fast delivery of the annual reports.

Each year the foundation rewards ten Nebraska school teachers with

$10,000 each in unrestricted rewards for outstanding teaching and one hundred Nebraska need-based college students receive $3330 each in scholarships.

Ancient Roman playwright Terence [190 B.C.] wrote, "Riches get their value from the mind of the possessor. They are blessings to those who know how to use them and curses to those who do not."

"For a person to build a rich and rewarding life for himself," once observed Earl Nightingale, "there are certain qualities and bits of knowledge that he needs to acquire. There are also things, harmful attitudes, superstitions, and emotions that he needs to chip away. A person needs to chip away everything that doesn't look like the person he or she most wants to become."

CONCLUSION

The takeaway exercise for this chapter is to:

- Realize what Proverbs 19:4 says, "that wealth maketh many friends." But it's important to realize what wealth will not do. You cannot *buy* the person you want to become.

- Keep in mind that although wealth is important, it is more than the accumulation of money and riches: it has to be about life, character, integrity, reputation, and giving back more than you take.

- Write down a description of the person you want to become, and more important, the character traits you need to become that person.

- Write down the things that you need to chip away, everything that doesn't look like the person you want to become.

- Remember the circle of wealth, no matter how modest or large your "wealth" to create, preserve, and pass along to future generations.

Next, we'll summarize the journey of a lifetime, noting that Buffett Wealth was not created overnight or instantly, but by the careful application of principles laid out by his mentors. First the *principle* and then the *principal.*

Chapter 12

The Journey of a Lifetime

"A journey of a thousand miles begins with a single step."

—Lau Tzu

The road to Buffett Wealth has been paved by applied principles. It has taken five decades for him to become one of the world's richest citizens by investing in other people's enterprises, and unborn generations from around the world may one day enjoy many of the benefits of this wealth. So goes the circle of wealth, after a lifetime journey. In an instant-oriented generation full of lofty expectations of quick wealth, the Warren Buffett story proves Aesop's fable that, indeed, the tortoise, not the hare, wins the race.

The good news is that Warren Buffett's wealth principles and methods are available to anyone who chooses them. This chapter summarizes and reviews what this book has covered. It is worth a study to understand how one man, through principles and hard work, developed and controls one of the most liquid sources of principal on earth.

In Chapter 1, we discussed how the Dow Jones Industrial Average in the beginning of last century started at 66 and grew to 11,000 in one hundred years. Beginning in 1965 through 2000, Buffett grew a less-than-$20-million investment in Berkshire Hathaway—a defunct New England textile mill—to more than $100 billion, without adding additional capital. It's been an extraordinary and mesmerizing tale.

FINDING OUT WHAT MAKES WARREN RUN

The main point of Chapter 1 was that to be the best, you should study the best. There's no need to buy the same stocks as Warren to be as wealthy as him; just understand and follow the same principles. The average investor and even the professional large mutual fund manager cannot buy whole companies and insurance enterprises that generate extra cash to purchase even more companies, as Warren has done and continues to do. However, the regular active investor with a smaller pool of capital has many more excellent investment choices.

What this book does is offer new wealth ideas that are not generally written or talked about—new terms for you to think about, like intrinsic value, circle of competence, and margin of safety. Hopefully, this book has taught you new ways, new terms, and new methods of looking at your investments through the wisdom and writings of the world's greatest investor. Warren has achieved this status without inheritance, managing a business, or taking the keys to any enterprise that he has purchased. (Oftentimes he doesn't even visit the businesses he's purchased.)

Hopefully you were entertained by the tales of Aesop and recognize that more than one way to build wealth is available. What is amazing is that Buffett has created his wealth without creating Federal Express, capturing the operating system of a personal computer, or innovating some new retail concept. He created wealth by *simply investing in part and in whole in other people's enterprises*—and these are boring, old-economy businesses, which Warren purchased at attractive prices and that were and still are managed by talented people. He purchases and manages them just like a small stock portfolio. There's no management advice, unless asked; no meetings; no budgets; not even CEO employment contracts. There are just simple monthly accounting reports. Warren's approach was, and still is, to pay a reasonable amount based on demonstrated earnings of quality companies and buy a dollar of assets for 50 cents and build permanent value for his shareholders. You, too, can do this if you, too, are fearful when others are greedy and greedy when others are fearful.

Warren's investing approach is easy to describe but difficult to practice. You don't need extraordinary intelligence to build wealth like Warren, but it doesn't hurt either. What is more important is that you temper your emotions while investing and that you invest with your head, not your glands.

Chapter 2, The Making of a Billionaire, described how a young boy from Omaha, Nebraska, became the world's foremost capitalist. He was gifted with intelligence and was born during capitalism's finest years. He had an early consciousness of business, money, frugality, industry, and stocks. His parents' gift was one of confidence, principles, character, and exposure to the stock market.

He purchased his first stock when he was eleven, and his first job was as a newspaper boy who eventually became the largest outside owner of the same newspaper. He was helped by his exposure at a young age by a mentor who taught him to invest intelligently, not emotionally.

After getting an IV (intrinsic value) and an Ivy League (master's in economics from Columbia) education, he went to work for his mentors; first his father for two years and then Ben Graham, now known as the dean of Wall Street, the father of value investing, and the author of *The Intelligent Investor* and *Security Analysis*.

Warren's lifelong frugality, hard work, discipline, mentor selection, insatiable reading, rational approach to investing, hands-off management attitude, inquisitive mind, photographic memory, patience, and self-effacing sense of humor were character traits that have served him well.

When he purchased his first home, at the age of twenty-seven, Warren bought 100 percent of his home ($31,500) for 10 percent of his net worth ($315,000). Investing in value stocks to build wealth and conducting your financial affairs in a conservative manner are the same principles that you, too, could employ.

DISCOVERING MORE ABOUT YOUR OWN ATTITUDES TOWARD MONEY AND WEALTH

In Chapter 3, we talked about defining yourself and answering the question, what kind of investor are you? Are you passive (defensive and don't have interest or time to invest) or active (enterprising and enjoy reading and research)? You may want to be like Don and Mid Othmer, who chose to be passive investors and invested $25,000 each with Warren Buffett, a sum that grew to $800 million. Although they had the good fortune to know of Warren Buffett and to invest in his company at an early enough stage, you, too, can be a successful passive investor by simply buying a low-cost index fund and putting a little bit away each month, quarter, or year.

Regardless of whether you are an active or passive investor, you still should be an independent thinker. Remember that stocks are not simply pieces of paper or blips on your computer screen; instead, they are pieces of a business. Value investors sleep better. Few consider retirement. The value-investing process is pure enjoyment for value investors. It's what they were born to do. It's their passion.

"There's only two times in a man's life when he should not speculate," wrote Mark Twain. "When he can't afford it and when he can."

Chapter 4 encouraged you to develop an investment philosophy. Yours could be as simple as two rules: Don't lose capital, and don't forget the first rule. Your investment philosophy could be more detailed, as Phil Fisher outlined in his book *Common Stocks and Uncommon Profits*: Buy for the long term and talk with management, and concentrate what you do own into a few stocks. The takeaway exercise in Chapter 4 was to sit down and write your investment philosophy.

LEARNING ALL YOU CAN ABOUT POTENTIAL INVESTMENTS

Chapter 5 explained the merits of knowing what you own. Do not follow stock tips from your barber or your neighbor. You should dive into and study a business, as Warren Buffett does, sometimes for a period of several decades before making an investment. You'll recall the story of how Warren, as a boy, bought six bottles of Coca-Cola for 25 cents total and sold them for 5 cents each, thereby earning a cool 20 percent profit. Fifty years later, he would become the largest owner of Coke. Berkshire, with an 8 percent ownership interest, enjoys the profit of one out of every twelve Coke beverages sold.

Furthermore, delivering the *Washington Post* while his father served in Congress helped Warren understand the newspaper business, and he eventually became the largest outside owner of the paper. His $11 million investment in the early 1970s is now worth more than $1 billion—without any additional investment.

Had you been schooled, like Warren, to understand that The Washington Post Company was trading at one-fifth its true or intrinsic value in 1973, an $11,000 investment would have turned into $1 million, just as a $110,000 purchase would have created $10 million.

The annual dividends from the Washington Post Company now return most of his original investment each year.

Another example can be found in Warren's early experiences with GEICO, which helped him not only because of a significant purchase he made when he was twenty-one years old, but eventually led him to be GEICO's largest shareholder, and now its owner in its entirety.

None of these investments would have happened unless Warren took the time to understand the businesses behind Coke, the *Washington Post*, and GEICO. Never invest in that which you don't understand.

Keep your investing simple. Only associate with business and management that is ethical. Ask the right questions. Remember the story of the dog that bit the stranger because the stranger didn't ask the right question.

Buy storybook and franchise stocks like Coke. If you gave Warren $100 billion to take away the Coca-Cola leadership in the beverage industry worldwide, he would give you the money back and say that it cannot be done. That's how strong Coke's brand and competitive advantages are. Warren knows what he owns and you can, too.

Chapter 6 emphasized the importance of investing in Main Street, not Wall Street. Warren first did business with the local retailers Nebraska Furniture Mart and Borsheim's Jewelry. Then he bought those businesses as long as management stayed on. He looks for managers who are passionate and fanatical about their business. He wants managers like Rose Blumkin who was so passionate about her business, Nebraska Furniture Mart, that she worked there until she died at age 104. Warren respects managers like Susan Jacques, of Borsheim's Jewelry, who is fanatical about her business even though she is the fourth generation of management, foreign born, and not even a member of the original founding family.

After Warren Buffett makes an investment, there are no layoffs, there's no talk of synergy. Most acquisition deals talk about 2 + 2 equaling 5, but end up where 2 + 2 equals 3. And then a subsidiary is quietly sold off. With Warren's acquisitions, 2 + 2 equals 4, and no purchases are made with the idea of laying off workers or combining efficiencies. Businesses are left alone to run just as if they were part of a small investment portfolio.

Imagine that you own shares of a large pharmaceutical company like Merck and part—a very small part—of Wal-Mart. It would be silly to suggest that Wal-Mart's pharmacy get together with Merck to sell their brands just because you happen to own both stocks. The same thing is true of Warren's multibillion-dollar portfolio of partly and wholly owned enterprises.

So Chapter 6 described Warren's viewpoint that the best investments are on Main Street, not Wall Street, and you should think about how your local grocery store, real estate office, or bank manages their respective businesses. If your local business changed ownership every few months, you would begin to wonder about the business. People are careful not to do business with an enterprise that suffers from a lack of loyalty by the owners. The same is true in the stock market. Loyalty given is loyalty received and Berkshire operates by that rare principle that Wall Street often overlooks. The average holding period of a typical NASDAQ stock, representing most technology investments, with 200 percent annual turnover, is just six months. On the New York Stock Exchange, with 100 percent annual turnover, the average holding period is just twelve months. There's not much loyalty there.

However, Buffett's loyal shareholders are the opposite and have been around for more than twenty years, as have the managers, employees, and customers of the businesses in which he invests. The average business that Warren has invested in started in 1909. Of the CEOs of the top fifty U.S. companies, on average, these CEOs enjoy tenure of just six years. In contrast, the Buffett CEOs have been around on average for twenty-four years and counting. With no retirement mandate, that number will certainly grow larger. Moreover, Warren has never lost a CEO to a competing enterprise—only to death or retirement.

Therefore, like Warren, you should do as follows:

- Look first at the business in which you're considering investing: Is it simple and easy to understand to you? Each person can understand different kinds of businesses.
- Then look at its managers. Are they of the utmost character? Are they rational? Do they make sensible, well-thought-out, well-researched business decisions? Are they candid when reporting to the owners of the business?
- Then look at the company's financials. What is its return on equity? What are the owner earnings, and is it a high profit-margin business?
- Then look at the stock market.

This four-step process used by Warren Buffett and his successor is the opposite approach of what most participants in the stock market do, and it's definitely the opposite of what the average trader and speculator does.

Most give some effort to understanding that which is easily measured about an investment (also known as quantitative analysis), but, unfortunately, too few consider the hard-to-measure and quality aspects (qualitative).

In Chapter 7, we talked about buying so well that you can keep your investments for a lifetime. What a novel, undersold idea that is. (If there is one thing to take away from this book it is the notion of treating your mind, education, health, and your investments as if they will be with you for the rest of your life.)

Be aware that Wall Street participants are easy and lawful prey to the transaction agents (stockbrokers) who are compensated by your trading activity, not by your length of ownership. Kind of like a doctor who is paid by how often he changes your medicine, not by prescribing what will cure you.

Another undersold investment principle is the concept of owning a concentrated amount of something you really like. You should have such strong convictions about the businesses in which you invest that you will want to own a lot of those businesses. The opposite of focus is blurred and the opposite of concentration is distracted. Make sure that everything in your financial life is focused and concentrated. Concentrate on and concentrate in your investments.

Warren Buffett has said, "We are quite content to hold any security indefinitely, so long as the prospective return on equity capital of the underlying business is satisfactory, management is competent and honest, and the market does not overvalue the business." Make fewer, better decisions. Or as Mae West said, "Too much of a good thing can be wonderful."

BENEFITING FROM MISTAKES AND DEBUNKING INVESTING MYTHS

We talked about Warren's investment mistakes in Chapter 8, and how you can learn from them. His mistakes were not from selling too soon, holding too long, or not buying enough. Instead, his biggest mistake was buying Berkshire Hathaway Textile Mills (original company that ultimately became the name of his investment conglomerate), because the textile industry suffered from cheap foreign labor and was unable to sustain itself. Fortunately, because Warren had bought Berkshire's assets for 50 percent off, he was able to redirect the assets and earnings from the textile mills and other subsidiaries to more profitable businesses. Another mistake he made was buying into the airline industry, an industry plagued with poor economics: as the old joke goes, "To become a millionaire is simple. Start out as a billionaire and buy an airline."

Remember what Warren said about the Wright Brothers, how he wished some capitalist had shot them down to save all the money that has been lost in the airline industry over the past century? Fortunately, Buffett was able to save his investors from his airline investment. Even more fortunately, Warren is coincidentally the largest operator of corporate jets—and if NetJets were a commercial airline, it would be the nation's sixth largest.

Another big mistake was investing in Dexter Shoes in Maine, because it suffered due to competition from inexpensive foreign labor. It seems like Mr. Buffett should have learned from his textiles experience and not repeated the mistake with footwear. But his mistake wasn't investing some $400 million in Dexter, which was a fine company with excellent management. Instead, his mistake was paying for the acquisition with stock, because the purchase price of Dexter will always represent 2 percent of the capital of Berkshire Hathaway, which is currently $2 billion and growing. Remember James Joyce's words, "A man of genius makes no mistakes. His errors are the portals of discovery." Even Ted Williams, baseball's greatest hitter, was successful only 40 percent of his time at bat.

Chapter 9 discussed some of the most common myths of investing, wealth, and Warren Buffett. Don't fall for the obvious. If it's too good to be true, it probably is. The way most of us invest is like driving a car using the rear-view mirror.

Wealth building is not an overnight proposition. With your investments, "trading for a living" is a contradiction of terms. Building wealth and investing is not complicated and it's actually simple, but not easy. Most think and make it more complicated than it is.

One of the myths is that Warren has been lucky. Another is that only Warren Buffett's methods work. In fact, many alternative investment methods are available. The biggest and most compelling myth is that others cannot duplicate what Warren has achieved. Employing the same principles and practical methods, anyone can be a value investor and a values manager.

BEYOND BUFFETT

In Chapter 10, the book turned to the next Warren Buffett: Lou Simpson, CEO of capital operations for GEICO Auto Insurance, Inc. (which is one of Berkshire's biggest investments; Simpson is Warren's hand-picked successor to run Berkshire Hathaway's investments after Warren is gone). Some of the things that Warren and Lou do are similar, and some are dissimilar.

Lou Simpson suggests five investment principles to help guide you in building wealth:

1. Think independently
2. Invest in high-return businesses run for the benefit of shareholders
3. Pay only a reasonable price, even for an excellent business
4. Invest for the long term
5. Do not diversify excessively

Lou is dedicated and hard working, and he reads everything. But you, too, can be like Warren and Lou if you, too, have the same character traits.

MORE THAN MONEY

Chapter 11 discussed the philosophy of wealth, Warren's lessons about life, and the circle of wealth. Warren believes that life is more than building wealth and wealth is more than money. Rather, it is about integrity, reputation, and character. Buffett Wealth is the principle, not the principal. Recall English philosopher James Allen who said, "Circumstance does not make the man. It reveals him to himself. Men do not attract that which they want, but that which they are." Warren Buffett did not attract wealth because he wanted it; he became wealthy because that's what he is.

"Character is power," noted the chaplain to British monarch John Howe [1630–1705]. "It makes friends, draws patronage and support, and opens the way to wealth, honor, and happiness."

An anonymous author wrote, "Men of genius are admired. Men of wealth are envied. Men of power are feared. But only men of character are trusted." Warren is a man of genius, so he is admired. He has created enormous wealth, so he is undoubtedly envied. He is the most powerful man in business, so he is feared. But the measure of the man is that he is trusted, so he is a man of character.

Mahatma Gandhi said, "There are seven sins in the world. Pleasure without conscience, knowledge without character, worship without sacrifice, science without humanity, politics without principle, commerce without morality, and wealth without work."

A longtime favorite and classic movie, *The Wizard of Oz*, uncovers characters searching for various character traits: intelligence, heart, and courage. They found out from the wizard that they had had these qualities all along. You, too, may be seeking certain character traits available to everyone, no matter your station in life. You may find out that you, too, have had them all along.

Plan to give back. Remember that Warren created wealth for himself, but at the same time, for every dollar he has built for himself, he has created $2 for his partners. And most of the total Buffett Wealth, currently exceeding $100 billion, will be passed on to current and future generations.

"To live content with small means," observed William Henry Channing, an eighteenth-century inspirational and spiritual American leader, "to seek elegance rather than luxury and refinement rather than fashion, to be worthy, not respectable, and wealthy, not rich, to study hard, think quietly, talk gently. Act frankly. To listen to stars and birds. To babes and sages with open heart, to bear all cheerfully, do all bravely, await occasions, hurry never. In a word, to let the spiritual unbidden and unconsciousness grow up through the common. This is to be my symphony."

Table 12.1 offers a summary of some of the more intriguing facts about Warren Buffett and Berkshire Hathaway's investing success and about Warren's strategies.

***Table 12.1* Intriguing Buffett Facts and Strategies**

- Buffett's conglomerate, Berkshire Hathaway, publicly traded on the NYSE under symbol BRKa and BRKb, is now the nation's twenty-fifth largest employer with over 165,000 employees.
- Berkshire Hathaway is the largest private employer in the state of Georgia.
- Buffett's NetJets subsidiary can be considered the sixth-largest private airline, based on number of corporate jets under management.
- Warren's company has no large headquarters staff (just 15.8), no options, no funny accounting, no yachts, no Rolls Royces, no mansions or typical trappings of wealth. Warren has one of the longest CEO tenures: thirty-eight years and counting.

Table 12.1 (continued)

- To give you a perspective of Warren's investment record, consider in the last century the DJIA went from 66 to 11,000. The NASDAQ, born in 1971, went from 100 to 2000.
- Beginning in 1965 when Warren bought control of Berkshire Hathaway, it has added one zero to its stock price every decade, from 7, to 70, to 700 to 7000 to 70,000. Now Berkshire Hathaway has the highest price of any stock on any stock exchange in the world, and he's proud of it.
- Buffett owns outright more than one hundred wholly owned businesses, including Dairy Queen, World Book Encyclopedia, and GEICO auto insurance.
- Buffett also owns more than $30 billion in stocks, including Coca-Cola, American Express, and Gillette.

The three qualities that Warren Buffett most admires are intellect, character, and temperament.

May you have the best of luck on your wealth-building journey of a lifetime. Hopefully you have enjoyed learning more about the principles and methods of an extraordinary investor. May you always act in such a way that you earn what you deserve. Here's hoping that you are inspired to create, preserve, and complete the circle of wealth for future generations. Good luck!

Appendix

"The Superinvestors of Graham-and-Doddsville"

by Warren E. Buffett

(This is an edited transcript of a talk given by Warren Buffett at Columbia University in 1984 commemorating the fiftieth anniversary of the book *Security Analysis*, written by Benjamin Graham and David L. Dodd. This specialized volume first introduced the ideas later popularized in *The Intelligent Investor*, written by Ben Graham.)

Is the Graham and Dodd "look for values with a significant margin of safety relative to prices" approach to security analysis out of date? I present to you a group of investors who have, year in and year out, beaten the Standard & Poor's 500 stock index. The hypothesis that they do this by pure chance is at least worth examining. If you found any really extraordinary concentrations of success, you might want to see if you could identify concentrations of unusual characteristics that might be causal factors.

I submit to you that in addition to geographical origins, there can be what I call an intellectual origin. I think you will find that a disproportionate number of successful coin-flippers in the investment world came from a very small intellectual village that could be called Graham-and-Doddsville. A concentration of winners that simply cannot be explained by chance can be traced to this particular intellectual village.

In this group of successful investors that I want to consider, there has been a common intellectual patriarch, Ben Graham. The children who left the house of this intellectual patriarch have called their "flips" in very different ways. They have gone to different places and bought and sold different stocks and companies, yet they have had a combined record that simply cannot be explained by the fact that they are all calling flips identically because a leader is signaling the calls. The patriarch has merely set forth the intellectual theory for making coin-calling decisions, but each student has decided on his own manner of applying the theory.

The common intellectual theme of the investors from Graham-and-Doddsville is this: they search for discrepancies between the value of a business and the price of small pieces of that business in the market. Essentially, they exploit those discrepancies without the efficient market theorist's concern as to whether the stocks are bought on Monday or Thursday, or whether it is January or July, etc. Our Graham & Dodd investors, needless to say, do not discuss beta, the capital asset pricing model, or covariance in returns among securities. These are not subjects of any interest to them. In fact, most of them would have difficulty defining those terms. The investors simply focus on two variables: price and value.

I always find it extraordinary that so many studies are made of price and volume behavior, the stuff of chartists. Can you imagine buying an entire business simply because the price of the business had been marked up substantially last week and the week before? I think the group that we have identified by a common intellectual home is worthy of study.

I begin this study of results by going back to a group of four of us who worked at Graham-Newman Corporation from 1954 through 1956. There were only four. I have not selected these names from among thousands. I offered to go to work at Graham-Newman for nothing after I took Ben Graham's class, but he turned me down as overvalued. He took this value stuff very seriously! After much pestering he finally hired me. There were three partners and four of us as the "peasant" level. All four left between 1955 and 1957 when the firm was wound up, and it's possible to trace the record of three.

The first example is that of Walter Schloss. Walter never went to college, but took a course from Ben Graham at night at the New York Institute of Finance. Walter left Graham-Newman in 1955 and achieved the record shown here over twenty-eight years.

He has total integrity and a realistic picture of himself. Money is real to him and stocks are real—and from this flows an attraction to the "margin of safety" principle.

Walter has diversified enormously, owning well over one hundred stocks. He knows how to identify securities that sell at considerably less than their value to a private owner. And that's all he does. He doesn't worry about whether it's January, he doesn't worry about whether it's Monday, he doesn't worry about whether it's an election year. He simply says, if a business is worth a dollar and I can buy it for 40 cents, something good may happen to me. And he does it over and over and over again. He owns many more stocks than I do—and is far less interested in the underlying nature of the business; I don't seem to have very much influence on Walter. That's one of his strengths; no one has much influence on him.

The second case is Tom Knapp, who also worked at Graham-Newman with me. Tom was a chemistry major at Princeton before the war; when he came back from the war, he was a beach bum. And then one day he read that Dave Dodd was giving a night course in investments at Columbia. Tom took it on a noncredit basis, and he got so interested in the subject from taking that course that he came up and enrolled at Columbia Business School, where he got the MBA degree. He took Dodd's course again, and took Ben Graham's course. Incidentally, thirty-five years later I called Tom to ascertain some of the facts involved here and I found him on the beach again.

In 1968, Tom Knapp and Ed Anderson, also a Graham disciple, along with one or two other fellows of similar persuasion, formed Tweedy, Browne Partners. Tweedy, Browne built that record with very wide diversification. They occasionally bought control of businesses, but the record of the passive investments is equal to the record of the control investments.

Table 3 describes the third member of the group, who formed Buffett Partnership in 1957. The best thing he did was to quit in 1969. Since then, in a sense, Berkshire Hathaway has been a continuation of the partnership in some respects. There is no single index I can give you that I would feel would be a fair test of investment management at Berkshire. But I think that any way you figure it, it has been satisfactory.

Table 4 shows the record of the Sequoia Fund, which is managed by a man whom I met in 1951 in Ben Graham's class, Bill Ruane. After getting out of Harvard Business School, he went to Wall Street. Then he realized that he needed to get a real business education so he came up to take Ben's course at Columbia, where we met in early 1951. Bill's record from 1951 to 1970, working with relatively small sums, was far better than average. When I wound up Buffett Partnership I asked Bill if he would set up a fund to handle all our partners, so he set up the Sequoia Fund. He set it up at a terrible time, just when I was quitting. He went right into the two-tier market and all the difficulties that made for comparative performance for value-oriented investors. I am happy to say that my partners, to an amazing degree, not only stayed with him but added money.

There's no hindsight involved here. Bill was the only person I recommended to my partners, and I said at the time that if he achieved a four-point-per-annum advantage over the Standard & Poor's, that would be solid performance. Bill has achieved well over that, working with progressively larger sums of money. That makes things much more difficult. Size is the anchor of performance. There is no question about it. It doesn't mean you can't do better than average when you get larger, but the margin shrinks.

I should add that in the records we've looked at so far, throughout this whole period there was practically no duplication in these portfolios. These are men who select securities based on discrepancies between price and value, but they make their selections very differently. The overlap among these portfolios has been very, very low.

Table 5 is the record of a friend of mine who is a Harvard Law graduate, who set up a major law firm. I ran into him in about 1960 and told him that law was fine as a hobby but he could do better. He set up a partnership quite the opposite of Walter's. His portfolio was concentrated in very few securities and therefore his record was much more volatile, but it was based on the same discount-from-value approach. He was willing to accept greater peaks and valleys of performance, and he happens to be a fellow whose whole psyche goes toward concentration, with the results shown. Incidentally, this record belongs to Charlie Munger, my partner for a long time in the operation of Berkshire Hathaway. When he ran his partnership, however, his portfolio holdings were almost completely different from mine and the other fellows.

Table 6 is the record of a fellow who was a pal of Charlie Munger's—another non-business-school type—who was a math major at USC. He went to work for IBM after graduation and was an IBM salesman for a while. After I got to Charlie, Charlie got to him. This happens to be the record of Rick Guerin. Rick, from 1965 to 1983, against a compounded gain of 316 percent for the S&P, came off with 22,200 percent, which, probably because he lacks a business school education, he regards as statistically significant.

One sidelight here: It is extraordinary to me that the idea of buying dollar bills for 40 cents takes immediately to people or it doesn't take at all. It's like an inoculation. If it doesn't grab a person right away, I find that you can talk to him for years and show him records, and it doesn't make any difference. They just don't seem able to grasp the concept, simple as it is. A fellow like Rick Guerin, who had no formal education in business, understands immediately the value approach to investing and he's applying it five minutes later.

Table 7 is the record of Stan Perlmeter. Stan was a liberal arts major at the University of Michigan who was a partner in the advertising agency of Bozell & Jacobs. We happened to be in the same building in Omaha. In 1965 he figured out I had a better business than he did, so he left advertising. Again, it took five minutes for Stan Perlmeter to embrace the value approach.

Perlmeter does not own what Walter Schloss owns. He does not own what Bill Ruane owns. These are records made independently. But every time Perlmeter buys a stock it's because he's getting more for his money than he's paying. That's the only thing he's thinking about. He's not looking at quarterly earnings projections, he's not looking at next year's earnings, he's not thinking about what day of the week it is, he doesn't care what investment research from any place says, he's not interested in price momentum, volume, or anything. He's simply asking: What is the business worth?

Table 8 and Table 9 are the records of two pension funds I've been involved in. They are not selected from dozens of pension funds with which I have had involvement; they are the only two I have influenced. In both cases I have steered them toward value-oriented managers. Very, very few pension funds are managed from a value standpoint. Table 8 is the Washington Post Company's Pension Fund. It was with a large bank some years ago, and I suggested that they would do well to select managers who had a value orientation.

Overall they have been in the top percentile ever since they made the change. The Post told the managers to keep at least 25 percent of these funds in bonds, which would not have been necessarily the choice of these managers. So I've included the bond performance simply to illustrate that this group has no particular expertise about bonds. They wouldn't have said they did. Even with this drag of 25 percent of their fund in an area that was not their game, they were in the top percentile of fund management. The

Washington Post experience does not cover a terribly long period but it does represent many investment decisions by three managers who were not identified retroactively.

Table 9 is the record of the FMC Corporation fund. I don't manage a dime of it myself, but I did, in 1974, influence their decision to select value-oriented managers. Prior to that time they had selected managers much the same way as most larger companies. They now rank number one in the Becker survey of pension funds for their size over the period of time subsequent to this "conversion" to the value approach. Last year they had eight equity managers of any duration beyond a year. Seven of them had a cumulative record better than the S&P. The net difference now between a median performance and the actual performance of the FMC fund over this period is $243 million. Those managers are not the managers I would necessarily select, but they have the common denominators of selecting securities based on value.

So these are nine records of "coin-flippers" from Graham-and-Doddsville. I haven't selected them with hindsight from among thousands. It's not like I am reciting to you the names of a bunch of lottery winners. I selected these men years ago based upon their framework for investment decision-making. I knew what they had been taught, and additionally I had some personal knowledge of their intellect, character, and temperament. It's very important to understand that this group has assumed far less risk than average; note their record in years when the general market was weak. While they differ greatly in style, these investors are, mentally, always buying the business, not buying the stock. A few of them sometimes buy whole businesses. Far more often they simply buy small pieces of businesses. Their attitude, whether buying all or a tiny piece of a business, is the same. Some of them hold portfolios with dozens of stocks; others concentrate on a handful. But all exploit the difference between the market price of a business and its intrinsic value.

I'm convinced that there is much inefficiency in the market. These Graham-and-Doddsville investors have successfully exploited gaps between price and value. When the price of a stock can be influenced by a "herd" on Wall Street with prices set at the margin by the most emotional person, or the greediest person, or the most depressed person, it is hard to argue that the market always prices rationally. In fact, market prices are frequently nonsensical.

Sometimes risk and reward are correlated in a positive fashion. If someone were to say to me, "I have here a six-shooter and I have slipped one cartridge into it. Why don't you just spin it and pull it once? If you survive, I will give you $1 million." I would decline—perhaps stating that $1 million is not enough. Then he might offer me $5 million to pull the trigger twice—now that would be a positive correlation between risk and reward!

The exact opposite is true with value investing. If you buy a dollar bill for 60 cents, it's riskier than if you buy a dollar bill for 40 cents, but the expectation of reward is greater in the latter case. The greater the potential for reward in the value portfolio, the less risk there is.

One quick example: The Washington Post Company in 1973 was selling for $80 million in the market. At the time, that day, you could have sold the assets to any one of ten buyers for not less than $400 million, probably appreciably more. The company owned the *Post, Newsweek*, plus several television stations in major markets. Those same properties are worth $2 billion now, so the person who would have paid $400 million would not have been crazy.

Now, if the stock had declined even further to a price that made the valuation $40 million instead of $80 million, its beta would have been greater. And to people that think beta measures risk, the cheaper price would have made it look riskier. I have never been able to figure out why it's riskier to buy $400 million worth of properties for $40 million than $80 million. And, as a matter of fact, if you buy a group of such securities and you know anything at all about business valuation, there is essentially no risk in buying $400 million for $80 million. Since you don't have your hands on the $400 million, you want to be sure you are in with honest and reasonably competent people, but that's not a difficult job.

You also have to have the knowledge to enable you to make a very general estimate about the value of the underlying businesses. But you do not cut it close. That is what Ben Graham meant by having a margin of safety. You don't try and buy businesses worth $83 million for $80 million. You leave yourself an enormous margin. When you build a bridge, you insist it can carry thirty thousand pounds, but you only drive ten-thousand-pound trucks across it. And that same principle works in investing.

In conclusion, some of the more commercially minded among you may wonder why I am writing this article. Adding many converts to the value approach will perforce narrow the spreads between price and value. I can only tell you that the secret has been out for fifty years, ever since Ben

Graham and Dave Dodd wrote *Security Analysis*, yet I have seen no trend toward value investing in the thirty-five years that I've practiced it. There seems to be some perverse human characteristic that likes to make easy things difficult. The academic world, if anything, has actually backed away from the teaching of value investing over the last thirty years. It's likely to continue that way. There will continue to be wide discrepancies between price and value in the marketplace, and those who read their Graham & Dodd will continue to prosper.

Table 1 Walter J. Schloss

Year	S&P Overall Gain, Including Dividends (%)	WJS Ltd Partners Overall Gain per year (%)	WJS Partnership Overall Gain per year (%)	
1956	7.5	5.1	6.8	Standard & Poor's 28¼ year
1957	−10.55	−4.7	−4.7	compounded gain 887.2%
1958	42.1	42.1	54.6	WJS Limited Partners 28¼
1959	12.7	17.5	23.3	compounded gain 6,678.8%
1960	−1.6	7.0	9.3	
1961	26.4	21.6	28.8	WJS Partnership 28¼ year
1962	−10.2	8.3	11.1	compounded gain 23,104.7%
1963	23.3	15.1	20.1	Standard & Poor's 28¼ year annual
1964	16.5	17.1	22.8	compounded rate 8.4%
1965	13.1	26.8	35.7	WJS Partnership 28¼ year annual
1966	−10.4	0.5	0.7	compounded rate 16.1%
1967	26.8	25.8	34.4	
1968	10.6	26.6	35.5	WJS Partnership 28¼ year annual
1969	−7.5	−9.0	−9.0	compounded rate 21.3%
1970	2.4	−8.2	−8.2	During the history of the Partnership it
1971	14.9	25.5	28.3	has owned over 800 issues and, at most
1972	19.8	11.6	15.5	times, has had at least 100 positions.
1973	−14.8	−8.0	−8.0	Present assets under management
1974	−26.6	−6.2	−6.2	approximate $45 million. The difference
1975	36.9	42.7	52.2	between returns of the partnership and
1976	22.4	29.4	39.2	returns of the limited partners is due to
1977	−8.6	25.8	34.4	allocations to the general partner for
1978	7.0	36.6	48.8	management.
1979	17.6	29.8	39.7	

Table 1 (continued)

Year	S&P Overall Gain, Including Dividends (%)	WJS Ltd Partners Overall Gain per year (%)	WJS Partnership Overall Gain per year (%)
1980	32.1	23.3	31.1
1981	6.7	18.4	24.5
1982	20.2	24.1	32.1
1983	22.8	38.4	51.2
1984 1st Qtr.	2.3	0.8	1.1

Table 2 Tweedy, Browne Inc.

Period Ended (September 30)	DOW Jones* (%)	S&P 500* (%)	TBK Overall (%)	TBK Limited Partners (%)
1968 (9 mos.)	6.0	8.8	27.6	22.0
1969	−9.5	−6.2	12.7	10.0
1970	−2.5	−6.1	1.3	−1.9
1971	20.7	20.4	20.9	16.1
1972	11.0	15.5	14.5	11.8
1973	2.9	1.0	8.3	7.5
1974	−31.8	−38.1	1.5	1.5
1975	36.9	37.8	28.8	22.0
1976	29.6	30.1	40.2	32.8
1977	−9.9	−4.0	23.4	18.7
1978	8.3	11.9	41.0	32.1
1979	7.9	12.7	25.5	20.5
1980	13.0	21.1	21.4	17.3
1981	−3.3	2.7	14.4	11.6
1982	12.5	10.1	10.2	8.2
1983	44.5	44.3	35.0	28.2

Total Return 15¾ years	191.8%	238.5%	1,661.2%	936.4%
Standard & Poor's 15¾ year annual compounded rate				7.0%
TBK Limited Partners 15¾ year annual compounded rate				16.0%
TBK Overall 15¾ year annual compounded rate				20.0%

*Includes dividends paid for both Standard & Poor's 500 Composite Index and Dow Jones Industrial Average.

Table 3 Buffett Partnership, Ltd.

Year	Overall Results from Dow (%)	Partnership Results (%)	Limited Partners' Results (%)
1957	−8.4	10.4	9.3
1958	38.5	40.9	32.2
1959	20.0	25.9	20.9
1960	−6.2	22.8	18.6
1961	22.4	45.9	35.9
1962	−7.6	13.9	11.9
1963	20.6	38.7	30.5
1964	18.7	27.8	22.3
1965	14.2	47.2	36.9
1966	−15.6	20.4	16.8
1967	19.0	35.9	28.4
1968	7.7	58.8	45.6
1969	−11.6	6.8	6.6

On a cumulative or compounded basis, the results are:

Year	Overall Results from Dow (%)	Partnership Results (%)	Limited Partners' Results (%)
1957	−8.4	10.4	9.3
1957–58	26.9	55.6	44.5
1957–59	52.3	95.9	74.7
1957–60	42.9	140.6	107.2
1957–61	74.9	251.0	181.6
1957–62	61.6	299.8	215.1
1957–63	94.9	454.5	311.2
1957–64	131.3	608.7	402.9
1957–65	164.1	943.2	588.5
1957–66	122.9	1156.0	704.2
1957–67	165.3	1606.9	932.6
1957–68	185.7	2610.6	1403.5
1957–69	152.6	2794.9	1502.7
Annual Compounded Rate	7.4	29.5	23.8

Table 4 **Sequoia Fund, Inc.**

| | Annual Percentage Change** | |
Year	Sequoia Fund (%)	S&P 500 Index* (%)
1970 (from July 15)	12.1	20.6
1971	13.5	14.3
1972	3.7	18.9
1973	−24.0	−14.8
1974	−15.7	26.4
1975	60.5	37.2
1976	72.3	23.6
1977	19.9	−7.4
1978	23.9	6.4
1979	12.1	18.2
1980	12.6	32.3
1981	21.5	−5.0
1982	31.2	21.4
1983	27.3	22.4
1984 (first quarter)	−1.6	−2.4
Entire Period	775.3%	270.0%
Compound Annual Return	17.2%	10.0%
Plus 1% Management Fee	1.0%	
Gross Investment Return	18.2%	10.0%

*Includes dividents (and capital gains distributions in the case of Sequoia Fund) treated as though reinvested.
**These figures differ slightly from the S&P figures in Table 1 because of a difference in calculation of reinvested dividends.
For returns since 1984, visit www.sequoiafund.com

Table 5 Charles Munger

Year	Mass Inv. Trust (%)	Investors Stock (%)	Lehman (%)	Tri-Cont. (%)	Dow (%)	Over-all Partnership (%)	Limited Partners (%)
Yearly Results (1)							
1962	-9.8	-13.4	-14.4	-12.2	-7.6	30.1	20.1
1963	20.0	16.5	23.8	20.3	20.6	71.7	47.8
1964	15.9	14.3	13.6	13.3	18.7	49.7	33.1
1965	10.2	9.8	19.0	10.7	14.2	8.4	6.0
1966	-7.7	-9.9	-2.6	-6.9	-15.7	12.4	8.3
1967	20.0	22.8	28.0	25.4	19.0	56.2	37.5
1968	10.3	8.1	6.7	6.8	7.7	40.4	27.0
1969	-4.8	-7.9	-1.9	0.1	-11.6	28.3	21.3
1970	0.6	-4.1	-7.2	-1.0	8.7	-0.1	-0.1
1971	9.0	16.8	26.6	22.4	9.8	25.4	20.6
1972	11.0	15.2	23.7	21.4	18.2	8.3	7.3
1973	-12.5	-17.6	-14.3	-21.3	-13.1	-31.9	39.5
1974	-25.5	-25.6	-30.3	-27.6	-23.1	-31.5	-31.5
1975	32.9	33.3	30.8	35.4	44.4	73.2	73.2
Compound Results (2)							
1962	-9.8	-13.4	-14.4	-12.2	-7.6	30.1	20.1
1962-3	8.2	0.9	6.0	5.6	11.5	123.4	77.5
1962-4	25.4	15.3	20.4	19.6	32.4	234.4	136.3
1962-5	38.2	26.6	43.3	32.4	51.2	262.5	150.5
1962-6	27.5	14.1	39.5	23.2	27.5	307.5	171.3
1962-7	53.0	40.1	78.5	54.5	51.8	536.5	273.0

1962–8	68.8	51.4	90.5	65.0	63.5	793.6	373.7
1962–9	60.7	39.4	86.9	65.2	44.5	1046.5	474.6
1962–70	61.7	33.7	73.4	63.5	57.1	1045.4	474.0
1962–71	76.3	56.2	119.5	100.1	72.5	1336.3	592.2
1962–72	95.7	79.9	171.5	142.9	103.9	1455.5	642.7
1962–73	71.2	48.2	132.7	91.2	77.2	959.3	405.8
1962–74	27.5	40.3	62.2	38.4	36.6	625.6	246.5
1962–75	69.4	47.0	112.2	87.4	96.8	1156.7	500.1
Average Annual Compounded Rate	3.8	2.8	5.5	4.6	5.0	19.8	13.7

Table 6 Pacific Partners, Ltd.

Year	S&P 500 Index (%)	Limited Partnership Results (%)	Overall Partnership Results (%)
1965	12.4	21.2	32.0
1966	−10.1	24.5	36.7
1967	23.9	120.1	180.1
1968	11.0	114.6	171.9
1969	−8.4	64.7	97.1
1970	3.9	−7.2	−7.2
1971	14.6	10.9	16.4
1972	18.9	12.8.	17.1
1973	−14.8	−42.1	−42.1
1974	−26.4	−34.4	−34.4
1975	37.2	23.4	31.2
1976	23.6	127.8	127.8
1977	−7.4	20.3	27.1
1978	6.4	28.4	37.9
1979	18.2	36.1	48.2
1980	32.3	18.1	24.1
1981	−5.0	6.0	8.0
1982	21.4	24.0	32.0
1983	22.4	18.6	24.8

Standard & Poors 19 year compounded gain	316.4%
Limited Partners 19 year compounded gain	5,530.2%
Overall Partnership 19 year compounded gain	22,200.0%
Standard & Poor's 19 year annual compounded rate	7.8%
Limited Partners 19 year annual compounded rate	23.6%
Overall Partnership 19 year annual compounded rate	32.9%

Table 7 **Perimeter Investments**

Year	PIL Overall (%)	Limited Partner (%)		
8/1–12/31/65	40.6	32.5	Total Partnership Percentage Gain	
1966	6.4	5.1	8/1/65 through 10/31/83	4277.2%
1967	73.5	58.8	Limited Partners Percentage Gain	
1968	65.0	52.0	8/1/65 through 10/31/83	2309.5%
1969	13.8	–13.8	Annual Compound Rate of Gain	
1970	–6.0	–6.0	Overall Partnership	23.0%
1971	55.7	49.3		
1972	23.6	18.9	Annual Compound Rate of Gain	
1973	–28.1	–28.1	Limited Partners	19.0%
1974	–12.0	–12.0	Dow Jones Industrial Averages	
1975	38.5	38.5	7/31/65 (Approximate)	882
1/1–10/31/76	38.2	34.5		
11/1/76–10/31/77	30.3	25.5	Dow Jones Industrial Averages	
11/1/77–10/31/78	31.8	26.6	10/31/83 (Approximate)	1225
11/1/78–10/31/79	34.7	28.9	Approximate Compound Rate of	
11/1/79–10/31/80	41.8	34.7	Gain of DJI including Dividends	7%
11/1/80–10/31/81	4.0	3.3		
11/1/81–10/31/82	29.8	25.4		
11/1/82–10/31/83	22.2	18.4		

Table 8 The Washington Post Company, Master Trust, December 31, 1983

	Current Quarter		Year Ended		2 Years Ended*		3 Years Ended*		5 Years Ended*	
	% Ret.	Rank	% Ret.	Rank	% Ret.	Rank	% Ret.	Rank	% Ret.	Rank
All Investments										
Manager A	4.1	2	22.5	10	20.6	40	18.0	10	20.2	3
Manager B	3.2	4	34.1	1	33.0	1	28.2	1	22.6	1
Manager C	5.4	1	22.2	11	28.4	3	24.5	1	—	—
Master Trust (All Managers)	3.9	1	28.1	1	28.2	1	24.3	1	21.8	1
Common Stock										
Manager A	5.2	1	32.1	9	26.1	27	21.2	11	26.5	7
Manager B	3.6	5	52.9	1	46.2	1	37.8	1	29.3	3
Manager C	6.2	1	29.3	14	30.8	10	29.3	3	—	—
Master Trust (All Managers)	4.7	1	41.2	1	37.0	1	30.4	1	27.6	1
Bonds										
Manager A	2.7	8	17.0	1	26.6	1	19.0	1	12.2	2
Manager B	1.6	46	7.6	48	18.3	53	12.7	84	7.4	86
Manager C	32.2	4	10.4	9	24.0	3	18.9	1	—	—
Master Trust (All Managers)	2.2	11	9.7	14	21.1	14	15.2	24	9.3	30
Bonds & Cash Equivalents										
Manager A	2.5	15	12.0	5	16.1	64	15.5	21	12.9	9
Manager B	2.1	28	9.2	29	17.1	47	14.7	41	10.8	44
Manager C	3.1	6	10.2	17	22.0	2	21.6	1	—	—
Master Trust (All Managers)	2.4	14	10.2	17	17.8	20	16.2	2	12.5	9

*Annualized

Rank indicates the fund's performance against the A.C.Becker universe.

Rank is stated as a percentile: 1 = best performance, 100 = worst.

Table 9 FMC Corporation Pension Fund, Annual Rate of Return (Percent)

Period ending	1 Year	2 Years	3 Years	4 Years	5 Years	6 Years	7 Years	8 Years	9 Years
FMC (Bonds and Equities Combined)									
1983	23.0								*17.1
1982	22.8	13.6	16.0	16.6	15.5	12.3	13.9	16.3	
1981	5.4	13.0	15.3	13.8	10.5	12.6	15.4		
1980	21.0	19.7	16.8	11.7	14.0	17.3			
1979	18.4	14.7	8.7	12.3	16.5				
1978	11.2	4.2	10.4	16.1					
1977	−2.3	9.8	17.8						
1976	23.8	29.3							
1975	35.0								
Becker large plan median									
1983	15.6								12.6
1982	21.4	11.2	13.9	13.9	12.5	9.7	10.9	12.3	
1981	1.2	10.8	11.9	10.3	7.7	8.9	10.9		
1980	20.9	NA	NA	NA	10.8	NA			
1979	13.7	NA	NA	NA	11.1				
1978	6.5	NA	NA	NA					
1977	−3.3	NA	NA						
1976	17.0	NA							
1975	24.1								
S&P 500									
1983	22.8								15.6
1982	21.5	7.3	15.1	16.0	14.0	10.2	12.0	14.9	
1981	−5.0	12.0	14.2	12.2	8.1	10.5	14.0		
1980	32.5	25.3	18.7	11.7	14.0	17.5			
1979	18.6	12.4	5.5	9.8	14.8				
1978	6.6	−0.8	6.8	13.7					
1977	7.7	6.9	16.1						
1976	23.7	30.3							
1975	37.2								

*18.5 from equities only

Source: Copyright Warren E. Buffett. Reprinted with permission.

Recommended Reading

Chapter 1

Warren Buffett, Letters to Berkshire Hathaway Shareholders
Larry Cunningham, *The Essays of Warren Buffett*

Chapter 2

Andy Kilpatrick, *Of Permanent Value, The Story of Warren Buffett*
Roger Lowenstein, *Buffett: The Making of an American Capitalist*

Chapter 3

Benjamin Graham, *The Intelligent Investor*

Chapter 4

Phillip Fisher, *Common Stocks and Uncommon Profits*. Philip Fisher published *Common Stocks and Uncommon Profits* in 1958 (Harper & Brothers). The Wiley Classic version also includes Fisher's 1975 publication, *Conservative Investors Sleep Well*, and his 1980 publication, *Developing an Investment Philosophy*.

Chapter 5

Janet Lowe, *Warren Buffett Speaks*
Simon Reynolds, *Thoughts of Chairman Buffett*

Chapter 10

Robert P. Miles, *The Warren Buffett CEO*

Also Recommended

Benjamin Graham and David Dodd, *Security Analysis*
Robert Hagstrom, *The Warren Buffett Way*, *The Warren Buffett Portfolio*
Barnett Helzberg, *What I Learned before I Sold My Business to Warren Buffett*
Janet Lowe, *Warren Buffett Speaks*; *Value Investing Made Easy*; *Benjamin Graham on Value Investing*; *The Rediscovered Benjamin Graham*; *Damn Right! Behind the Scenes with Berkshire Hathaway Billionaire Charlie Munger*
Robert P. Miles, *101 Reasons to Own the World's Greatest Investment*

Index

About the Author

Robert P. Miles (www.robertpmiles.com) is an investment advisor, international speaker, author, and acclaimed Warren Buffett expert. He is a long-term shareholder of Berkshire Hathaway. Miles is also the author of *101 Reasons to Own the World's Greatest Investment: Warren Buffett's Berkshire Hathaway* (Wiley) and *The Warren Buffett CEO: Secrets from the Berkshire Hathaway Managers* (Wiley), which was recommended reading by Warren Buffett in his famed letter to shareholders. Known for his subtle wit and entertaining stories, Robert Miles has shared his *Buffett Wealth Workshops* with enthusiastic audiences on three continents. His keynote address, *Reflections of a Billionaire CEO: How to See You in the Image*, has been heard in over twenty-five countries throughout the world. He is also the author and presenter of Nightingale-Conant's audio series entitled *How to Build Wealth Like Warren Buffett*. He is the host of Buffett CEO Talk, video interviews with the Berkshire Hathaway managers. Miles is a graduate of the University of Michigan Business School. He resides in Tampa, Florida.